First-Year Baby Care

An Illustrated Step-by-Step Guide

Fully revised and expanded
by Paula Kelly, MD

Meadowbrook Press
Distributed by Simon & Schuster
New York

Library of Congress Cataloging-in-Publication Data

First-year baby care : an illustrated step-by-step guide for new parents / edited by Paula Kelly. -- Rev. & updated.
    p. cm.
  ISBN 978-1-4516-2990-3
  1. Infants--Care--Handbooks, manuals, etc. I. Kelly, Paula, 1949-
  RJ61.F47 2011
  618.92'02--dc23
                    2011019573

Medical Editor: Paula Kelly, MD
Editor: Alicia Ester
Creative Director: Tamara JM Peterson
Illustrations: Karen Martin, Patricia Carey, and Susan Spellman
Index: Beverlee Day

Published by Meadowbrook Press
6110 Blue Circle Drive, Suite 237
Minnetonka, Minnesota 55343

www.meadowbrookpress.com

BOOK TRADE DISTRIBUTION by Simon and Schuster
a division of Simon and Schuster, Inc.
1230 Avenue of the Americas
New York, New York 10020

The contents of this book have been reviewed and checked for accuracy and appropriateness by medical
doctors. However, the authors, editors, reviewers, and publisher disclaim all responsibility arising from any
adverse effects or results that occur or might occur as a result of the inappropriate application of any of the
information contained in this book. If you have a question or concern about the appropriateness or application
of the treatments described in this book, consult your healthcare professional.

18 17 16 15 14 13 12 11   10 9 8 7 6 5 4 3 2

Printed in the United States of America

Contents

Introduction v

Chapter One: Your Newborn 1

Chapter Two: Caring for Your Baby 19

Chapter Three: Feeding Your Baby............................55

Chapter Four: Your Baby's Safety............................. 91

Chapter Five: Your Baby's Development 115

Chapter Six: Medical Care for Your Baby 129

    Appendix 186

    Growth Charts 190

    Index... 192

In Memory
of Beth Winters

Acknowledgments

Special thanks to Melissa Avery, CNM, MSN; Pamela Barnard; Mavis Brehm, RN, BSN; Rachel Bye, MD; Mitch Einzig, MD; Kristine Ellis; Robert and Lindsay Collins; Jackson and John Gehan; Michael Grady; Alvin Handelman; Robin, Gregory, and Jasmaine Harris; Elizabeth Hass, CPNP, LC; Carol K. Jacobs, RN, CPNP; Gail and Kevin Ketter; Bonnie Kinn; Pat, John, and Kevin Sevlie; Kate and Lily Shank; Sue and Diane Sherek; Peg and Meghan Short; Nancy and Nicholas Wood; Sue and Sara Veazie; and Christine Zuchora-Walske.

Thanks also to Great Starts Birth & Family Education of Seattle for permission to reprint the material on baby exercises. Some of the material in the medical care section first appeared, in a slightly different form, in *The Parent's Guide to Baby and Child Medical Care*, edited by Terril H. Hart, MD (Meadowbrook, 1982).

Introduction

Becoming a new parent is one of the most thrilling experiences you'll ever have. It's also one of the most challenging. *First-Year Baby Care* will guide you through your new parenting responsibilities when you'll likely need it most—during your baby's first year. This book's tips and instructions will hopefully boost your confidence to care for your baby as best as you can.

Today, many new parents spend little time in the hospital or birth center after their babies are born. They often can't rely on the hospital or birth center staff to teach them all they'll need to know about caring for newborns. Newborn classes can provide important information, but many parents still find themselves wondering and worrying about how to keep their babies healthy and safe.

This book's goal is to help fill in the gaps. As a pediatrician, I've found that new parents often raise the same questions about baby care. They wonder about everyday matters, like how to bathe a baby or childproof a home, and more complicated ones, like finding daycare, monitoring child development, and handling medical problems. To answer such questions, we've drawn on current research and medical recommendations—as well as the wisdom of contemporary parents—to update *First-Year Baby Care* for today.

This third edition builds on the practical, easy-to-follow information found in the first two editions. In it you'll still find illustrated step-by-step instructions and essential facts on caring and feeding your baby and keeping him safe and healthy, alongside the latest knowledge on a variety of parenting topics, from breastfeeding, sleeping, and introducing solid foods to buying baby gear, choosing the best daycare, and traveling with your baby. We've added key facts on topics like nutrition and vaccinations, and included new resources (including trustworthy websites) to help busy (and possibly bewildered) new parents manage their new roles.

Your baby's first year will test your resolve and give you many moments of great joy. I hope this book helps you rise to the challenges and appreciate the wonderful new addition to your family.

Paula Kelly

Paula Kelly, MD

P.S. In recognition of the fact that children do indeed come in both sexes, and in an effort to represent each, the use of masculine and feminine pronouns will alternate with each chapter.

Before Your Baby Arrives

You have lots to do before your baby is born—choose a name, decorate the nursery, buy supplies. The following tasks, however, may be the most important, because they'll benefit your baby's well-being—and yours—before and after he's born.

Take Care of Yourself

Birth defects are the leading cause of infant death. By taking care of yourself during pregnancy, you help prevent birth defects. Here's what you can do:

- Eat well. Try to eat the recommended number of servings from each of the five main food groups. Strive for variety in your diet. Drink at least eight glasses of water daily. Consume salt in moderation. Consult the latest dietary guidelines from the United States Department of Agriculture (http://nutrition.gov). Talk to your caregiver about taking a prenatal vitamin to make sure you're getting essential nutrients, minerals, and vitamins—especially calcium, iron, and folic acid (a B vitamin that helps decrease the incidence of spina bifida and other birth defects). You may want to increase your omega-3 fatty acid and vitamin D intake as well, to encourage optimum brain and eye development and build strong bones and teeth for your baby. Avoid consuming seafood high in mercury, raw fish and shellfish, saccharin, unpasteurized milk and cheese, and lunch meats, and talk to your caregiver about other foods to limit or avoid. Reduce your caffeine intake.

- Have regular checkups, to assure you get the recommended prenatal blood tests and ultrasounds. Your caregiver will follow your weight and blood pressure and screen for diabetes and, later in your pregnancy, the presence of Group B streptococcus (GBS) bacteria. GBS is the most common cause among newborns of blood and brain infections. Taking antibiotics before delivery can prevent transmission to your baby.

- Make sure your vaccinations are current, especially the rubella (German measles) vaccination. Acquiring an infection from this disease during early pregnancy can result in serious heart, vision, and hearing problems for your baby.

- Alert your caregiver to any illnesses you are exposed to during pregnancy, including fifth disease (parvovirus B19), chicken pox (varicella), and cytomegalovirus (CMV). Though uncommon, some illnesses can cause problems for your fetus.

- Exercise regularly. Talk to your caregiver about what kinds of exercise are right for you and in what amounts.

- Avoid alcohol, cigarettes, and recreational drugs. These substances can affect your fetus's physical and emotional development. Also, talk to your caregiver before taking any prescription medications.

- Avoid environmental hazards, like chemicals found in industrial plants or even in some household cleaning products, and don't drink water that contains high levels of lead or pesticides. Also avoid contact with litter boxes and rodent droppings. Both cat and rodent feces are linked to diseases (toxoplasmosis and lymphocytic choriomeningitis virus, respectively) that can cause birth defects, physical or mental delays, or miscarriage.

- Assess your family history and your partner's for risk factors. A family health history questionnaire is available at the March of Dimes website (http://www.marchofdimes.com/pregnancy/trying_healthhistory.html).

Choose the Right Birthplace

When selecting your maternity care provider and birthplace, ask plenty of questions about their policies and procedures. Knowing what to expect will help ease your mind and prepare you for the birth. Find out about their rooming-in policy (Will it be possible for your baby to stay with you after the birth to bond and breastfeed?) and learn their emergency procedures. Although it's unlikely that something will go wrong, if you need an emergency cesarean or your baby arrives earlier than expected or ill, you'll want to know that your birthplace has proper newborn resuscitation capabilities and appropriate nursery care for premature and sick babies. Be sure you're comfortable with your provider and birthplace, so you and your baby get the best care possible.

Some parents list their goals and desires for the birth in a birth plan. Consider creating your own with consultation from your caregiver.

Choose a Health Caregiver for Your Baby

Around the twenty-fourth week of your pregnancy, you'll be encouraged to select a health caregiver for your baby. You'll spend a great deal of time at the caregiver's office for well-child visits during the first year, so it's important that you trust, respect, and feel comfortable with him or her.

The following is a list of different types of pediatric caregivers. Make sure the caregiver you choose is covered by your insurance plan.

- Pediatrician—a Doctor of Medicine (MD) who specializes in children's healthcare

- Family physician—an MD who provides care for the entire family

- General practitioner—an MD or a Doctor of Osteopathy (DO) who can provide pediatric or family healthcare

- Pediatric or family nurse practitioner—registered nurse with additional training and certification in pediatric or family healthcare

- Physician's assistant—graduate of two-year training program in primary medicine who provides pediatric services under the supervision of a physician

- Naturopathic physician—a Doctor of Naturopathic Medicine (ND) who provides well-child care, emphasizes the non-medical treatment of illnesses, and refers seriously ill children to medical doctors

- Perinatologist—a specialist in newborn medicine who's needed when it's known though prenatal testing that a baby will have a birth defect or other special needs

- Neonatologist or a neonatal nurse practitioner—a medical specialist who cares for newborns (such as premature babies) who are sick or require non-routine newborn care.

You can find a caregiver using the following resources:

- Your own primary caregiver, if you intend to choose a different caregiver for your child

- Birth center of a hospital or clinic, especially postpartum and nursery nursing staff: Nurses see the caregivers at work with both mothers and babies and can therefore give you excellent advice and information.

- Health insurance provider directory: Your selection might be confined to a specific group of healthcare providers.

- Friends with children: Parents usually have strong feelings about their pediatric caregivers. Consider both positive and negative comments.

- Online caregiver locators, such as the American Academy of Pediatrics (AAP) Pediatrician Referral Service at http://www.aap.org, or Angie's List at http://www.angieslist.com.

- County health association or board of health

- *The Official ABMS Directory of Board Certified Medical Specialists* (available at your local library or online at http://www.abmsdirectory.com)

- Local chapters of caregiver associations, such as the AAP, AAFP, or the American Medical Association (AMA)

- Teaching hospitals

- Telephone directory yellow pages, under *Physicians, Family Practice, or Pediatrics*

- Local magazine listings of "Top Doctors."

It's important to interview your child's caregiver. Some caregivers accept only newborns into their practices, and it may be difficult to change caregivers if you're unhappy with the care your child receives. When choosing a caregiver, take into account your philosophy and approach to healthcare. Do you want to play an active role in your child's healthcare or do you want to rely on the caregiver's authority? Are you okay with a caregiver who's in a solo, small group, or large clinic practice? Do you want to go to an office that just sees children or one that sees all ages? Do you prefer an office that does only primary care or one that also offers multispecialty care?

What are your views on breastfeeding? Circumcision? Infant sleep? Vaccination? Once you've answered these kinds of questions, ask a potential caregiver several questions (like those that follow) about his or her:

- Training, experience, and affiliations (*When and where did you receive your medical training?*)

- Medical philosophy (*How do you view the parent's role in a child's healthcare?*)

- Standard care (*How soon after my baby's initial exam would you like to see him again?*)

- Availability (*When are you at the office?*)

- Office staff and resources (*What other professional staff are available at your office? What are their roles?*)

- Office management (*How are well-child appointments scheduled?*)

Do the caregiver's answers match your philosophy and approach to healthcare? If they don't, move on to the next potential caregiver. If they do, double-check with parents of current and past patients. Are they satisfied with the caregiver's quality of care? After considering all the information, trust your own feelings about a caregiver. If you feel comfortable with him or her, your child likely will, too.

Decide Whether to Breastfeed or Formula-feed Your Baby

A slew of studies in recent years have shown how important breastfeeding is to the well-being of babies, mothers, and society. This has fueled a resurgence of breastfeeding in North America, which was a formula-feeding culture for several decades. Both options are open to you as a new mom in the new millennium. See Chapter 3 for a full discussion of breastfeeding and formula-feeding.

Before your baby is born, it's a good idea to decide how you'll feed him. Deciding before the birth gives you time to borrow or buy supplies (for example, breast pump or bottles) and, if you choose to breastfeed, arrange to take breastfeeding classes and build a breastfeeding support system.

Your baby should "room in" or stay with you as much as possible while you're at the hospital or birth center, but especially if you plan to breastfeed. Some hospitals have a special designation as being "Baby Friendly" to declare their commitment to keeping mom and baby together as much as possible. Make your breastfeeding plans and wishes very clear to the birthing staff. If you have a cesarean birth, you might not be able to breastfeed immediately after the surgery, but you can start as soon as you recover.

Learn about Newborn Exams and Procedures

After the birth, a caregiver will examine your newborn thoroughly and perform exams to evaluate his well-being. (See page 11.) While these routine procedures are no cause for alarm, it may ease your mind to discuss any concerns or questions you have about them beforehand. In most states, parents have the right to refuse any or all of these tests.

One procedure you may want to think about in advance is umbilical cord clamping. It can be prearranged to collect a sample of cord blood by leaving the placenta side of the cord unclamped. Cord blood contains stem cells that can be sent to a private or public bank for use by family members or strangers. For more information on this procedure, see page 11.

Decide about Circumcision

If you're expecting a baby boy, you may want to weigh the pros and cons and seek advice before his birth on whether you want him circumcised. Circumcision is a surgical procedure that removes some of the skin that covers the tip of the penis (foreskin). This procedure is performed by an experienced person (medical professional or religious officiant), and it usually happens before the baby leaves the hospital or birth center but sometimes in an outpatient clinic or during a religious or cultural ceremony at a later date.

Circumcision is a controversial issue. Once a routine procedure in the United States, questions about the necessity of circumcision have risen in the past few decades. A longtime belief that supports circumcision is its potential medical benefits, like its ability to lower the risk of urinary tract infections, penile cancer, and some sexually transmitted infections, including human immunodeficiency virus (HIV). In 2007, the World Health Organization (WHO) and the Centers for Disease Control (CDC) issued statements that male circumcision significantly reduces the acquisition of HIV by men during penile-vaginal sex (though the protection is only partial and should not replace other preventive interventions).

Other reasons for circumcision stem from religious traditions (such as the Jewish bris), social customs (for example, circumcision makes many boys look like their fathers), and cultural beliefs (for example, some people think circumcision makes hygiene easier).

Those who oppose circumcision believe that its risks outweigh its potential benefits. Like the risks associated with any surgery, possible risks of circumcision include pain, infection, bleeding, mutilation, interference with breastfeeding, and (rarely) death. Also, some have raised concern that circumcision interferes with sexual pleasure and function.

The American Academy of Pediatrics (AAP) has remained neutral on the issue, suggesting parents learn the facts and make the decision best for their family. They've stated, "Existing scientific evidence demonstrates potential medical benefits of… circumcision; however, these data are not sufficient to recommend routine… circumcision…. To make an informed choice, parents of all male infants should be given accurate and unbiased information and be provided the opportunity to discuss this decision." Ask your caregiver about the pros and cons of circumcision before your baby's birth. Research the topic on your own. If circumcision is part of your culture or religious tradition, talk to a respected leader about the meaning behind and reasons for the procedure. Talk to other parents of boys about their feelings toward circumcision. Consider as much information as you can before making your decision.

If you decide to have your baby circumcised, the AAP recommends that he be given an analgesic before the procedure to block pain. This is done via injection of a numbing drug at the base of the penis. To help dull pain during the procedure, he may be given an oral sugar solution. A premature or ill baby, or one with an abnormally developed penis, should not be circumcised. Bleeding problems and infection are more likely to occur. Also, make sure you notify your caregiver ahead of time if your family has a history of bleeding problems.

If you decide to leave your baby's penis natural, know that he won't be alone. In the United States, it is estimated that less than sixty percent of newborn boys are circumcised, and the number of non-circumcised boys has risen steadily over the last few decades. In other countries around the world, non-circumcised boys greatly outnumber circumcised boys.

Consider Home Healthcare

Because many new families are sent home shortly after childbirth, many parents feel that their babies could benefit from additional healthcare during the first few days at home. Newborn jaundice, umbilical cord care, skin care, and feeding issues are common concerns. If you think you'd like some professional postpartum support, consider arranging a home healthcare visit shortly after you arrive home from the hospital or birth center. Nurses with maternal-newborn training can help you care for your baby and advise you when further medical attention is needed. Some healthcare plans cover all or a portion of the expense; check to see whether yours does. Other helpful professionals include lactation consultants, who can help you learn to breastfeed, and postpartum doulas, specially trained laypeople who take care of you and your home so you can focus on your baby.

Establish a Support System

After you give birth, you'll discover a new world with your baby. The physical and emotional changes you'll experience, along with the increased responsibility, may leave you feeling overwhelmed. And the desire to do everything "right," from feeding and bathing your baby to keeping the toilets scrubbed, can only increase the pressure.

Don't feel you have to brave parenthood alone. Arranging for help and setting up a support system *before* your baby arrives will ensure that you can manage—and enjoy—the first few weeks with your little one. Think now about the kind of help you'll need. For example, you may want:

- Help with baby care, including breast-feeding, bathing, comforting, and so on
- Help with household tasks, like meal preparation and laundry
- Transportation to medical appointments, the grocery store or pharmacy, and so on
- Companionship

Ask for help whenever you need it; this isn't the time to be reserved. And always remember this advice: If someone trustworthy offers you help, whether it's to watch your baby so you can take a quick shower or to drive you to the grocery store, *take the offer*!

If your baby arrives earlier than expected or has unanticipated issues, such as fever or jaundice, make sure you are clearly informed about the special care and support that will be necessary. See appendix for recommended resources.

Take Care of Practical Needs

Make sure you've borrowed, bought, or acquired as much as you can before the birth, because taking a newborn on shopping trips or outings can be daunting! Throughout this book, you'll find information to help you make safe, sensible choices that'll best prepare you for parenthood. On pages 25–27 you'll find tips to help you decide what type of diapers to use. On pages 44–48 are recommendations for dressing a new baby. On page 38, you'll read about outfitting a crib, and on pages 101–09, you'll learn about what to look for when buying equipment for your child. Read about car safety on pages 98–101, and have an approved car seat properly installed before your baby's birth.

Chapter One

Your Newborn

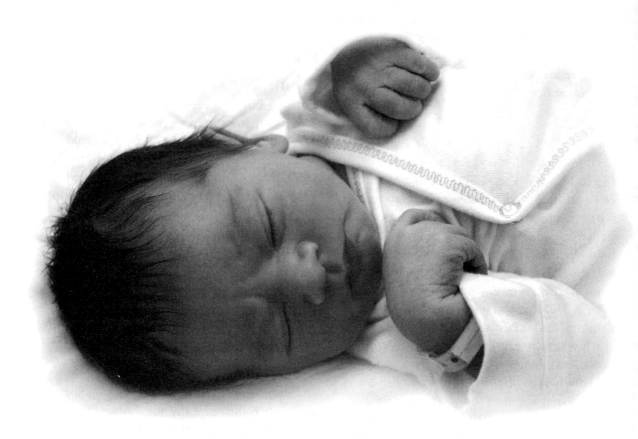

If you're a new parent, you probably spent lots of time learning about pregnancy and childbirth and worrying how you'd handle labor and delivery. You longed to hold your healthy baby in your arms. These memories of pregnancy and childbirth won't soon fade. (In fact, you might tell any willing listener the detailed story of your child's birth!) But once your child is born, you realize childbirth was the beginning of parenthood, not just the end of pregnancy.

This year with your baby will be full of firsts—the first smile, the first tooth, the first word, and maybe even the first step. Your baby will need a lot of your care and attention as she accomplishes these and other firsts. A year from now, you'll be amazed by how much your child has grown and changed (likely more than any other year of her life), and you'll be proud of how much you've learned and accomplished as a parent.

Changes for the Family

A new baby is notorious for making life unpredictable. In the middle of a quiet dinner, or long-overdue lovemaking, or a much-needed phone conversation with a supportive friend, your baby suddenly needs you *now*. And you go to her—gladly. Few things in life are more satisfying than comforting and nurturing your child.

Here are some changes you and your family can expect when your newborn arrives.

Parents

Let's face it: Becoming a parent means you'll have less free time and fewer opportunities to be spontaneous. Going to a movie or a restaurant will almost never happen without a lot of preplanning. You'll need to arrange childcare and work around your baby's schedule, not just your own. Plus, you'll wonder how long you can stay away from your little one. Once you walk out the door without your baby, you'll find yourself thinking and talking of nothing but her.

If you're parenting with a partner, a newborn can test a couple's relationship—especially if the baby is your first. To you both, it may seem as though the entire day—and night—consists of diapering and feeding and rocking and burping. You may feel as though you're losing touch with each other. Your partner may even feel a bit jealous of the attention you're giving the baby. Know that it takes time to adjust to parenthood. Once you've grown used to your roles as parents, find ways and time to nurture your relationship. Remember: You're in this together!

If you're parenting without a partner, you might feel overwhelmed at first. You may be exhausted, and not having anyone to share the work and frustrations (and joys) may make your new role seem that much more difficult. Be sure to establish a support system. Having family and friends to look after your baby occasionally, or just listen to you will help greatly. You might also consider joining a single mothers group. See appendix to learn more about single mother support networks.

Mom

Both parents experience emotional ups and downs during the first weeks of their baby's life, but moms are especially vulnerable during the postpartum days. Lack of sleep, tremendous hormonal changes, and feelings of being overwhelmed can cause bouts of depression.

For some, these emotional fluctuations are mild and subside within a few weeks ("baby blues"). Eating right, gradually exercising more often, and sleeping when the baby sleeps usually help chase away baby blues. Supportive family, friends, and other new parents also can help new moms feel back on track.

For others, however, the emotional fluctuations are overwhelming, long-lasting, and may require treatment. These women may suffer from postpartum mood disorders (PPMDs) or postpartum psychosis. Talk with your caregiver if your depression concerns you or those around you. He or she will have ways to help you.

Dad or Other Parent

Although a new dad or other parent doesn't experience the hormonal and physical changes that a new mom does, he or she may experience a range of emotions. Confusion, ambivalence, fear, depression—these are all emotions a new dad or other parent can feel about his or her new role, even while feeling an intense love for the baby.

Just as with new moms, supportive family, friends, and other new parents can help these parents.

Siblings

If you have an older child, no matter how well you've prepared her for the baby's arrival, she may still have trouble accepting the fact that she's no longer the baby. She may suddenly want to start nursing again. Her sleep patterns may change. She may start sucking her thumb or wetting herself. These regressions are normal and simply her way of seeking the love and attention she fears the baby will steal from her. To help reassure her, spend (and see that your partner spends) some uninterrupted one-on-one time with your older child every day. Listen carefully to her feelings about the baby and the changes in your family. Point out the benefits of being an older child, like choosing what to eat, being able to go the park and play, and having friends.

Today, many babies are born into families that don't fit the once traditional mold—that is, a working dad and a stay-at-home mom who are happily married. Lots of moms return to work after their maternity leave, and more and more dads are choosing to care for their babies full-time at home. Many single men and women want to know the joys of parenting and choose to adopt a child, or perhaps become pregnant by a procedure like in vitro fertilization. An increasing number of same-sex couples are becoming loving parents, and the number of blended families is also on the rise.

Furthermore, not every baby born to a family is without problems. A baby may be born prematurely or have some kind of medical problem, like alcohol or street drugs in her system. She may be born with a genetic condition or a congenital problem, like Down syndrome or a cleft palate.

Whatever the family's structure and however a baby joins the family, every parent should pledge to provide a loving, safe, and healthy environment for the little one as she enters our increasingly global community. (For further helpful information, see the recommended resources in the appendix.)

Changes for the Baby

While parents must adjust to life with their newborn, a baby must adjust to life outside her mom's womb. Being born, whether vaginally or by cesarean section, is an exhausting physical experience. In fact, after an initial alert period at birth, most newborns fall into a deep sleep for about six hours. Here are other changes a baby undergoes after birth:

- At birth, a baby normally weighs between six and eight pounds (2.7 and 3.6 kilograms) and is eighteen to twenty-two inches (45.7 to 55.9 centimeters) long. Typically, she'll lose up to 10 percent of her weight in the days following birth, then start to regain that weight by the end of the first week.

- While in the womb, a baby receives all her nourishment through the umbilical cord. She doesn't have to swallow to satisfy her hunger. In fact, she doesn't know what hunger is! Once born, swallowing becomes a reflex, and the baby feels hunger and knows she must act to satisfy it.

- Before birth, a baby doesn't breathe. She receives all her oxygen through her mom's blood. At birth, her circulation is sluggish, and her breathing may be shallow and irregular (although her heart may beat 120 times per minute). She'll also sneeze, gasp, hiccup, and cough.

These aren't cold symptoms; they're just her way of clearing mucus from the respiratory system.

- While in the womb, amniotic fluid kept a baby at a constant comfortable temperature. Once born, however, her temperature drops rapidly. To warm her, she's placed on her mom's chest or abdomen and covered with a blanket or swaddled. (Alternatively, she may be placed in or under a warming table.)

- While in the womb, the surrounding fluid, blood, and tissue muffled outside sounds for a baby and kept her "in the dark." Once born, however, she experiences sounds much more loudly and clearly, and she's exposed to direct, bright light. Before birth, her sleeping and waking schedules were her own and weren't influenced by the light of day and dark of night.

- Before birth, a baby was constantly and gently rocked by her mother's movements, a motion she found calming and reassuring. After birth, she must rely on others to remember to provide this motion. (This is why rocking a fussy baby can calm her.)

With all these changes, it's little wonder that babies spend much of their first few weeks sleeping and adjusting to their new surroundings and their new abilities.

What Does a Newborn Look Like?

Contrary to popular belief, not all newborns are cute. In fact, many can look downright peculiar. Following are descriptions of a typical newborn's features in the days immediately following birth.

Head, Hair, and Neck

A newborn's head is large in proportion to her body—about one-fourth of her body's length—making her quite "top heavy" with little or no head control. Her neck is short and creased. Her head may look lopsided, and the top of it may appear pointy (this "molding" is caused by the skull bones shifting to allow for a smoother passage through the birth canal). The head usually regains a rounded shape a couple of days after birth. A tough membrane protects the head's two soft spots, called fontanels, where the skull bones haven't yet fused (allowing brain growth to continue). Your caregiver will monitor brain growth and ventricle (fluid chambers within the brain) size by measuring your baby's head circumference in addition to height and weight. The anterior fontanel, the larger one at the top near the front, closes after eighteen to twenty-four months. It is not abnormal to be able to see pulsing at the site of the anterior fontanel. The posterior fontanel, at the top near the back, closes by six months.

It's impossible to predict how much hair newborns will have or keep. Some have lots of locks and may never lose them. Others have no hair or a short crop that'll fall out and regrow after about six weeks, sometimes in a completely different color. Some newborns have wrinkly scalps and will eventually grow into the extra skin. Others may have peeling scalps (cradle cap).

Face

A newborn's eyes often appear red and puffy, and there may be broken blood vessels in her eyeballs. This is caused by pressure exerted on them during birth or by the drops or ointment she received after birth to prevent infection. Light-skinned babies usually have blue-gray eyes, and dark-skinned babies usually have brown eyes. Permanent color might not develop for about six months. Some babies can produce tears from birth, but most don't for six weeks or so.

A newborn's nose appears flat and broad. For the first five months or so, she is an "obligate" nose breather, meaning she needs to breathe primarily through her nose.

Occasionally babies are born with teeth, called natal teeth. They can cause pain and interfere with breastfeeding; your baby's caregiver or dentist may need to remove them. Blisters may be present on the lips from in utero sucking; these are normal and aren't painful. Babies are often born with a white spot on the center of the roof of the mouth, called an Epstein pearl. This is normal and will resolve spontaneously over the next few weeks.

A newborn usually has fat cheeks, and she may appear chinless.

Skin/Fingernails

A newborn's skin is wrinkled and loose, and it may begin to look dry and start to peel after a few days. Her body may be covered with vernix caseosa, a white, waxy substance that eased her movement through the birth canal. She also still may have lanugo, a downy fuzz covering her shoulders, back, and cheeks. This soft hair will disappear within a few days.

Skin color usually changes during the first few days, ranging from bluish purple to pink to gray. Newborns of African, Asian, or Mediterranean descent often have light skin that will darken eventually. A blue color of the lips, gums, or skin around the mouth may represent a deficiency of oxygen in these tissues and should be evaluated.

Fingernails can be long and sharp, and grow fast, and are likely to result in scratches on the face as the newborn has little control over stray movements. (See page 36 on how to trim your baby's nails).

Body

A newborn's body curls into itself, and her abdomen is large and her hips narrow. After birth, a metal or plastic clamp is placed on her umbilical cord below where it was cut. The clamp stops the bleeding from the umbilical vessels and is removed before she leaves the hospital or birth center. The remaining stump of tissue will fall off on its own. Your baby's caregiver or the staff at the hospital or birth center will tell you how to care for the stump. (See page XX to learn more.) Whether your baby ends up with an "innie" or "outie" bellybutton depends on how the cord heals and is out of your control.

Whether a girl or a boy, a newborn's breasts and genitalia may be swollen, and the nipples may even leak a milky substance, sometimes referred to as "Witch's milk." Baby girls may slightly bleed or discharge mucus from the vagina. The presence of mom's hormones in the newborn causes these effects, which most often disappear in a few days or weeks. Newborns usually pee or poop within the first twenty-four hours. (See page 23.)

Some babies are born with extra nipples (called supernumerary or accessory nipples) or extra breast tissue located on the chest or abdomen below the regular nipple line. These are no cause for concern.

Arms

A newborn's arms are flexed. The hands, which are generally cool and curled into fists, may look blue because of an immature circulatory system. The wrists may be fat and creased.

Legs

A newborn's knees are bent, and the legs are bowed. Like the hands, a newborn's immature circulatory system may make the feet look blue. A newborn's feet are also mottled and may appear flat because of fat pads on the soles.

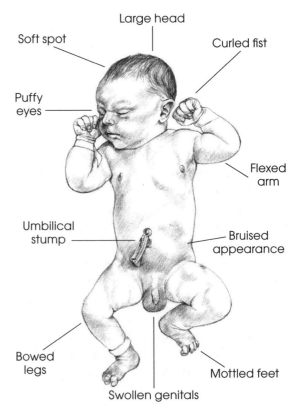

Large head
Soft spot
Curled fist
Puffy eyes
Flexed arm
Umbilical stump
Bruised appearance
Bowed legs
Mottled feet
Swollen genitals

Conditions That May Be Present at Birth

Even after an uncomplicated birth, your baby may have one or more of the following conditions. These conditions may be present at birth, and they most often heal or disappear with time.

Birthmarks

Some birthmarks may be present at birth, while others may develop in the first month. They're very common and shouldn't cause concern. Most birthmarks disappear or fade on their own by the time a child is five or six.

Nevi (moles)

These are usually small, dark brown to black spots that can be present at birth or appear later. They can be flat or raised. Very rarely, a baby's born with a large nevus, which a dermatologist should check. Nevi can grow as the child grows, and while they rarely become cancerous later, it's a good idea to make monitoring their appearance a lifelong habit.

Café-au-Lait Spots

Light brown marks known as "café au lait" spots also may be present. These usually require no intervention, but may need further evaluation if they're unusually large or more than six are present.

Hemangiomas (blood vessel malformations)

- Flat angiomata ("salmon patches"): Often called "angel kisses" or "stork bites," these flat, pink or light red patches are the most common birthmarks. They're usually on or around the eyelids, forehead, bridge of the nose, or on the back of the head and neck. They may darken with crying or straining, but they usually fade in a few months.

- Raised "strawberry" marks: These bumps aren't usually noticeable at birth but appear in the first month as small raised dots. They grow fairly rapidly during the first six months and then begin to shrink, eventually disappearing most often by age five or six.

- Port-wine stains: These are irregularly shaped, darker red or purple spots that sometimes fade but don't disappear completely. If they're around the eye or forehead, they may need further evaluation because of potential health problems.

- Mongolian spots: These flat, black or bluish areas are common on darker-skinned newborns, most frequently on the back or buttocks. These spots can be large or small, and most disappear by age five or six. These spots can look like bruises, but they're not caused by trauma.

Lip Blisters

Your baby's intense sucking may cause a blister on her lips. Don't worry; these are normal and not painful.

Tears and Blocked Tear Ducts

The lacrimal system that makes and drains tears (which serve an important function in protecting the eye's surface) is not fully developed at birth, and it may be months before your baby cries "real tears." Some babies are born with a condition called dacryostenosis, in which the tear ducts are blocked and don't drain effectively, leading to excessive tearing or even discharge in the affected eye(s). Usually the ducts open on their own. Sometimes massaging the ducts (ask your caregiver how to do this) or cleaning them with moist compresses will help clear the discharge. If the blocked ducts persist, a minor surgical procedure may be needed near the end of the first year to open the ducts.

Broken Clavicle (Collarbone)

A vaginal birth sometimes breaks a baby's clavicle. It'll heal in a few weeks, even without special treatment. A small lump will probably appear at the fracture at the site of the break, but it'll later disappear on its own. Being aware of the break when lifting a newborn will prevent her discomfort.

Developmental Dysplasia of the Hips

Babies may be born with developmental abnormalities involving instability or looseness of the hip joint. Babies, especially girls, who have been in a breech or bottom first position are at a higher risk. The condition may be detected on the first exam or in the days and weeks following birth. You should notify your baby's caregiver if you have a family history of early childhood hip problems. During well-child visits, the caregiver will continue to examine for this condition and evaluate further and treat it if necessary.

Cephalhematoma/ Caput Succedaneum

A cephalhematoma or a caput succedaneum is a swelling of blood beneath the scalp. Bruising may be present as well. It occurs when a baby's head presses against the pelvic bone during birth or when a baby is delivered by vacuum extraction or forceps. Your newborn may have one or several big "goose eggs" at the top or back of the scalp and some may become hard. These may increase bilirubin production, and can be a contributing factor for jaundice, but

shouldn't cause other problems. They usually disappear in about a week.

Milia/Miliaria

Milia are undeveloped or blocked sweat glands that usually look like white, pinpoint spots on the nose, chin, and cheeks. They disappear over time.

Miliaria is another name for heat rash, which can show up as fine pink pimples usually on the face or in skin folds. If your baby is affected, give her frequent, cool baths or sponge baths to help open her pores. Sweating from overwrapping may cause miliaria, so the best prevention is to keep your baby dry and cool.

Newborn Jaundice

Jaundice is a common condition in newborns. It's caused by the liver's inability to efficiently process the by-products of old, broken-down red blood cells (bilirubin), giving the skin and the whites of the eyes a yellowish color. Newborns are born with lots of red blood cells and often immature livers that are slow to process large amounts of bilirubin. (After processing through the liver, bilirubin is eliminated in the stool.) This condition often appears within a few days after birth and disappears once the liver becomes more efficient (usually a week after birth).

If jaundice appears within the first twenty-four hours after birth, it might be related to a difference in blood types between you and your baby, and may need closer monitoring and more aggressive treatment. Regardless, your baby will be observed closely in the hospital or birth center for the development of jaundice. It usually presents in a head to toe direction. It's felt that the lower on the body the jaundice appears, the higher the level of bilirubin is.

Because jaundice often appears after babies leave the hospital or birth center, your baby's caregiver should check her a few days after the birth and look for signs of jaundice. Sometimes a caregiver will monitor a newborn's bilirubin level with blood tests. In many cases, no treatment is necessary. Parents need only to make sure their child is feeding well and peeing and pooping often, and to watch for any signs that the condition is worsening (for example, the skin and eyes stay or become more yellow, the baby develops a high-pitched cry, or she becomes sluggish and irritable). If the jaundice persists or worsens, the newborn may be covered with a special blanket to lower the level of bilirubin or placed under special lights. These "blue lights" are a particular wavelength that has been shown to speed up bilirubin breakdown. Indirect sunlight through a non-tinted window will also hasten bilirubin breakdown. Although rare, if left untreated severe jaundice can cause hearing loss, mental retardation, and behavior problems.

Although breastfed babies may acquire jaundice more often than formula-fed babies, *this is not a reason to discontinue breastfeeding.* Sometimes the condition results when the baby doesn't consume enough breast milk and becomes dehydrated, either because she's having trouble latching on or because the milk supply is low. In either case, more frequent feedings and getting help with breastfeeding should increase the baby's milk consumption. Other times, the condition results when breast milk affects the elimination of bilirubin (breast milk jaundice). Usually, the jaundice gradually decreases, but breastfed babies can have mild jaundice for several weeks. This condition is rarely harmful, and most often caregivers recommend that moms continue to breastfeed exclusively, although

it's possible a caregiver may recommend that a mom interrupt breastfeeding for a day or two to let her baby's bilirubin levels decrease. In this case, she should pump her breasts to maintain a steady milk supply. (See pages 63–64.)

Newborn Rashes

Within a few days after birth, many newborns have a common rash called erythema toxicum. These splotches or pimples often appear on the chest, back, or face and disappear without treatment.

Another benign newborn rash is neonatal pustular melanosis. It produces small blisters that dry and peel, leaving freckle-like marks.

It is normal for the skin to become dry and crack and peel within the first week. This will resolve by itself.

Sacral Dimple

It's not uncommon for a baby to have a dimple located at the top of or just below her buttock crease. Usually this is shallow and of no consequence, but it may be an indicator of underlying developmental problems of the spine or spinal cord. Your care provider will let you know if any further evaluation is indicated.

Hernia (Groin or Inguinal)

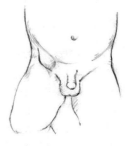

A groin or inguinal hernia develops when a small opening in the lining or wall of the abdomen allows part of the intestine to bulge outward—in boys into the scrotum (testicular sac) and in girls into the groin. It is much more common in premature babies and in boys. The groin or scrotum will appear larger than usual on one or both sides and will likely enlarge even further when the baby is crying due to pressure from within. Surgery is usually done to prevent the intestine from becoming stuck, swollen, or twisted outside the abdomen.

Hernia (Umbilical)

Some babies will have a persistent opening in the abdominal wall muscle where the umbilical cord was, called an umbilical hernia. Tissue from within the abdomen may bulge outward especially when the baby cries from the pressure within. Most of the time, this opening gradually closes on its own. There is no need to try to keep the tissue from coming in and out.

Hydrocele

A hydrocele is a swelling from excess fluid around a baby boy's testicle(s). It can mimic a hernia because the testicle appears large. To uncover whether your baby has a hydrocele or a hernia, your caregiver may hold a light next to the scrotum. If it glows, it will suggest the swelling is from fluid, not the intestine. Your caregiver may continue to observe it, but hydroceles usually disappear without treatment within the first year.

Hypospadias

Some baby boys are born with the penile opening for urine (the urethra or meatus) located on the underside, rather than at the tip, of the penis. This often requires corrective surgery at a later time (most commonly done around twelve to eighteen months of age). These babies should not be circumcised because the foreskin tissue may be needed for the procedure.

Undescended Testes

Normally, a baby boy's testes descend into the scrotum in utero and their presence can be felt at birth. Sometimes, however, one or both of the testicles is slow to descend and is located higher in the groin or even in the abdomen at the time of birth. If the testicles do not proceed to descend on their own, surgery may be indicated later in the first or second year.

Misshapen Feet/Curved Legs

Having feet that appear turned, misshapen, or "pigeon toed" is common in newborns because of their position in the uterus. This condition (also called intoeing) usually corrects itself before the end of the first year. Most caregivers don't recommend treatment in the first year unless there are also other foot deformities. If the feet are rigid or can't be straightened with movement, or if there are underlying bone abnormalities, casting or surgery may be necessary.

Tongue-tie

With this condition, the cord of tissue (frenulum) attaching a newborn's tongue to the floor of her mouth may be shorter and tauter than usual, limiting the tongue's forward movement. Rarely, cutting the frenulum may be suggested to correct the problem if it interferes with suckling.

Wrist Lesions

Newborns can produce lesions by sucking on their wrists while in the womb. They'll disappear without treatment over time.

Newborn Exams and Procedures

Your newborn will be examined in the hospital or birth center for a variety of reasons. Some exams and procedures take place immediately after birth, and some are delayed until just before you head home, when your baby is more settled. These routine procedures are no cause for alarm, and what ones are required varies from state to state. Contact your state's department of health to learn what tests it requires. Discuss and research any concerns or questions you may have about these tests. In almost every state, parents have the right to refuse any or all tests for their newborns.

Drying Off and Skin-to-Skin Contact

If you have a vaginal birth, your baby will be dried off immediately after the birth and should be placed onto your stomach. This skin-to-skin contact will help warm your baby and start the bonding process. If you plan on breastfeeding, this is a good time to begin. In many hospitals, evaluations can take place while you hold your baby.

If you have a cesarean birth, your baby likely will be dried off by a member of the medical staff while you're getting stitched up. Once the staff suctions her mouth and nose, and performs the necessary evaluations, your baby can be placed onto your stomach for skin-to-skin contact. If you're too tired, your partner may be able to hold your baby to his or her skin. You can begin to bond with your baby and breastfeed once you've recovered.

Cord Clamping

After delivery, the umbilical cord will still be attached to the placenta. It may pulsate as it continues to provide oxygen to your baby, who is beginning to take her first breaths. Once your baby is breathing on her own, the cord will be clamped and cut. The clamp will be removed in the next day or two, after it has dried. The remaining stump will fall off in the next weeks.

Cord Blood Banking

It can be prearranged to collect a sample of cord blood by leaving the placenta side of the cord unclamped. Cord blood contains primitive early blood cells (stem cells) that can be sent in a pre-ordered kit to a cord blood bank where the cells are separated and stored cryogenically. There are both private, for-profit and public nonprofit banks that list with a national registry. If you have a close family member or relative with a disease that may require a bone marrow transplant as treatment, it might be helpful to arrange to store blood in a private bank. Otherwise, the American Academy of Pediatrics (AAP) does not recommend collecting and storing cord blood in private banks at this time. You may want to consider sending blood to a public registry if the option is available, but be aware that this blood would not be available for your child in the future.

Eye Care

When a baby passes through the birth canal, her eyes may catch any infections the mother is carrying there. Some infections can cause blindness, so to prevent them a caregiver commonly administers eye drops or erythomycin ointment in the newborn's eyes.

Vitamin K Shot

Shortly after birth, a caregiver will inject your baby with vitamin K, which increases her body's ability to clot blood. This shot is meant to prevent serious bleeding problems until your baby can process vitamin K on her own.

Apgar Tests

Immediately after the birth, a caregiver will evaluate your baby using the Apgar scale (see below), which indicates your baby's well-being. The caregiver will observe your baby's heart rate, respiratory effort, muscle tone, reflex irritability (or response), and skin color. Then he or she will record a score of zero to two for each of these five areas, first at one minute and again at five minutes after birth. Don't be overly concerned about your baby's performance: A perfect score of ten is unusual, and scores over seven are just fine. Even lower scores are seldom cause for alarm.

Sign	0	1	2
Heart Rate	Absent	Slow (under 100 beats per minutes)	Normal (over 100 beats per minute)
Respiratory Effort	Absent	Slow, irregular	Good, crying
Muscle Tone	Limp, floppy	Some flexing of extremities	Active, spontaneous motion
Reflex Irritability (Response to catheter or bulb syringe in nostril)	No response	Grimace	Cough or sneeze
Color	Blue, pale	Body pink, extremities blue	Completely pink

Identification

Soon after delivery, a nurse will put a bracelet or tag on you and your baby for identification purposes. She or he also may take a footprint of your baby.

Newborn Exam

Typically, a caregiver will examine your baby thoroughly within twenty-four hours of birth. If you're in the hospital more than one day, your baby will likely get a full discharge examination before heading home. Exams provide an excellent opportunity for you to ask questions and learn. The caregiver will check your baby from head to toe for birthmarks, check her eyes to make sure there are no cataracts, listen to her heartbeat, feel her pulses, test for developmental problems of the hips, check her reflexes (see pages 16–17), and examine the inner organs that can be felt through her soft skin. The caregiver may also conclude whether your baby is preterm or post-term by determining more exactly what her gestational age is.

Hepatitis B Vaccination

Hepatitis B is a serious disease that attacks the liver and can lead to cirrhosis or liver cancer. Since vaccination started in 1991, rates of infection in children have dropped by more than 95 percent. Vaccination guidelines state that babies should receive the first dose of the vaccine at birth, the second dose between ages one and two months, and the third dose between ages six and eighteen months. Babies whose mothers test positive for hepatitis B should be given an additional shot (hepatitis B immune globulin). Consult with your baby's caregiver.

Screening Blood Tests

A caregiver will check your baby for several diseases that could cause serious damage but don't have any visible symptoms. He or she will obtain a blood sample by pricking your baby's heel sometime after twenty-four hours of age and send it to a state public health laboratory for analysis. Which specific tests and how many are screened for varies from state to state. Check with your state's department of health or The National Newborn Screening and Genetics Regulation Center (NNSGRC)'s website: http://genes-r-us. uthscsa.edu/. The March of Dimes also has information and a video at their website (http://www.marchofdimes.com) that discusses the importance of newborn screening.

Following are the most common diseases that are screened.

- Phenylketonuria (PKU): Affecting one infant in twelve thousand, PKU is a hereditary disease that's caused by the body's inability to digest protein normally. Unaffected parents can pass on PKU, which causes mental retardation and organ damage if not treated. Newborns with this disease shouldn't be breastfed (although consuming a very small amount of breast milk may be okay with a caregiver's approval). Instead, they're put on a special formula that's low in phenylalanine, the part of the protein that the body can't digest.

- Galactosemia: This hereditary disease occurs when the body can't use milk sugar (lactose) normally, causing mental retardation, cataracts, and an enlarged liver. Unaffected parents can pass on the disease, which affects one infant in fifty thousand. Newborns with this disease can't be breastfed and must drink a lactose-free formula.

- Hypothyroidism: This condition affects one infant in four thousand and causes growth problems, mental retardation, and lethargy. A defect in the thyroid gland causes hypothyroidism, which is treatable with hormone medication.

- Congenital Adrenal Hyperplasia: This disease is a genetic disorder that results in a hormonal imbalance and affects one infant in fifteen thousand. It can cause sexual development problems, hormone problems, and death if not treated with replacement hormones.

- Hemoglobinopathy: This disease causes changes in red blood cells. Sickle cell disease is the most common form of hemoglobinopathy, and it can cause anemia (a low red blood cell count) as well as other serious problems. Sickle cell disease usually affects those of African, Mediterranean, Indian, or Middle Eastern descent, but anyone is susceptible. This test can also detect other forms of hemoglobinopathy. Treatment of some forms of the disease requires medical monitoring and intervention, while others require no treatment.

- Other metabolic disorders: Screening tests can also detect other diseases, including cystic fibrosis and many metabolic conditions like maple syrup urine disease, biotinidase deficiency, and fatty acid oxidation disorders.

Newborn Hearing Screening

The American Academy of Pediatrics (AAP) recommends that all newborns get tested for hearing loss before leaving the hospital or birth center. Severe to profound hearing loss affects one to six newborns out of one thousand, and many affected babies don't have any risk factors that would prompt screening. Intervention for hearing loss is available and recommended by six months of age. A caregiver will use one of the two following procedures to test your baby's hearing:

- Auditory brainstem response (ABR): This test measures how the brain responds to sounds.

- Otoacoustic emissions (OAE): This test measures sound waves produced in the inner ear.

Both procedures are quick (about five to ten minutes), painless, noninvasive, and can be done while your baby is sleeping or lying still. If you don't receive the results before heading home, call your caregiver's office to confirm them. If you can't have your newborn's hearing screened at the hospital, you should have it done before she is three months old. See page 168 for possible warning signs of hearing loss.

Your Newborn's World

Until recently, researchers thought newborns were naturally passive and uninterested in their environment. Today, they're learning that newborns are remarkably responsive and perceive the world almost as well as adults—and in some cases, better than adults. Here are brief descriptions of a newborn's senses and faculties.

Touch

Before birth, touch lets a baby relate to her surroundings more than any other sense. Once born, a newborn is still very sensitive to touch, probably more so than adults. She can perceive small changes in texture or temperature, and she loves warm, soft, firm pressure, especially on the front of her body. Being swaddled (see page 22) or held closely often calms her, and your baby may find a light, gentle massage extremely soothing and comforting (see page 36).

Attachment Parenting

Attachment parenting is a philosophy that supports children forming strong ties with their parents to foster lifelong emotional development and well-being. Birth bonding, breastfeeding, and co-sleeping are a few components of this philosophy. For more information, visit Attachment Parenting International's website at http://www.attachmentparenting.org/.

Close physical contact between parent and baby in the first weeks can promote a newborn's sense of well-being and aids her development in ways that can be measured several years afterward. Breastfeeding lets a mother begin to bond with her child within minutes or hours of birth. Cuddling, kissing, stroking, lots of eye-to-eye and skin-to-skin contact, and other affectionate interactions are wonderful ways for both parents to begin their relationship with their newborn. Because contact is so important, many hospitals and birth centers have relaxed routine procedures so they don't interfere with this bonding. Before you choose your birthplace, ask your caregiver whether rooming-in will be possible.

Sight

Although newborns can see at birth, they best see objects that are about eight to twelve inches (20.3 to 30.5 centimeters) away. This is the distance between a baby's face and her parent's face during feeding or cuddling. Beyond that distance, newborns see only brightness and movement, and many have crossed eyes, a normal condition in early infancy (see page 154).

Newborn eyes may track an object moving slowly from side to side or, with more difficulty, an object moving up and down. By the time your baby is two months old, her eyes should track objects that move slowly in any direction. If you have any concerns about your baby's sight, ask her caregiver to test her vision. Crossed eyes, however, are usually normal during the first two months.

Newborns observe the world with unlimited interest. They'll often stop feeding to stare at objects, especially patterned objects and those with sharply contrasting colors. Soon they'd rather look at faces than anything else. (To a newborn, an object is a face if it's round and seems to have a hairline, eyes, and a mouth.)

Hearing

Most babies are born with well-developed hearing. Within ten minutes after birth, a baby can locate a sound source, and she seems to prefer high-pitched voices and rhythmic, soft sounds. Loud noises should startle a newborn or make her move (see page 16). She seems to respond to sounds that last at least ten seconds. Sometimes, a sound will intrigue her so much that she'll stop feeding to pay more attention to it.

Most states require hospitals and birth centers to test a newborn's hearing shortly after birth. Parents should receive the results of the test before heading home. (If you don't, ask for them.) If you have any concerns about your child's hearing, talk with her caregiver. (See pages 168–69.)

Smell and Taste

Researchers know little about a newborn's sense of smell or taste, mostly because it's difficult to tell when a baby discriminates between one smell or taste and another. Foul odors usually upset a newborn. And she seems to react to sweet, sour, and salty tastes, and can differentiate among plain, slightly sweetened, and very sweet water.

Intelligence

Babies are born with a keen, discriminating interest in their environment. They can choose to pay attention to one object and ignore others. They soon can combine touch, sight, and hearing into meaningful patterns.

At first, a newborn's short memory won't let her remember an object if it doesn't reappear within two-and-a-half seconds. She reacts to various stimuli in the same way, like sucking a finger, but she often reacts with her whole body to a change in her environment, like a drop in temperature.

Sociability

Although babies are aware of only their existence, they find people interesting. They crave eye, vocal, and physical contact with others, especially their parents. By the end of the first week, a newborn might recognize a parent's voice, and by two weeks she can know her parents by sight. By the end of the first month, she may behave differently with her parents than with other people. Some babies smile either during sleep or when awake, though it's likely not intentional.

Reflexes during the First Year

A newborn's reflexes are her spontaneous, automatic responses to external or internal stimuli. They're the building blocks of intelligence and the foundation of physical coordination. Some reflexes, like gagging and blinking, are lifelong. Others, like grasping and stepping, disappear or "go underground" only to reappear later as consciously controlled activities. Your baby's caregiver will check for these reflexes to make sure she has a healthy nervous system.

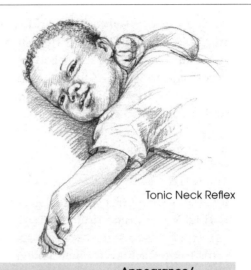

Tonic Neck Reflex

Reflex	What Triggers It	Description	Appearance/ Disappearance
Startle (Moro)	External stimuli, like sudden changes in light, noise, movement, or position. Internal stimuli, like crying or muscle twitches during sleep	A newborn will fling out the arms and legs, then quickly pull them into the chest while the body curls, as if to cling.	Tapers off in 1 to 2 months and disappears by 3 to 6 months.
Sucking	Touching a part of the baby's mouth or cheek with a nipple or finger.	The baby's lips pucker while her tongue curls inward.	Is present before birth and strongest in the first 2 months. After this it fades, merging gradually with voluntary activity.
Rooting (Searching)	Stroking a cheek or an area around the mouth.	The baby's head turns in the direction of the stroking and searches with the lips for a nipple. The baby uses this reflex to seek food.	Continues while the baby is nursing, but usually gone by 4 months.
Tongue Thrust (Extrusion)	Touching the baby's lips.	The baby's tongue automatically moves forward when her lips are touched. This protects her from choking, and aids feeding from the breast or bottle.	Often fades around 4 months.
Grasping (Palmar, Plantar)	Stroking the palms of the hands or pressing the balls of the feet at the bases of the toes.	The baby's fingers or toes curl as if to hold onto an object.	Decreases noticeably after 10 days and usually disappears around 4 months. May continue in the feet until 8 months.
Stepping	Holding the baby in a standing position and pressing down a little.	The baby lifts each foot in turn, as if to walk.	Diminishes after 1 week and will disappear in about 2 months.
Placing	Holding the baby's shins against an edge.	The baby tries to step upward to put her feet on the surface of a table or bed.	Disappears in about 2 months.

Reflex	What Triggers It	Description	Appearance/ Disappearance
Tonic Neck (Fencing)	Laying the baby on her back	The baby's head is turned to one side while lying on her back. The arm on the side that the face is turned toward extends straight out, and the other arm flexes in a kind of fencer's pose.	Most obvious at 2 to 3 months and disappears at around 4 months.
Blinking	Bright light, touching an eyelid, or sudden noise.	The baby's eyelids open and close rapidly.	Permanent.
Gagging	Foreign matter in the respiratory system.	The baby chokes, gasps, spits up, and may turn blue. (Even when the head is under water, the reflex in most cases prevents infants from breathing in.)	Permanent.
Swallowing	Food in the mouth.	The baby's trachea closes while the esophagus opens.	Permanent.
Withdrawal	Pain, cold air.	The baby tries to pull away while drawing in her limbs close to the body.	Permanent.
Parachute	"Diving" the baby toward the floor.	The baby extends hands out for protection.	Appears around 7 months after birth.

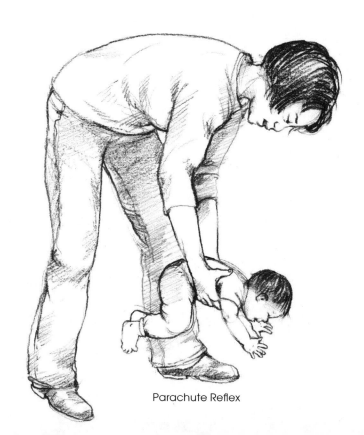

Parachute Reflex

Chapter Two

Caring for Your Baby

Here are a few activities that are part of daily life with a newborn: feeding him, changing his diapers, dressing and undressing him, comforting him when he's fussy, and putting him to sleep. This routine won't change much during the first year. On his first birthday, your child will be just as incapable of changing his own diaper as he was when he was a week old.

When you change that first diaper, you may feel as helpless as your baby. You're nervous (especially if someone besides the baby is watching you), and each movement seems awkward and unnatural. Bath time may also give you the shakes, and dressing your baby for his first outing may seem to require at least four hands.

This chapter will help you handle these everyday tasks. With practice, you'll soon be dressing your baby in no time, calming him in seconds, and changing his diapers in your sleep. While doing these basic tasks for your baby, you'll also develop patience, the ability to multitask, and the resourcefulness needed to amuse a baby during his umpteenth diaper change.

These tasks give you the chance to bond with your baby. Bathing and diapering let you hold him, make plenty of eye contact with him, sing him special songs, and play silly games with him. Rocking him to sleep can be one of the most blissful activities of your day. Soon you'll find that doing these tasks lets you experience the joys of parenthood.

At the end of this chapter, parents who will eventually return to work can learn how to find reliable, competent daycare for their baby.

Handling Your Baby

Healthy babies aren't as fragile as you may think. Don't be afraid to touch, hold, rock, and cuddle your baby as often as possible. And don't let the soft spots (fontanels) on his head prevent you from holding, stroking, and caressing him. The thick membranes covering them are designed to protect his head until the skull bones fuse. You may notice pulsing veins under the skin of the soft spots—don't worry; that's normal.

Holding Your Baby

Holding your baby gives him physical and emotional security, and aids his development. Touching and talking to him will make you comfortable with each other, so don't worry about spoiling your child by holding him whenever possible. (Besides, you *can't* spoil a newborn because every "demand" he makes is really a need, not a want.) Here are the best ways to hold your baby:

Option 1: Cradled in your arms.

Option 2: With your baby's head nestled against your shoulder while you support his back with one hand and his bottom with the other.

Option 3: Carrying him as you would a football. Lay your baby on his back along one of your arms, close to your side, and cradle his head with your hand.

Picking Up Your Baby

During the first three or four months, it's important to support your baby's head when you pick him up and lay him down. He can't support his own head; his neck is too weak and his head is too heavy. Also, if you pick him up slowly and gently, you're less likely to startle him.

Option 1: If he's lying on his back, slide one hand under his neck and spread your fingers to cradle his head. Bend at the waist so you can comfortably slide your other arm under him. Lift him slowly in a compact bundle. Don't let his arms and legs dangle.

Option 2: If he's lying on his stomach, put one arm under his shoulder and neck. Cup his chin with your hand. Slide your other arm under his middle and spread your fingers to support his belly and thighs. Lift him slowly in a compact bundle. Or it may be easier to roll your baby gently onto his back and follow the instructions in option one to pick him up.

Note: It's okay for babies to be on their stomachs while they're awake and supervised. In fact, having some "tummy time" every day is important because it encourages a baby's neck and upper body muscle development. But to help prevent sudden infant death syndrome (SIDS), the American Academy of Pediatrics (AAP) recommends that babies *always* sleep on their backs. (See page 40.)

To put down your baby: Lower his head and back while keeping your arms under him. Make sure you support his head. Lower his bottom, then gently slide both your arms from underneath his body.

Swaddling and Rocking

For the first month or two, most babies like being snugly wrapped in a receiving blanket, shawl, or wrapper-type sleep sack. Swaddling provides warmth and resembles the sensation of being in the womb. It can help calm a baby, and it's a particularly good way to soothe a colicky infant (see pages 147–48), especially when you combine it with rocking. Rocking recreates the motion your baby felt while in the womb. Don't rock too slowly; about sixty rocks per minute is a good pace. As they grow, babies eventually won't like to be swaddled and will prefer to move freely.

Step 1: Set a square blanket in front of you so it looks like a diamond. Fold down the top point so that the folded corner comes almost to the middle of the blanket. Lay your baby on his back on the blanket so his head is just above the fold.

Step 2: Take one of the side points, pull it snugly across your baby's chest, and tuck it under his thighs. Then bring the bottom point up over his feet and tuck it under one of his shoulders. Fold this edge down if it comes up too high above the shoulders.

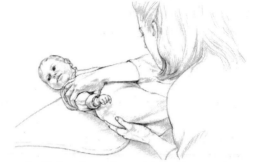

Step 3: Take the other side point and stretch it across your baby. Tuck it under his thighs. At first, you'll probably want to confine his arms so he won't flail them about and excite himself. Later on, you may want to leave them free so he can suck on his fingers and move his arms freely. Make sure your baby's hips aren't too tightly wrapped. He must be able to move, to develop his joints properly.

A Note about Shaking Your Baby

Shaking a baby so his head jerks back and forth rapidly can break his blood vessels and cause irreversible brain damage. If you feel angry or frustrated with your baby, never shake him. Take a deep breath and count to ten, or ask someone to watch him until you can regain control. If you're alone with your baby, put him in a safe place (like his crib) and leave the room for a few minutes to calm down. For more information on this issue, see page 42.

Elimination

Changing diapers will probably never be your favorite task. Diapers leak and can stain clothing. Your baby may even pee on you in the middle of a diaper change. These things will happen, so keep your sense of humor and try not to make comments such as, "Yuck!" Your baby can't control his peeing and pooping (and won't for at least a couple of years), so showing your disapproval or disgust may send him the message he's done something wrong. Remember that the passage of urine and stool "from below" is an important indicator that things are going in well "from above."

Urination

The Early Weeks

Don't be surprised if your newborn seems to always have a wet diaper. It's normal for a newborn to pee within twenty-four hours from birth and then up to thirty times a day. If your newborn stays dry for four to six hours or longer, call his caregiver. The darker your baby's urine color, the more concentrated it is. Dark yellow urine can signify that your baby is not getting enough to drink. A baby's urine can also have a salmon-colored or pinkish tinge to it (referred to as "brick dust" urine). This is not blood, but rather urate crystals, which also can suggest dehydration. Urinating should never be painful. If it ever seems that your baby is uncomfortable, have your caregiver examine him.

The First Year

Starting from the third or fourth day after birth, your baby should wet at least six to eight diapers a day. If he wets fewer, make sure he's getting enough liquid. If he's breastfed, nurse him more often. If he's formula-fed, it's okay to supplement his formula with water (no more than four ounces per day) in very warm weather. If he still isn't wetting enough diapers, have his caregiver examine him. He may be dehydrated (see page XXX).

Bowel Movements

Right after Birth

A greenish-black tar-like substance called meconium builds up in a baby's intestines before he's born. After birth, he'll poop out the meconium, usually beginning within the first day and continuing over the next one to two days, before normal digestion can start. Next to appear are browner, pastier stools referred to as "transitional" stools. The subsequent type of stool varies depending on if your baby is breast- or formula-fed.

The Early Weeks

As your baby adjusts to feeding from the breast or bottle, his digestive system learns to function outside the womb. At first, he'll poop pretty frequently (and sometimes quite explosively), probably after every feeding or even more often. His stools will be loose and seedy or curd-like, and the color may vary. As long as your baby is feeding well and seems content, all these features are normal and don't suggest that he has diarrhea. (See pages 158–59 for more on diarrhea.) By the time he's three weeks old, his stools will have predictable characteristics, and he may poop less frequently.

Red, white, or black stools aren't considered normal. Consult your baby's caregiver if his stools are any of these colors.

The First Year

- The breastfed baby: A breastfed baby's stools are usually mild-smelling, mustard yellow, and loose. They may be greenish or brownish and appear seedy or watery; if they do, there isn't a problem with his digestion as long as he seems otherwise healthy. Because breast milk is so perfectly suited to your baby, it's almost impossible for him to become constipated as long he's breastfed exclusively.

  Be aware that constipation refers to stool consistency only, not frequency (that is, how hard and difficult to pass they are, not how often they are passed. See page 150 for more on constipation.) After the first month, don't worry if he doesn't poop for several days. Even if he strains a bit when he finally does, the poop should be soft. Some babies poop several times day; others, one time every several days. Both situations are normal, and it's also normal for babies to adjust their pooping patterns often. As long as your baby is thriving, there's no need to worry.

- The formula-fed baby: Because formula is less digestible and creates more waste than breast milk, the consistency of a formula-fed baby's stools is more solid than a breastfed baby's. The stools are usually brown or gold with a texture that resembles peanut butter, and they often smell like normal adult stools. A formula-fed baby can poop as often as six times a day early on, but then taper off to once a day (and sometimes once every few days) as he grows. If a formula doesn't agree with your baby, you'll probably first notice irritability and perhaps a change in his stools' consistency.

- When solids are introduced: The American Academy of Pediatrics (AAP) recommends introducing solid foods when a baby is four to six months old. Any solid food that's new to your baby's digestive system may change the smell of his stools, and it may change their color to match the color of the new food (orange stools after eating carrots, for example). In older babies, undigested food may appear in the stools.

Diapers and Other Necessities

Disposable Diapers

Disposable diapers have a waterproof outer liner, an inner core layer with absorbent materials that trap moisture into the middle, and a soft layer next to the baby's skin that keeps moisture away. Some disposables add lotion to help protect the baby's skin. Disposables have tab fasteners and elastic around the legs and waist to further prevent leaks. Have lots on hand when you bring home your newborn, because you'll probably use between 150 and 200 the first month. (Buy a few different brands to start; you'll want to compare them to learn which works best for you and your baby.)

Cloth Diapers

Nearly all cloth diapers are made entirely of cotton (some may include a bit of polyester). Cloth diapers let moisture evaporate and air circulate freely, allowing your baby's body to cool when heat builds. They usually come prefolded (with a center strip more absorbent than the outer strips) or fitted. Although not as popular, flat diapers can be folded in different ways to fit your baby as he grows. Moisture-resistant diaper wraps cover the diaper snugly, and Velcro or snaps fasten most of them. Pull-on diaper wraps are usually looser; they require the diaper to be fastened by snaps, clips, or pins. All-in-one cloth diapers come with the diaper covers attached. If used exclusively, you'll need two to three dozen cloth diapers and three to six diaper wraps.

Changing Area

You'll change your baby's diaper thousands of times before he's toilet trained, so it's important to have a safe, comfortable, organized place for this task. Here are some options for a changing area.

- Changing table: Check that it's sturdy and has a high guardrail, secure safety straps, and a place to store diapers, wipes, and creams. (Open shelves are more convenient than small, high-sided baskets, but make sure the shelves are out of reach of crawling or walking children.) Be wary of ones with flip-open changing areas that extend beyond the main table. The table may topple when a baby is placed near the edge of the overhang.

- Combination dresser and changing table: Again, be wary of ones with flip-open changing areas that extend beyond the main dresser. The dresser may topple when a baby is placed near the edge of the overhang.

- Rail rider changing table: This space saver attaches to the rails of a standard crib. When not in use, one end detaches, and the table hangs flat against the side of the crib. Check for stability and secure safety straps.

- Wall-mounted fold-out changing table: Here's another space saver that can be used for babies up to thirty pounds. Check for stability and secure safety straps.

- Play yard changing area: This removable pad attaches to the rails of a play yard. Check for stability and secure safety straps.

- Contoured changing pad: This thick, waterproof pad comes with safety straps and screws for attachment to a standard changing table. It also can be placed on the floor, dresser top, or elsewhere. If using on an elevated surface, make sure the surface is wide, sturdy, and a comfortable height. Because you can't anchor the changing pad to the surface, be sure the surface is nonslip.

- Portable changing pads: Typically used on-the-go, these waterproof fabric squares or fold-up nylon, vinyl, or plastic changing kits also can be used at home. They're best used on the floor, since they usually don't come with safety straps.

Diaper Wipes, Creams, and Powders

- Store-bought, disposable baby wipes are convenient but expensive. They're fine to use as long as they don't irritate your baby's skin (avoid those with alcohol or fragrance). A cheaper option is to clean your baby with a washcloth and warm water.

- Some parents use a wipe warmer, a heated tub that holds and heats disposable wipes. This isn't a necessity, but your baby may enjoy it.

- Purchase a diaper barrier cream for everyday use. If your baby gets diaper rash, you'll also need a rash cream or ointment (see page 157).

- If you use a powder, make sure it doesn't contain talcum, which can damage your baby's lungs if inhaled.

Diaper Pails

- If you use a diaper service, they'll supply you with a hamper that's lined with heavyweight plastic and includes a professional-quality deodorant.

- If laundering your own cloth diapers, you can use a plastic wastebasket with a flip-up lid, lined with a waterproof nylon laundry bag.

- For disposables, you may want to use a diaper disposer that compacts and deodorizes the diapers. Otherwise, a plastic wastebasket with a flip-up lid will work.

Choosing Diaper Care

Here's a quick look at the advantages and disadvantages of the three main options for diaper care: laundering cloth diapers, using a diaper service, and using conventional disposables. What option you choose will depend on a number of factors, including your schedule, your budget, your feelings about the environment and natural resources, and of course your baby's reaction to various kinds of diapers.

Method	Advantages	Disadvantages
Laundering cloth diapers	• Requires no toxic chemicals (phosphates, bleach, and so on), so won't leave chemical residues that can irritate baby's skin. • Requires water and energy to launder, but less than are used in the manufacture of disposables. • Is often the least expensive option of the three.	• Must be stored until laundered as well as laundered. • Few daycare providers will use cloth diapers. • Can be inconvenient when you're traveling.
Using diaper service	• Saves time. • Requires no rinsing or soaking. • Is less expensive than using disposables. • Laundered in accredited and inspected laundries, so you know diapers are clean.	• Is more expensive that laundering your own diapers. Is inconvenient when you're away from home. • May be hard to locate a service in some areas.
Using disposable diapers	• Ready to use from the package. • Can be tossed in any garbage receptacle (after contents have been flushed down the toilet). • Most daycare providers insist on disposables. • Are very absorbent.	• Is usually the most expensive option. Infrequent changes, perfumes, and other chemicals may contribute to diaper rash and allergic reactions. • Require large amounts of wood, plastics, energy, and water to manufacture. Fill up landfills and take hundreds of years to decompose.

Note: Some parents choose less-common options, like "green" disposables or a diaper-free method called "elimination communication." For information on the former, check out manufacturers such as Seventh Generation (http://www.seventh generation.com) and Tushies (http://www.tushies.com). For info on the latter, see http://www.diaperfreebaby.org

Note: Despite the popular belief that disposable diapers are more hygienic than cloth diapers in daycares, both kinds of diapers can be equally contaminating if they're handled improperly. Daycare providers must consistently monitor and follow strict hygiene procedures (like hand washing and proper storage of soiled diapers) to reduce the transmission of germs.

Diaper Care

Obviously, cloth diapers require more care than disposables, if you wash your own. But laundering cloth diapers doesn't have to be time-consuming or complicated (see the following laundering suggestions). If you use a diaper service, you won't have any diaper care. Simply empty the contents in the toilet, then toss the soiled diaper (no rinsing or soaking required) in the supplied hamper that's lined with heavyweight plastic and includes a professional quality deodorant. A driver will regularly pick up the soiled diapers and leave you clean ones.

Soaking Cloth Diapers

Some parents prefer to presoak cloth diapers before laundering them to help reduce stains. They toss the soiled diapers into a diaper pail or washing machine with cold water and a cleaning agent (usually baking soda, vinegar, or borax), then let them soak for several hours or overnight. Other parents find soaking diapers unnecessary, especially if they use disposable diaper liners to protect the cloth. Some parents figure that diapers don't need to be spotless—they are, after all, *diapers*!

Laundering Cloth Diapers

There are various methods for laundering cloth diapers, but here's a particularly easy, effective routine:

1. Set up a dry diaper pail (a plastic wastebasket with a flip-up lid, lined with a waterproof nylon laundry bag), and toss in the soiled diapers. Keep the lid closed to contain odors.

2. Run the diapers through one cold water rinse (without detergent), then one hot wash cycle using a detergent without bleach (disintegrates fabric), fabric softener (ruins absorbency), or perfume (may irritate baby's skin). Toss in any diaper wraps that need washing during the hot cycle.

3. Machine-dry the diapers or hang them outside to dry. (Sunshine will bleach them naturally.) If line-dried diapers are stiff, toss them in the dryer and run the air-fluff cycle for a few minutes.

4. To dry the diaper wraps, lay them on top of the dryer while the diapers are drying inside, machine-dry them on the air-fluff cycle, or line-dry them. (Don't machine-dry them in a hot dryer; this may ruin them.)

Disposable Diapers

To get rid of a disposable diaper, dump as much of its contents into the toilet as possible. Then roll up and fasten the diaper in a compact bundle and toss it in the garbage, a diaper pail, or a diaper disposer that compacts and deodorizes the diapers.

Diapering Your Baby

Tips

- Change your baby's diaper whenever he has pooped or is fairly wet. Don't feel as though you must change him if he's just slightly wet. Babies pee a lot, and you'll drive yourself crazy if you try to change him every time you detect wetness. As it is, you'll change ten to twelve diapers a day.

- Unless your baby has an especially bad case of diaper rash, you don't have to change his diapers during the night. If he's sleeping peacefully and is covered, a wet diaper won't chill him.

- See page 157 to learn how to treat diaper rash.

- If you're using cloth diapers and your baby pees a lot while he's asleep, double-diaper him (fasten one diaper over another) before putting him down so you don't have to wake him for a change.

- While your baby's navel heals, fold the front edge of the diaper below the navel so it can't chafe and irritate the tender area.

- Always keep a hand on your baby while he's on an elevated changing area. Even a newborn can wiggle to an edge and fall off.

- If you must leave the room in the middle of a diaper change, take your baby with you or lay him in a crib or other safe place.

- Avoid using talcum powder, which can damage a baby's lungs if inhaled. Talcum-free powders, if used, should be rubbed on your hands and then applied to your baby's bottom, not shaken directly on.

Materials

- Diapers with waterproof outer layer
- Cotton balls or soft washcloth
- Warm water
- Diaper barrier cream for everyday use
- Diaper rash cream or ointment
- Cloth or disposable baby wipes (Store-bought baby wipes, which are convenient but expensive, are fine to use as long as they don't irritate your baby's skin.)

Step-by-Step

Step 1: Place your baby on his back on a changing area. Unfasten the diaper and remove it. If the diaper is soiled, roll it up and empty it into the toilet later. With a clean end of the diaper, wipe away any remaining poop from your baby's bottom.

Step 2: Holding your baby's legs, lift his bottom and clean it with a warm washcloth or baby wipe, always wiping from his front to his back. Let your baby's bottom air-dry. Apply a diaper barrier cream. If he has diaper rash, apply diaper rash cream or ointment.

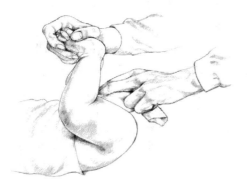

Step 3: Lift his bottom again and place the fresh diaper beneath, with the top edge of the diaper at waist level. With disposable diapers, make sure the tabs are behind your baby. With cloth diapers, fold over any extra material in front for a boy or in back for a girl.

Step 4: Bring the tabs up over the front of the diaper, then fasten them securely at each side. Make sure the back overlaps the front. If you're using pins with cloth diapers, put your hand between the diaper and your baby's skin to avoid sticking him.

Sponge-Bathing Your Baby

Tips

- When you baby first arrives home, give him sponge baths. Don't bathe him in a tub until his umbilical cord has fallen off and the navel has fully healed. Also, if he's been circumcised, wait until his penis has completely healed before giving him a tub bath.

- You don't have to bathe or shampoo your child every day. As long as you keep his face, hands, and genitals clean, two or three baths a week is often enough.

- Newborns sometimes don't like being completely naked. If being naked annoys your baby, wrap him in a soft towel (unclothed or with just a diaper on) and uncover one part of his body at a time to wash it. Or leave him clothed, and remove clothing only when you want to wash the skin beneath it.

- Some newborns don't like to lie still long enough for a complete sponge bath. If your baby squirms, try bathing a different part of him throughout the day; for example, wash a different part each time you change his diaper.

Materials

- Bowl of warm water
- Soft washcloths and a soft towel
- Cotton balls
- Mild, unscented soap
- Cotton swabs
- Gentle baby lotion (optional—some advise no lotions for the first month, to prevent allergic reactions)
- Sponge cushion (optional)

Step-by-Step

Step 1: Place your baby on a sponge cushion or changing area. Moisten a cotton ball with warm water and wipe from the inside of one eye to the outside. Do the same to the other eye with a fresh cotton ball. Moisten another cotton ball and wipe around your baby's ears. Dampen a washcloth and clean around his mouth, chin, and neck.

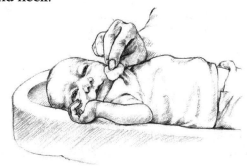

Step 2: Hold your baby's head over a bowl of warm water and gently wet his scalp. Shampoo it with a mild soap, massaging gently with your fingertips, not your fingernails. (Gentle rubbing can help prevent cradle cap—see page 153.) Rinse his head and pat it dry.

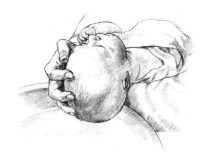

Step 3: Gently wash his chest, arms, and legs. Make sure to get into all the creases in his skin, including those around his neck and under his arms and knees. Wipe his hands and feet; check for lint between his fingers and toes. Also look for long or sharp fingernails and toenails. (See page 36 to learn how to trim nails.)

Step 4: Support your baby's head and gently turn him on his side. Wash and rinse his back. Pat it dry. Dampen a fresh washcloth and wash the genitals. For a girl, spread the labia and gently wash the skin from front to back, then pat it dry. For a boy, gently wash the penis and scrotum, getting into the surrounding creases. Wash carefully around a circumcised penis. If the penis is not circumcised, don't retract the foreskin to wash it.

Step 5: Check the navel for redness or swelling (signs of infection). Know, though, that it's normal for the base of the cord to ooze and stink a bit as it dries up. If your baby's skin is prone to dryness, warm some gentle baby lotion in your hands and massage it into his skin. Put a fresh diaper and a fresh outfit on him, and your baby's sponge bath is done.

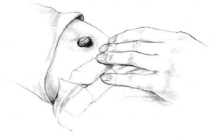

Tub-Bathing Your Baby

Small Tubs

Tips

- At first, your baby might not like taking baths. Continue giving him sponge baths until he's a little older, then try giving him a tub bath. Eventually, most babies love taking tub baths.

- As with sponge baths, you don't need to bathe or shampoo your baby every day. As long as you keep his face, hands, and genitals clean, two or three baths a week is often enough.

- Never take your eyes off your baby while he's in the tub, no matter how short a time and how little water you're using. If you must interrupt the bath to answer the door or phone (or whatever), quickly wrap him in a towel and take him with you.

Materials

- Portable baby tub with sponge cushion (A plastic dish tub will work for a smaller baby. You can also bathe your baby in the kitchen sink as long as you can rotate the faucet away from the sink.)

- Table or countertop at a convenient height

- Soft washcloths and a soft towel

- Gentle, unscented soap

- Baby shampoo

The Big Tub

- When your baby is too big for his baby tub and he can sit up steadily on his own, he's probably ready to bathe in a regular bathtub.

- Run only a few inches of water in the tub to reduce the risk of drowning or even unintentional dunking. *Never leave your baby unattended in the bath.*

- Always test the bath water before putting your baby in the tub. It should feel pleasantly warm. Keep him away from the faucets; one turn of the hot water tap and he could scald himself. After drawing the bath, run a little cold water so the faucet won't burn your baby if he touches it.

- At first, you may want to bathe with your child so you can better keep a hand on him. (This way, you also don't have to kneel on a hard tile floor and bend over throughout his bath.) Later on, you can place nonslip strips on the bottom of the tub to help keep your baby steady.

- When your baby can stand, don't let him do so in the tub without keeping a hand on him.

Step-by-Step

Step 1: Run about two inches (5 centimeters) of warm water in the tub, then check the water temperature to make sure it's pleasantly warm. Extreme temperatures can scald, burn, or shock an infant. Gently ease your baby into the tub, bottom first.

Step 2: Wash your baby's face, ears, and neck with a soft washcloth and gentle soap. Work your way down his body, washing him just as you would with a sponge bath. (See page 31.) Rinse well.

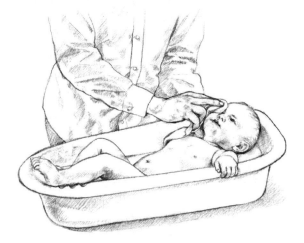

Step 3: Support your baby in a reclining position and shampoo his head, working from front to back so the shampoo doesn't get into his eyes. Rub the scalp firmly but gently with your fingertips. Rinse well, then pat him dry with a soft towel.

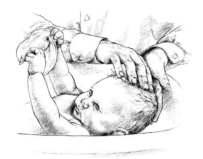

Skin Care

An occasional bath with a mild, unscented soap, a thorough rinse, and being patted dry with a soft towel is all the skin care your baby needs. Some parents apply powders and lotions to make their babies smell good and keep the skin from drying out or chafing. These products aren't necessary (and some caregivers advise against their use in the first month); the best way to avoid dry skin is to not bathe your baby too often. In general, use skin care products sparingly and heed the following warnings:

- Baby (talcum) powders and cornstarch: Baby powder can get into your baby's lungs, swelling and irritating them and possibly causing breathing problems. It can also inflame the skin affected by a diaper rash. Some research suggests that cornstarch can cause or exacerbate yeast infections.

- Baby lotions and natural oils: While these products aren't needed, your baby may love being gently massaged with a little lotion or oil after his bath. (See page 36.) Avoid mineral oils: They can cause a rash on some babies.

Navel

Before your baby's umbilical cord stump falls off, make sure you keep the area clean and dry. Give him sponge baths only, and make sure his diaper is turned down away from the area. You don't need to clean the area with rubbing alcohol; in fact, many hospitals no longer recommend this treatment.

The stump usually falls off between two and fourteen days after birth. (If it doesn't fall off by three weeks, have your baby's caregiver examine it.) When it does, it leaves a raw spot that can take several days (or even weeks) to heal. There's no need to bandage the area. Keep it clean and dry to prevent infection. A little secretion or pinkish discharge from the navel is normal, but tell your baby's caregiver if there's any bloody discharge that continues for more than a week, any profuse bleeding, or any red swelling. Sometimes the cord will continue to ooze a moist yellow discharge. This is an umbilical granuloma; it usually can be treated in the caregiver's office with a silver nitrate cautery stick. If this doesn't work, the caregiver may use surgical thread to remove it.

Penis

Circumcised

The tip of the penis will be red and swollen up to a week after circumcision. A yellow or gray coating may appear on the tip of the penis where the foreskin was cut. If a scab is present, let it fall off on its own. It's normal for the wound to ooze a few drops of blood. Until it's completely healed (usually within a few days but possibly up to a week), wash the tip by dripping warm water on it, then pat it dry. When you change your baby's diaper and after every bath, dab the tip with a barrier jelly or place a piece of gauze smeared with barrier jelly on it. Once it's healed, you can wash it normally and can stop using the jelly.

Contact your baby's caregiver if you notice any of these warning signs:

- Your baby doesn't pee normally within six to eight hours after the circumcision.

- The tip of the penis is persistently swollen, bleeding, or red.

- The tip leaks foul-smelling fluid or develops crusted, fluid-filled sores.

Natural (Non-circumcised)

The natural penis requires no special care. Wash it as you would any other part of your baby's body. Don't try to retract the foreskin; the head of the penis doesn't need cleaning. Natural secretions clean it very efficiently. These white secretions aren't dirt or pus; they're healthy skin debris that'll eventually separate the foreskin from the head by the time your child's five or six years old (but possibly not until adolescence).

As with any other part of his body, contact your baby's caregiver if the penis and foreskin is very discolored, emitting an unusual discharge, or bleeding.

Vagina

There may be some blood passed through your baby's vagina in the first few weeks. These "mini-periods" are from maternal hormones and will go away on their own. It is not necessary to scrub away all of the whitish secretions that accumulate in the folds of the vaginal tissue.

Baby Massage

Babies are especially sensitive to touch, so your baby may find a light, gentle massage extremely soothing and comforting. You can massage a little baby lotion or natural oil into your baby's skin after his bath. (Set the bottle in his bath water to warm the lotion or oil.) Slowly, gently, and rhythmically massage his neck, then massage down his body to his feet. Don't forget his arms and hands. Turn him over and massage his shoulders, back, and buttocks. Finally, massage his forehead and down his face. Many hospitals and community centers offer classes on baby massage.

Trimming Fingernails and Toenails

Keeping your newborn's fingernails and toenails short protects him—and you! As he explores with his hands and feet, long and ragged nails can scratch his face and body as well as yours. Short fingernails are also a health precaution; dirt collects under long fingernails, and it'll be years before your baby quits putting his fingers in his mouth.

Here's what to do when you cut your baby's nails:

- Use baby nail clippers. Make sure there's enough light to see what you're doing. Before clipping, press the skin away from the nail to avoid clipping the fingertip.

- Trim the fingernails or toenails when your baby is asleep or after a bath, when his nails are softer and easier to cut. You may even be able to peel away the edge of the nail.

- Cut fingernails and toenails straight across. Make sure you leave no ragged edges.

- Some moms nibble their babies' nails, especially while nursing.

If you do clip a fingertip, don't worry. Nearly every parent does it at least once. Wrap a facial tissue around your baby's finger and hold it above his heart. The bleeding will likely stop in a couple of minutes. If it takes longer than that, your child is probably still okay. Put him someplace safe where you won't mind some possible bloodstains. Although putting on a bandage seems logical, try not to do so, especially on a fingertip. Bandages can easily come off fingers and toes, and can become choking hazards to babies.

Sleep

Functioning on less sleep is one of the biggest adjustments parents of newborns have to make. As your baby grows during the first year, he'll sleep through the night more often, which means you will, too. But it may take a few years before your sleeping is back to its prebaby schedule.

Sleep needs and habits vary among babies. Your newborn may sleep for twenty-two hours a day or only twelve. He may sleep for several uninterrupted hours or for only one hour at a time. (Keep in mind that newborns usually need to feed every two to four hours around the clock.)

Even though you may think he sleeps too little or too much, he's probably getting enough if he's healthy. You probably can't resist checking on your baby as he sleeps, especially if you hear his snuffling and fretting. Don't let these normal noises alarm you.

As the first year progresses, your baby may take a couple naps during the day, then sleep for a stretch of time at night. (See page 40 to learn more about sleeping through the night.) Not long after his first birthday, he may even give up one nap. The older your baby gets, the more active he'll be during the day, especially when he starts crawling and walking. And the more energy he expends during the day, the easier he may fall asleep at night.

Bed Options

Your newborn will need a safe place to sleep. Many parents use cribs, but other options work just as well. Even a lined basket, padded drawer, or sturdy cardboard box will work, as long as the sides are high enough to prevent the baby from rolling out. Some parents choose to have their babies sleep in the same room with them, a practice called co-sleeping. Research suggests that co-sleeping promotes bonding and breastfeeding and perhaps prevents sudden infant death syndrome (SIDS).

It is not recommended, however, for babies younger than six months to sleep in the same bed as parents (bed-sharing), as this may increase the risk of SIDS and accidental smothering. There is also a risk of the baby falling, or getting wedged between the bed and the wall or headboard.

There are specially designed baby beds (co-sleepers) that fit next to the parent's bed and make for easy access for feeding and comforting. (See below and page 103.)

Beds

- Crib: A crib can be your child's bed until age two or older. (See page 101 for what to look for in a crib.)

- Bassinet or cradle: Both are compact and portable, but your baby will outgrow them quickly. Babies about one month old or ten pounds will usually need a crib. (See page 102 for what to look for in a bassinet or cradle.)

- Bedside co-sleeper: These are perfect for parents who want their baby to sleep in the same room as them. Some bedside co-sleepers can convert into freestanding bassinets, changing tables, and play yards. (See http://www.arms-reach.com for more information).

- Play yard: This convenient, portable product is great for travel because it can be used as a crib, bassinet, changing table, and play area.

Bedding

- Mattress for crib, bassinet, or cradle: Use a firm, nonallergenic mattress, because a soft mattress can suffocate a baby. (An inner-spring mattress will hold its shape longer than a foam mattress.)

- Waterproof mattress pads: You'll want one or two of these pads to place between the mattress and the fitted sheet.

- Fitted sheets for crib, bassinet, or cradle: Make sure the sheet fits tightly and securely around the mattress.

- Bumper pads: Bumper pads aren't recommended because they can suffocate your baby (and can be used as steps to climb out), but if used they should be thin and anchored tightly to the sides of the bed.

- Blankets and pillows: These are also suffocation hazards. Don't use pillows, and if you use blankets, they should be lightweight.

- Mobile: A wind-up mobile can soothe baby to sleep, but make sure it meets safety standards.

Environment

- If your baby's bed isn't in your bedroom, begin a routine of putting him to sleep in his bedroom. He'll gradually connect the routine with sleep time and settle down. Plus, if he's sleeping in another room, his restless sleep periods won't distract you.

- Keep the temperature of your baby's room around 70°F (21°C). A room that's warmer than 70°F may overheat the baby and possibly lead to SIDS. If you're trying to conserve energy or cut your heating bills, turn your thermostat down at night and put your baby in a blanket sleeper. (*Don't* use an electric blanket.) Also, don't position his bed next to a cold window. Instead, set it as close to the heating vent or radiator as safety permits without overheating your baby.

- Besides overheated environments, other factors that can lead to SIDS are soft or loose bedding and co-sleeping on waterbeds or with parents who've consumed drugs or alcohol before going to bed or who smoke while in bed.

- When necessary, use a cool-mist humidifier or vaporizer in winter and a fan in summer, but don't set them too close to your baby's bed. Follow the manufacturer's guidelines to clean the humidifier or vaporizer so it won't contaminate the air with molds. Also, use the purest water you can so any waterborne contaminants won't be spread.

- Your entire household doesn't need to keep silent while your baby sleeps. He'll easily get used to the normal sound levels. Try to avoid, however, abrupt changes in the noise level, which can startle and awaken him.

- To block out outside light as well as summer heat and winter cold, install shades or curtains in your baby's bedroom.

- In comfortably warm weather, your baby can take naps outside, but don't put him in direct sunlight. Drape netting over his bed to ward off insects.

- Always place your baby on his back to sleep to reduce the risk of SIDS.

- Never cover his head while he's sleeping.

- Don't use pillows, comforters, quilts, or other soft or plush items.

- The American Academy of Pediatrics (AAP) currently does *not* recommend that babies younger than six months share a bed with parents. However, if you do choose to bed-share, follow these precautions:

  - Make sure your bed's headboard and footboard don't have openings or cutouts. Your baby's head could become trapped in them.

  - Make sure your mattress fits snugly in the bed frame so he won't become trapped between the two.

  - Don't place him to sleep in your bed alone.

  - Make sure your mattress is firm. Your baby could roll into a depression in the mattress onto his stomach.

  - Don't drink alcohol or take medications or drugs that may keep you from waking and may make you roll over onto him, possibly suffocating him.

  - Don't set your bed near draperies or blinds. Their cords could strangle him.

Getting Your Baby to Sleep

Newborns seem to have three kinds of sleep:

- Quiet sleep (deep and calm)

- Active sleep (accompanied by sucking, grimacing, and rapid eye movements)

- Drifting sleep (drowsily floating in and out of sleep).

Early in his first year, your baby may need help falling asleep. A newborn often has trouble learning to shut out outside stimuli. The best way to help settle your baby down so he can prepare for sleep is to nurse him or give him a bottle. If he's not hungry, try the following ideas:

- Swaddle or rock him until he falls asleep. When he's four months old or so, set him in his bed before he's completely asleep so he learns to drop off by himself.

- Car rides, stroller rides, swings, and holding him as you walk will often lull an excited baby to sleep.

- Use soft, rhythmic background noise. Soft music will work, but so will the drone of a fan, vaporizer, dishwasher, or air conditioner. If you play a recorded heartbeat over and over right after birth, it may remind your baby of life in the womb and calm him. Lullaby recordings with a heartbeat in the background are also available.

- Lay your baby across your lap on his belly and give him a gentle back rub.

- Fresh air often makes babies sleepy. Take your baby outside for a while or put his bed at a safe distance near an open window if it's not too chilly.

Sleep Positions

The American Academy of Pediatrics (AAP) recommends that babies sleep on their backs. Research shows this sleeping position significantly reduces the risk of sudden infant death syndrome (SIDS). (The risk of your baby choking on spit-up or vomit while sleeping on his back is very minimal.)

Staying Awake at Night

Babies don't know that they're supposed to sleep at night and be awake during the day. Some sleep more during the day, which usually means these babies are wide awake and ready to play at 4 A.M.! Here are some things you can try to get your baby sleeping at night:

- During the day, let your baby take his naps anywhere in your home. At night, put him in his own room.

- Don't let him sleep more than four uninterrupted hours during the day.

- Stimulate him during the day by singing or massaging him. But at night, be quiet and calm while attending to him and keep the room dark.

Sleeping through the Night

Some babies seem to master sleeping through the night from very early on and others seem to struggle endlessly with it. In a study of a group of nine-month-olds, less than 20 percent slept without waking at least once between midnight and 5 A.M. Also, because breast milk is easier to digest than formula, breastfed babies often wake during the night to feed.

Parents wonder what to do when their baby wakes at night, if they're sure he isn't sick or hungry. When the baby is younger than four months or so, everyone seems to agree that he must have some need, and it's best if the parents attend to him promptly so everyone can get back to sleep as soon as possible. But when the baby is older than four months, parenting "experts" disagree on the best way to handle the situation. Some believe that the baby should cry himself back to sleep; if parents respond to his crying, he'll expect them always to respond and won't learn to soothe himself. Others feel that parents should always respond to their baby's cries and soothe him back to sleep.

Talk with other parents and your caregiver before deciding how to handle this situation. Babies have different temperaments, and no single solution will work for everyone. You need to feel comfortable with whatever decision you make.

Comforting a Crying Baby

One challenge for new parents is to figure out why a baby's crying and how to stop it. Most times, you can comfort your baby by satisfying a basic need—feeding him, changing his diaper, entertaining him. The following paragraphs describe reasons why a baby may cry and offer some suggestions for comforting him.

Hunger

Often a crying baby is a hungry baby. Crying is his last resort to get someone to feed him. Babies give earlier, calmer cues to show they're hungry, like sucking on a fist or rooting (see page 16), and it's wise for parents to respond to these cues. Food may be what a crying baby wants, but it can be difficult to feed him when he's upset.

Gas in Stomach

To burp your baby, use one of the techniques described on pages 81–82. Some babies need one burp for every three to five minutes of feeding. Some babies are delayed burpers; a half-hour may pass from the end of a feeding to the first burp. If your baby is a delayed burper, be patient and keep trying. He'll eventually pass that gas!

Need to Suck

Most babies are born with an intense sucking reflex. They suck not only to get nourishment, but also to soothe and comfort themselves. If you're nursing your child, the breast is the best source of comfort for him. But if he's clearly not hungry, help him find his (clean) fingers to suck or offer one of your own. Don't give him a pacifier for the first few weeks; sucking on it may interfere with his latch on your breast.

Wet or Soiled Diapers

As you can imagine, having a wet, stinky mess next to your skin is uncomfortable. On average, newborns wet or soil ten to twelve diapers each day. If your baby is cranky, he really may be demanding a diaper change. (Even if a diaper change doesn't stop his crying, at least it's reduced the chances he'll acquire a diaper rash.)

Temperature Extremes

Babies, like adults, don't like to be too hot or too cold. Don't overdress your baby, leave him in drafts, or take him out into cold weather if he's not properly bundled. Dress him as you would to keep yourself comfortable in any environment.

Boredom

Babies, also like adults, can become bored. Your baby's crying may be his way of requesting some stimuli. (See pages 123–25 for ways to entertain a bored baby.)

Overstimulation

A baby's senses can get overloaded if there's *too much* stimuli, however. Loud noises, bright lights, and crowds in particular can overwhelm your baby, causing him to cry. Placing him in a dim, quiet room should solve the problem.

Inadequate Physical Contact

Newborns need lots of physical contact with their parents and other caregivers, and they'll cry if they don't get enough. Remember: It's impossible to hold, stroke, or caress your baby too much. Placing your baby in a front carrier or sling is a great way to keep your baby close to you while keeping your hands free.

Colic

Many babies younger than three or four months have a fussy period almost each day or for several hours at a time when nothing seems to comfort them. If your baby fits this description, he may have colic. See page 147 to learn more about colic and find suggestions for coping with it.

Warning about Shaking Your Baby

Although you may become frustrated by your baby's crying or irritability, *never* shake your baby. Serious injuries (including blindness, brain damage, and abnormal development) occur when a baby is severely or violently shaken or when his head is struck. This represents a serious form of child abuse.

A baby suffering from non-accidental head trauma (or NAHT, also called shaken baby syndrome) may vomit, have tremors, convulsions, or breathing trouble, and become very listless or fussy or even comatose as a result of the injuries. It's urgent that you seek immediate medical attention for your baby if there is any chance that he's suffering injuries from shaking or being hit in the head.

If you're worried that you might be capable of losing control when your baby is crying or irritable, put him down in a safe place such as his crib and let him cry alone. Take a deep breath and count to ten. Seek help from family and friends to give yourself a break and have your baby's care provider examine him to see if there's a reason he's irritable.

Non-nutritive Sucking

Babies are born with a need to suck. Some babies even sucked their thumbs or fingers while in the womb. Sucking lets a baby soothe himself (non-nutritive sucking) or get nourishment. When your baby is fussy and you know he isn't hungry, bored, tired, or in need of a diaper change, having him suck on his thumb or fingers or on a pacifier (but only if breastfeeding is well established) may calm him.

Thumb and Finger Sucking

According to the American Dental Association (ADA), thumb and finger sucking won't harm the development of a baby's teeth or mouth if the sucking isn't too frequent or intense. Most children give up thumb and finger sucking when they're between two and four years old, but they may revert to the habit if they're tired, stressed, or afraid. This is a natural reaction and isn't a reason for concern. If your baby prefers to suck on his fingers or thumb, try to always keep them clean. If your baby is upset and doesn't naturally suck on his fingers or thumb, you can gently guide it to his mouth and see if he'll take it and calm down.

Pacifiers

Essentially, sucking on a pacifier has the same effects and poses the same potential dental problems as thumb and finger sucking. But pacifier use can also make early breastfeeding difficult, because sucking on it may interfere with how a newborn latches onto the breast. Always wait until a baby can breastfeed easily before introducing a pacifier. Pacifiers may reduce the incidence of SIDS, but there's no reason to try to force your baby to take a pacifier. Some parents and experts claim that pacifier use is an easier habit to break than thumb or finger sucking (but kicking the pacifier habit might lead to thumb or finger sucking as a replacement behavior).

Here's some advice about pacifier use:

- Make sure the pacifier is in one piece and has a soft nipple. (Don't use the nipples from bottles. Alone, they're too small to be safe. Even when attached to a ring collar, a bottle nipple may be pulled loose by strong sucking.)

- Check that the shield is at least 1½ inches (3.8 centimeters) across and is made of firm plastic with air holes.

- Use a pacifier that's dishwasher safe.

- Make sure the pacifier is the right size for your child. (Pacifiers come in two sizes: one for the first six months and one for older children.)

- Check that the pacifier doesn't have ribbons attached to it. (Tying a pacifier to a crib or to your child poses the risk of strangulation.)

- Replace the pacifier when the rubber has changed color or becomes torn.

- Don't pop a pacifier in your baby's mouth whenever he's fussy. First make sure he doesn't need something else: food, dry clothes, warmth, cuddling, or whatever.

- If your baby needs to suck a pacifier to fall asleep, he'll probably wake up and cry when it falls out of his mouth. To solve this problem, try to remove the pacifier when he gets sleepy.

- Never dip a pacifier in honey. Your baby may get botulism (a type of food poisoning) from the honey.

Clothing and Shoes for Your Baby

Clothing

Babies grow quickly during the first year, so don't be surprised if your baby rapidly outgrows his clothes. On average, babies double their birth weight in four to six months and triple it by the end of the year. Babies also generally grow eight inches (20.3 centimeters) during their first year.

Baby clothes can be expensive, and it's hard to get your money's worth when your baby is growing like a weed and staining everything in sight or when the clothing is poorly made. Following are some strategies for stretching your baby's clothing budget:

- Borrow clothing from friends and family.

- Use saved clothing worn by your other children (and save clothing worn by this baby for any future children).

- Buy smart:
    - Buy baby clothes at consignment or thrift stores, where you'll often find high-quality, gently used items at great prices.
    - Buy clothes on sale or at outlet stores.
    - Buy big, and keep shrinkage from washing in mind when you buy.
    - Choose multipiece outfits: They provide more flexibility. Larger pieces of the outfit can still be worn when smaller pieces do not fit.
    - Buy clothes that allow for simple adjustments as baby grows larger; clothing that can be let out by snaps, straps, buckles, and cuffs.
    - Cut the feet out of stretchies and have baby wear booties.
    - Look for fabrics that give, like terry cloth and knits.

Unfortunately, baby clothing manufacturers don't adhere to a standard sizing system. Some companies use the labels *small, medium, large,* and so on; others label their clothes by months of age; still others by weight. To make matters worse, the same term can mean different things to different manufacturers. When shopping for baby clothes, look for clothes labeled by weight, or take your baby with you so you can eyeball items for proper fit. If neither of these strategies is possible, use one the following charts to help you choose clothes that will (hopefully) fit your baby.

Size	Height	Weight
General		
Newborn	up to 24 in.	up to 14 lbs.
Small	24.5 to 28 in.	15 to 20 lbs.
Medium	28.5 to 32 in.	21 to 26 lbs.
Large	32.5 to 36 in.	27 to 32 lbs.
X-Large	36.5 to 38 in.	33 to 36 lbs.
By Age		
0 to 3 mo.	up to 22 in.	up to 10 lbs.
6 mo.	22 to 24 in.	11 to 14 lbs.
9 mo.	24 to 25 in.	14 to 16 lbs.
12 mo.	25 to 27 in.	17 to 20 lbs.
18 mo.	27 to 30 in.	21 to 24 lbs.
24 mo.	30 to 33 in.	25 to 28 lbs.

Look for the following features when buying, reusing, or borrowing baby clothing. These features will better ensure the clothes are practical, safe, and comfortable for your baby.

Practical Features

- Long wrist and ankle cuffs to accommodate growing limbs

- Front opening, crotch opening, and/or encased elastic for easy dressing, undressing, and diapering
- Fasteners minimal and easy to manipulate
- One-piece design for speedy change of outfit
- Colorfast dye, including trim
- Machine washable and dryable fabric
- Wrinkle-free fabric
- Sturdy construction
- Full cut, extra limb length, and/or adjustable snaps for growing room
- Accessories (for example, matching bibs, vests, hats, or blankets) usable after baby has outgrown other parts of outfit
- Gender-neutral design that can be handed down to a baby brother or sister

Safety Features

- No drawstrings, toggles, straps, sashes, or belts that hang loosely and pose strangulation hazards
- Roomy but not-too-loose fit (Loose-fitting coats and capes, and oversize or baggy clothing can get caught on furniture, in doors, and so on.)
- Flame retardant fabric or snug fit for fire safety. If your baby must wear clothing that isn't flame retardant, make sure it fits snugly so there's little air between the fabric and your baby's skin. (Air feeds a flame if the fabric is on fire.)
- Absent or securely fastened bows, buttons, appliqués, and/or other trim to prevent choking
- No loose threads that could entangle baby's fingers or toes and cut off circulation
- Generous neck, arm, and leg openings for easy breathing and circulation
- Clearly identified manufacturer in case of questions, complaints, or recall

Comfort Features

- Seams flat, smooth, and minimal in number
- Absent or minimal trim
- Collars, buttons, bows, appliqués, snaps, and/or seams soft, non-bulky, and located where baby won't be lying on them
- Fit that's not too loose or too tight
- Soft, breathable fabric
- No features on inside of clothing (embroidery backing, zippers, stiff tags, and so on) that might irritate baby's skin

Keeping Your Baby Cool or Warm

Babies can have a difficult time maintaining their body temperatures. They produce heat from birth, but need time to develop the ability to conserve that heat. Until he learns to regulate his internal thermostat, here are some tips for dressing your baby so he's at a comfortable temperature:

- In cold weather, dress your baby in layers so you can add or take off clothes as the temperature warrants. For a newborn, a short trip in cold weather is usually fine if he's bundled properly. For a longer trip, your baby may become chilled, especially if he falls asleep. Also, make sure his cheeks aren't exposed for a long time; they get cold quickly.
- In warm weather, parents often mistakenly overdress their baby. Overdressing can cause rashes and dehydration through excess sweating. When you're out of an air-conditioned environment, dress your baby in as little clothing as possible and keep him out of the sun.

Dressing Your Baby

As your baby grows and becomes more active, he's not likely to keep still while you dress him. With practice, you'll learn how to wrangle him into an outfit. But you'll probably also rely on games and songs to keep him quiet and perhaps a special toy to keep him amused.

- To put on a shirt, gather the neck opening into a loop. Slip it first over the back of your baby's head, then forward. Stretch the opening as you bring it down gently past the forehead and nose so you don't scratch his face.

- To pull on sleeves, put one of your hands through the wrist opening and up the sleeve, then grab your baby's hand. With your other hand, pull the sleeve over his arm.

- To take off a shirt, take your baby's arms out of the sleeves first, then stretch out the neckline. Lift the neckline over the nose and forehead, then slip the shirt off toward the back of the head.

- To put on a one-piece outfit, start by spreading it out on a flat surface, then laying your baby on top the outfit. Slide his legs in first, then his arms, and zip or snap it closed.

Shoes and Socks

Before your baby walks, he doesn't need shoes (except to protect his feet on rough or hard surfaces and for warmth). Even when he starts walking, bare feet will help him master the task faster. Babies are born with relatively flat arches. By walking on his bare feet, your baby builds up his arches and strengthens his ankles. Plus, he can use his bare toes for balance. When you decide your baby needs shoes, here are some things to keep in mind:

- A baby just learning to stand may have trouble balancing while wearing shoes. He may fall often until he gets used to them.

- For walking on uncarpeted floors, avoid socks or booties that don't have slip-resistant soles.

- To ensure a good fit, take your baby along when you buy him shoes. Measure the width and length of his feet, then look for shoes that match those measurements. Check the size of your baby's shoes every three months.

- Try on shoes with the appropriate socks for the season. Socks should also fit well. (If they're too small, they can constrict your baby's toes.)

- Have your baby stand or walk in the shoes to see how they fit. There should be ½ inch (1.25 centimeters) of space beyond his longest toe to allow for growth.

- Baby shoes can be expensive, but you don't need to buy the priciest, sturdiest shoes. As long as they fit well and your baby's comfortable wearing them, a pair of inexpensive shoes will work. Sneakers, for instance, are just fine for babies. They're soft, flexible, and less expensive than leather shoes.

Clothing Checklist

Following are the kinds of clothing your baby most likely will wear during the first year. You might not need all of the items, and what and how many items you'll need will depend on how often you do laundry, the season, your baby's age, among other factors.

Item	Number	Description
Soft cotton shirts (with snaps at neck) or undershirts	4–7	These shirts provide extra warmth when worn under other clothing. In warm weather, your baby may be comfortable wearing just an undershirt and a diaper. Some styles come with side snaps, which work great while your baby's navel heals.
Onesies	4–8	These one-piece cotton bodysuits that snap at the bottom make dressing your baby easy.
Stretchies or coveralls (and overalls)	6	These one-piece suits cover your baby from neck to toe and can be worn day or night. The front snaps make it easy to change them, and the stretchy material is comfortable and allows room for growth. Overalls are practical and comfortable for older babies who are starting to creep or crawl. A crawling baby needs extra padding, especially on his knees and bottom.
Dresses		In general, dresses aren't practical for babies. They don't keep the legs warm and often bunch up. If you want your baby to wear a dress, choose shorter ones. Longer dresses tend to get in a crawling baby's way. In cooler weather, pull on stretch tights under the dress.
One-piece pajamas or sleep sacks	4–7	One-piece pajamas are like coveralls made of soft material that's great for sleeping. Avoid those that have plastic on the bottoms of the feet; these can make your baby's feet sweat. A sleep sack is like a cozy sleeping bag for your baby, except it's fitted over his shoulders and has cutouts for his arms. Many come with a wrap piece that helps keep your baby swaddled. Unlike pajamas with feet, a sleep sack can come off and go back on quickly for easy diaper changes.
Socks or booties	4–7	These are used only for keeping your baby's feet warm in cooler temperatures. Babies' feet are naturally cool, so let the temperature guide whether your baby needs them.
Bibs	4	Some bibs slip over your baby's head, and some fasten around the neck. Some even have long sleeves that'll help keep his clothes clean. Some plastic ones have a pocket at the bottom designed to catch falling food.
Caps, bonnets, or hats	1–3	Cotton or synthetic caps or wide-brimmed bonnets work well in warm weather to protect your baby's head and face from direct sunlight. Knitted hats will keep your baby's head and ears warm in cool or cold weather.
Sweater or jacket	1	Usually made of Orlon or acrylic, sweaters are available in front- or back-opening styles. (Wool sweaters are scratchy and can be a pain to launder. Plus, some babies are allergic to wool.)

Item	Number	Description
Snowsuit (or one-piece fleecewear) or bunting	1	Snowsuits are made of heavy, durable material. Many have optional snap-on mittens and hoods. Choose one that's a little big because it'll have to cover your baby's clothes. Avoid slippery fabric—it's hard enough to hold onto a wiggly baby! Buntings are bags made of soft, heavy fabric. They're usually quilted or lined and have front zippers. They're great for outings in cooler weather. Look for one that has a slit for a car seat buckle.
Mittens	1 pair	Baby mittens are knit bags with drawstrings around the cuffs, making them easy to get on and off your baby's hands.
Receiving blankets	4	These soft, lightweight blankets can swaddle or cover a newborn; act as a changing area; and become extra padding when rolled up in a car seat.
Warmer blankets	2	Knitted shawls or blankets, often made of Orlon or acrylic, are warm and washable. They wrap easily and stay tucked around your baby.

Finding a Daycare Provider

The right childcare for your baby depends on your family's needs. You may choose to stay at home and provide the care yourself. Or you may plan to return to work full-time or part-time and arrange for childcare during your working hours.

Childcare options include formal or licensed daycare (daycare center and home daycare) or informal daycare (nanny, au pair, care by a relative, or share care, in which two or more families share the cost of and care by a nanny). Each type of childcare has advantages and disadvantages. You must weigh the pros and cons of each before choosing the childcare that best ensures your baby's safety and well-being, meets your family's needs and budget, and gives you peace of mind.

If you decide to use a daycare center or home daycare, follow these steps to find the best one for your baby. Be patient and prepared to visit many providers. This search may take a lot of time and energy, but don't settle for a less-than-perfect daycare. Remember: Your baby deserves the best care you can find. (For information on babysitters, see Chapter 4.)

Separation Anxiety

At first, your baby might not mind being separated from you and having another care for him. Once he's about seven months old, however, he may develop separation anxiety and stranger fear. If your baby doesn't want you to leave him in a new environment, try to make the transition gradual by not leaving him and walking away suddenly until he seems more at ease.

1. Know what you want. Are you looking for a daycare near your home or your work? Do you want your baby around lots of other kids or just a few? How much can you afford to pay? Will you need a lot of flexibility?

2. Broadcast your search and research your options. Ask friends, family, healthcare providers, coworkers, and houses of worship to help you find the most reputable daycares. Some employers offer childcare referral benefits; check with yours. Call the Child Care Aware hotline at 800-424-2246 to find the phone number of your local childcare resource and referral agency, which can refer you to licensed and accredited centers and home daycares in your area. Check online resources, too. Visit http://www.naeyc.org or http://www.nafcc.org to find daycare guidelines and contact information. If all else fails, check the phone book. The yellow pages will list daycare centers and home daycares in your area.

    If a daycare sounds promising to you, note its name and phone number, the name of the person who referred it, his or her evaluation of it, and what he or she paid for its services.

3. Visit and interview daycares. You can ask basic questions over the phone (for example, about fees and available openings), but you won't know what a daycare is really like until you visit it. The more time you spend interviewing a potential daycare center or home daycare provider, the better. At each interview, note the name of the daycare, the name and position of the person you're interviewing, the daycare's address and phone number, and the date. Trust your intuition and pay close attention to how

the center's staff or the home daycare provider answers the questions on pages XX–XX. After the interview, ask for a copy of policies and a schedule of the day's activities, then record your observations and impressions of the daycare.

> ### Background Checks
> To find companies you can pay to do child abuse, criminal, driving, credit, and social security or work authorization background checks on potential caregivers, use the keywords *background check* in an online search. Another option is to check the Yellow Pages under *investigators* or *security*.

4. Check references. Ask parents why they love a certain daycare. Nothing provides a ringing endorsement of a daycare like other parents' positive evaluations. Ask parents specific questions. Don't simply ask whether they *like* the daycare or provider; ask what exactly they like about the care and what they don't. Here are other good questions to ask:

    *   How old are your kids, and how long have they been enrolled in the daycare?

    *   If your children are no longer enrolled, why did you remove them?

    *   How did you select the daycare?

    *   How has the daycare helped you with normal developmental issues and concerns?

    *   Have you had any problems with the daycare? How have you resolved differences?

    *   Have your children ever been hurt in daycare or not wanted to attend daycare? What happened?

    *   Have you had your children in other care? How do the daycares compare?

    *   What's the best feature about the daycare? Any weak points?

    *   For added assurance, call your state's Better Business Bureau to find out whether any complaints have been filed against the daycare.

5. Make an unscheduled visit. Dropping in unannounced can provide you with a more accurate picture of the daycare's day-to-day operations. Does the care seem as excellent as it did during your formal visit?

6. Visit the daycare with your child. See how he or she and the caregiver(s) interact. Does your child seem comfortable in the environment?

7. Get on the waiting list, if it's an option. If the perfect daycare doesn't have space for your child, securing a spot on the waiting list nearly always means that your child will get in—eventually. In the meantime, ask the daycare to recommend other similar places, and arrange for other care (share care, relative care, or other) until a spot becomes available.

Daycare Interview
Fundamentals and Philosophies

*   When did the daycare open for business?

*   Is the daycare licensed and inspected? Is the license current? Is the daycare accredited?

*   How many children are enrolled? What's the age range?

*   Is there a separate room for infants? How many babies are in the room (preferably six or fewer)?

*   Is the infant-to-provider ratio no more than three to one (two to one for home daycares)? Will the same person care for my baby every day?

- How does the provider stimulate babies throughout the day? Will my baby be kept in a swing or bouncer seat? For how long? Will my baby be allowed on the floor? Is the floor padded? Is the floor cleaned daily?

- What's the daily schedule of activities? Does it include outdoor play? Does it include TV viewing? If so, how much?

- How does the provider and any assistants respond to crying infants? How do they discipline disruptive children? What are some examples? How willing is the provider to follow my discipline guidelines?

- What does the daycare expect from parents?

Provider Qualifications

- What are the providers' educational background, credentials, and training? How about interests, experience, or church or social affiliations?

- How are candidates for positions screened?

- Do all employees undergo federal background checks, including criminal and child abuse checks?

- Must employees pass regular physical examinations and have up-to-date vaccinations?

- Are providers first-aid and CPR certified (including infant training)?

- How much are assistants paid? Any benefits?

- What is the provider turnover rate? What's the average term of employment? (Children need consistency and will form strong relationships with their caregivers.)

- Will I be notified if a new provider takes over care of my baby? Can I request a particular provider?

- Who can I regularly talk to about my baby's development, behavior, and needs? Will my baby's activities be recorded daily? Can I review the log?

- Are visits (expected and unexpected) from parents welcome?

Health and Safety

- What's the daycare's sick-child policy? What if the illness is minor? How will I be notified when my baby is ill?

- How often does the daycare experience outbreaks of serious contagious illness? How will I be notified of an outbreak?

- Does the daycare require a physical examination before accepting a child?

- Does it accept children who aren't vaccinated?

- Has a child ever been hurt while in the daycare's care? What happened?

- Has anyone pulled a child out of the daycare's care? If so, why?

- What is the policy on biting and other child-inflicted injuries?

- What's the protocol if the daycare suspects a child is being hurt at home or school?

- How does the staff manage children with allergies or special needs?

- Will my child's medical records and emergency information be posted in plain sight? Will the staff dispense prescription medications? Where will medications be stored?

- What security measures does the daycare have in place? Does it have a sign-in and sign-out sheet? Are the entrances monitored? What's the policy for having someone other than a parent pick up a child?

- Are fire extinguishers and smoke and carbon monoxide detectors present and in working order? Where are the fire exits? Are monthly fire drills performed?

- What's the cleaning schedule?

- Are cleaning products and other toxic substances locked out of children's reach?

- Are the food preparation and diaper changing areas sanitized frequently?

- How old are cribs, changing tables, and other equipment? How is the daycare notified of product recalls?

- Will babies have their own cribs?

- How often are linens changed? How are they laundered?

- Does the staff make sure babies sleep on their backs, to help prevent SIDS?

- Does the daycare have an enclosed play yard?

- Are the toys age-appropriate? How old are they and how often are they cleaned and replaced?

- Are providers required to wash their hands after diapering and feeding each child?

- How often do they wash the children's hands?

Sleeping, Feeding, Diapering

- Can my baby be fed breast milk? How will breast milk be stored? Will my baby be held during feeding?

- Does the daycare have a place for nursing moms to breastfeed?

- Is there a feeding schedule? A napping schedule? Will my feelings about scheduling be respected?

- Does the daycare provide meals and snacks or should I bring food for my child? What food is served?

- Where and how often are diapers changed? How are diapers disposed? Is the daycare willing to use cloth diapers?

Fees and Operation

- What are the daycare's hours and holiday schedule?

- What's the policy for closing due to inclement weather?

- What are the fees for babies? Are the fees for older children less? How often are fees raised? Are there any additional fees? Will I be charged when I'm on vacation or my child is sick at home?

- Are pickup and drop-off times flexible?

- Will I be charged a late pickup fee? How much?

- How and when will I be billed?

- Will I need to provide supplies for my baby, like diapers and bottles?

- Will the daycare advise me of childcare tax credits and provide receipts?

- Is there an opening for my child? How do I apply?

- Is there a waiting list? How long a wait can I expect?

- Does the daycare give preference to siblings, if I choose to have more children?

References

- May I have a list of families I can call for references? (Make sure the list contains both families currently enrolled in the daycare and families no longer enrolled.)

Observations and Impressions

- Does the daycare have definite rules and regulations, a firm sick-child policy, emergency backup care plan, and staff members with solid, current credentials?

- Are the providers' CPR and first-aid training adequate? Do they appear responsible, enthusiastic, and well prepared? Do they seem to share your philosophies on key parenting issues like sleep, discipline, and feeding?

- Is the provider-to-child ratio acceptable? (See next page.) Do the providers appear to care for the children without difficulty? Keep in mind that an acceptable ratio is compromised if toddlers are always in the infant room, if a baby caregiver leaves to help with the toddlers, or if one of the babies has special needs.

- Do the provider and children seem happy and engaged? Is the general mood joyful and playful?

- Are the children under constant, attentive supervision?

- Do the providers hold the babies? Talk and sing to them? Do they respond to crying babies immediately? When you ask them about individual children, do they seem to know each one and his or her needs and personality?

- Is the daycare inviting and clean? Clutter-free and organized? Does it seem overcrowded?

- Are the rooms adequately heated, air-conditioned, ventilated, and lighted? Are the food preparation, sleeping, eating, and changing areas impeccably clean? How about the restrooms?

- Is the daycare childproofed? (Open cupboards and crawl on the floor—your baby will.) Does the staff observe basic safety rules? Do you notice any safety problems like cords or tripping hazards? Do the crib sheets fit tightly (to reduce risk of sudden infant death syndrome or SIDS)? Is the play area fenced in and away from streets?

- Is emergency information clearly posted? How about phone numbers for the police, fire department, and poison control? Where are the first-aid supplies located?

- Is the environment stimulating? Is the schedule of activities varied? Does TV play a minimal role?

- If the daycare serves meals and snacks, are they nutritious?

- What's the noise level? Is the napping area quiet? Is there background music?

- Does each infant have his or her own crib and cubby space (for pacifiers and other personal items)?

- Do the children's charts appear current, complete, and packed with detailed entries?

- Does the provider seem willing to listen to my concerns and happy to answer my questions?

- Will I feel at ease knowing my child is in this setting?

Caregiver-to-Child Ratios

The ratio of caregivers to children can vary, depending on group size and state licensing requirements. (Contact your state's health and human services department to learn the caregiver-to-child ratios for your state.) The National Association for the Education of Young Children (NAEYC) has set these guidelines:

Daycare Centers

- For infants, the ratio is 1 caregiver for every 3 children if a group has 6 babies, 1 for every 4 if a group has 8 babies.

- For toddlers (age 12 to 24 months), the ratio is 1:3 for 6 children, 1:4 for 8 children, 1:5 for 10 children, and 1:4 for 12 children.

- For children between ages 24 and 36 months, the ratio should be 1:4 for a group of 8 children, 1:5 for a group of 10, and 1:6 for a group of 12.

Centers aren't required to follow NAEYC's guidelines, so ask what each center's ratio is and decide whether it's okay for you. A good center will keep the groups of children small regardless of staff size.

Home Daycares

The NAEYC recommends that a home daycare provider should care for no more than 2 babies (under age 30 months), 5 preschoolers (age 30 months to 5 years), and 2 school-age children (age 5 or older) at once.

Chapter Three

Feeding Your Baby

Feeding a baby is one of the greatest joys of early parenting. There's no more cherished feeling than providing your baby nourishment as she lies nestled warm and relaxed in your arms.

A baby grows more during her first year than at any other time in her life. Her weight generally triples by her first birthday, and she typically grows eight inches (20.3 centimeters) over her first twelve months. (See the weight and length charts on pages 190–91.) What your baby eats determines how well she'll grow.

Research continues to affirm that breastfeeding is immensely important to babies, mothers, and society. The American Academy of Pediatrics (AAP), the World Health Organization (WHO), and many other organizations and experts recommend that babies breastfeed for at least the first one to two years of life. Furthermore, babies should ideally consume only breast milk for at least the first six months. These studies and recommendations have fueled a resurgence of breastfeeding in North America, which was a formula-feeding culture for several decades. Now at least 70 percent of new mothers try to breastfeed.

Breast milk meets a baby's nutritional needs perfectly, and no formula can match it. Plus, no bottle can exactly imitate the breast as the perfect way to deliver milk. If breastfeeding is impossible, however, formula provides adequate nutrition. And it's certainly true that there are formula-fed babies who are just as happy and healthy as breastfed babies. But the evidence strongly suggests breastfeeding betters the chances a baby will enjoy great health, now and for the rest of her life.

To help you make the best choice for your family, the following table outlines the primary pros and cons of breastfeeding and formula-feeding. You'll want to choose a feeding method well before your baby's birth. Both breastfeeding and formula-feeding require some preparation and planning.

Breastfeeding and Formula-feeding: A Fact-based Comparison

Breastfeeding

Pros

- Provides milk that's all-natural, guaranteed safe, and made for individual baby. As the saying goes, "Breast is best."

- Provides optimum nutrition for baby: Breast milk contains just the right amount of fatty acids (DHA and ARA), lactose (milk sugar), water, probiotics and prebiotics, and amino acids for proper human digestion, brain and eye development, and growth.

- Promotes optimum emotional, cognitive, behavioral, and physical development of baby.

- Results in less stinky spit-up and bowel movements.

- Provides baby with antibodies and other cells that help protect against infections of the ears, lungs, and gastrointestinal tract. Newborns are born with immature immune systems that make these substances of special importance. Breastfed babies have fewer physician visits and hospitalizations for illnesses.

- May help protect baby against allergy development.

- Is easy to digest, which means less constipation, diarrhea, and gas in baby.

- Encourages baby's proper jaw and tooth development.

- Provides colostrum to newborn, which strengthens immunity against infection and disease and helps prevent jaundice.

- Adapts to baby's needs, which is especially important for premature or ill babies who require more calories and nutrients. Breastfed premature babies have lower rates of infection than formula-fed premature babies.

- Lets baby decide how often and how much to eat, which lowers the risk of childhood and adult obesity.

- Helps protect baby against a number of terminal and debilitating diseases, like sudden infant death syndrome (SIDS), childhood leukemia, Crohn's disease, meningitis, and juvenile diabetes.

- Helps mom's uterus return to normal size by stimulating production of the hormone oxytocin.

- Burns mom's calories (about five hundred per day).

- Is economical—costs only as much as mom's appetite.

- Is convenient—baby's nourishment is always on hand and ready to eat.

- Is environmentally sound—requires no manufacturing or packaging and produces no waste.

- Is emotionally satisfying and enjoyable for mom and baby.

- Enhances mother-baby bonding.

- Makes traveling with baby easy.

- Helps protect mom against ovarian, uterine, cervical, and breast cancers.

- Protects maternal iron stores due to delay of menstruation.

- Helps protect mom against heart disease and osteoporosis.

- Ensures mom sits or lies down regularly to rest.

- Gives mom regular surges of the "happy, calming" hormones, prolactin and oxytocin.
- The nutritious qualities of breast milk change to match the needs of the growing infant.

Cons

- Must be learned. Though natural, breastfeeding is rarely "automatic." Mastering breastfeeding can be difficult for both mom and baby. Especially in the first days and weeks, breastfeeding can require immense patience and persistence. It is a potential source of inadequate feelings and frustration. *But support and guidance from knowledgeable, empathetic groups, professionals, and family and friends can help moms and babies achieve and continue breastfeeding success.*

- May seem difficult if mom had a cesarean birth. Cesareans can cause milk delay, and the baby might press on mom's incision while feeding. *But with continued feeding attempts, mom's milk will come in, and she can use different positions (such as lying down or the football hold) to keep her baby off of her belly. Women who had cesareans are very likely to be successful at breastfeeding.*

- May draw unwanted attention in public. *But with a little practice, it's easy to breastfeed discreetly. Plus, with more and more women breastfeeding, the sight of a woman nursing in public is becoming more frequent and less shocking. In addition, federal and state lawmakers are currently passing laws that support breastfeeding in public (and in general).*

- May cause mom physical discomfort, like cracked nipples and engorged breasts. *But these problems can be managed or prevented by proper positioning, frequent feedings or pumping, and beneficial routines like breast massage and nipple cream application.*

- Only mom can breastfeed. *It's true that only moms can feed babies at the breast. But today's breast pumps allow moms to express and bottle breast milk anywhere easily and quickly, which lets others enjoy feeding babies mothers' milk and lets moms maintain their milk supply—and nourish their babies with breast milk—after returning to the workplace.*

- May make it hard to tell how much the baby has eaten. *But if the baby is wetting four to six disposable (or six to eight cloth) diapers and soiling three to four diapers in twenty-four hours, then she is probably consuming an adequate amount of food.*

- There are many different ways to learn how to breastfeed, which can frustrate and confuse mom if she feels like she's getting conflicting advice. *But with continued practice, she will eventually find her own personal style and succeed.*

There are times, despite all efforts, that breastfeeding just doesn't work or, rarely, isn't advised (if the mother is too ill and in need of certain medications—your caregiver will let you know if this is the case). If you've done your best and can't breastfeed, don't worry. Your baby will get adequate nutrition through formula-feeding and you can still bond by holding her close during feedings.

Formula-feeding

Pros

- Provides adequate infant nutrition when mother's milk is unavailable (due to mom's absence or illness) or when the baby is unable to metabolize or digest it (if she has a rare condition such as galactosemia).

- Can be fed to baby by anyone without mom's involvement.

Cons

- Is nutritionally inferior to breast milk. Today's formula is still missing about a hundred nutritional components found in breast milk.

- Provides no antibodies.

- Can't be guaranteed safe. Contamination may occur at the manufacturing plant, in the bottles, and on the nipples.

- Can be time-consuming and inconvenient. Toting bottles and preparing and heating formula takes a lot of planning and time.

- Raises baby's risk of illness. Formula-fed babies are ten to fifteen times more likely to become hospitalized when ill.

- Is expensive. The average American family spends between thirteen hundred and three thousand dollars per year to formula-feed a baby. This amount includes the cost of the formula, bottles, nipples, and expected medical visits to care for illnesses.

- Doesn't help mom's postpartum physical recovery.

- Often doesn't promote mother-child bond as effectively as breastfeeding.

Breastfeeding Basics

Physical Preparations

Your pregnant body will naturally prepare your breasts for breastfeeding. Early in pregnancy, your areolas (the base of the nipples) darken. Your breasts enlarge, and your body stores extra fat throughout the pregnancy for the energy it'll need for breastfeeding.

Here are some things you can do to prepare your body for breastfeeding:

- Wash your nipples with water only, not soap. Soap can wash away natural protective oils.

- Don't "toughen" your nipples. Aggressive nipple tweaking may damage the tiny glands in the areola and in late pregnancy could release a hormone that starts labor contractions. (Gentle tweaking—during sex, for example—is fine.)

- Don't use lotions and ointments on your nipples. They can clog pores and cause irritation.

- Wear a well-fitted bra to help prevent future sagging. You can even wear adjustable nursing bras before delivery.

- If you've had breast cancer or breast surgery, especially breast reduction surgery or nipple transplantation, consult a breastfeeding specialist and your surgeon about whether you can breastfeed. You will want to find out if the milk ducts or major nerves were affected by your surgery.

- If your nipples are inverted, talk with your caregiver about breastfeeding. He or she will help you decide if you need to take steps during your pregnancy to prepare your nipples.

- Keep in mind that the size of your breasts has absolutely nothing to do with your ability to nurse. Milk is produced in glands deep within the chest; the fatty tissue that makes breasts doesn't influence milk production in any way.

Emotional and Mental Preparations

While your body prepares physically for breastfeeding, you can prepare mentally and emotionally. First and foremost, it's important to have a positive attitude. Breastfeeding can be difficult at times and your postpartum hormones may make your mood changes more severe, so be sure to avoid naysayers and seek support systems that'll help you initiate and maintain successful nursing. Ask your caregiver or childbirth educator about breastfeeding classes in your area and available lactation consultants (breastfeeding experts who are trained to care for breastfeeding mothers and babies). You can also contact your local La Leche League group or the International Lactation Consultant Association (http://www.ilca.org) for breastfeeding support.

First Feeding

Ideally, you should begin to breastfeed as soon as possible after giving birth—within the first hour assuming all goes well with your delivery. Babies are in an alert stage immediately after birth followed by a sleepy stage for several hours. Your baby should "room in" or stay with you as much as possible while you're at the hospital or birth center. Some hospitals have a special designation as being "Baby Friendly" to declare their commitment to keeping mom and baby together as much as possible.

Make your breastfeeding plans and wishes very clear to the birthing staff.

If you have a cesarean section or difficult delivery, the first feeding may be delayed while you recover, but breastfeeding is still very possible. Ask to hold and nurse your baby as soon as you can.

Colostrum

At first, your breasts produce a thin, rich, yellowish fluid called colostrum. (You can express colostrum by squeezing the areola as early as sixteen weeks into your pregnancy.) This substance is packed with nourishing proteins and antibodies that protect babies from harmful infections. Early and frequent nursing sessions are very important to ensure that the breasts will eventually produce milk. Colostrum isn't voluminous, and you may worry that your baby isn't getting much for all her nursing. Don't worry; a newborn's stomach is the size of a walnut, and it takes only about a quarter-ounce of colostrum to fill it up. Don't supplement her feeding with formula unless her caregiver or a lactation consultant recommends it.

Transitional and Mature Milk

Your breasts start producing milk usually two days (if this isn't your first baby) to six days (if this is your first baby) after giving birth. If you've had a caesarean section, your milk may come in later than after a vaginal delivery. (In this case, keep trying to feed your baby and consult with her caregiver or a lactation consultant.) The milk gradually transitions from colostrum to mature milk. How much milk you produce changes to meet your baby's needs. Breast milk looks a lot like skim cow milk (thin, clear, white), but unlike skim milk, it will separate if stored in the refrigerator. (Gently swirl the milk to mix it.)

Successful Latch

A baby's sucking is a reflex. (See page 16.) Latching on to a breast and suckling, however, might not come as naturally to some babies. These babies must learn how to position themselves correctly on the breast, grip, suck, and swallow while nursing. If a baby frequently sucks on an artificial nipple or a pacifier in the first one to two weeks, she may have trouble latching on properly for nursing (nipple confusion). A correct latch shouldn't be painful (although at first, you may feel some pain for about a minute), should stimulate a healthy milk supply, make milk flow better, keep your baby content, and prevent engorgement. In a successful latch-on, the tongue needs to be positioned under the breast with the nipple and areola drawn in. The lips should not be pursed but turned outward and the mouth opened wide. You may need to express a few drops of milk onto your nipple or stroke your baby's cheek or lower lip. If your baby has trouble latching on, ask your caregiver or a lactation consultant for help. He or she may suggest using a breast pump or nipple enhancers.

"Let-down" Reflex

Generally, milk doesn't flow from your breast the moment your baby begins to suck. Often it takes a few minutes for the sucking to trigger the let-down reflex, which lets the milk flow. When your baby sucks at your breast and you begin to relax, a surge of the hormone oxytocin in your body prompts your milk glands and ducts to let down the milk.

Many women experience this reflex as a tingling, prickling, almost electrical feeling in their breasts. Besides a baby's suckling, it may be triggered by a crying baby, pumping milk, nipple stimulation, sexual arousal, warm showers, or seemingly nothing at all! This sensation fades as the nursing session progresses, and it frequently disappears altogether after breastfeeding for several months. Whether or not you feel this sensation, you'll know your milk is flowing by listening to your baby's regular, satisfied swallows.

During the first few days or weeks of nursing, the same hormone that makes your milk flow will also make your uterus contract and shrink in size. These "afterpains" are normal when you nurse, and they'll stop once your uterus has returned to its original size. They can be a useful indicator of a successful latch-on, and help decrease uterine bleeding. In many cases, afterpains are worse for women who've given birth before.

Supply and Demand

Your milk production is based on supply and demand. The more your baby nurses and the more she empties your breasts, the more milk you'll make. During the first weeks after the birth, let her nurse as often as she wants to build up your breasts' milk production. If she sucks on an artificial nipple or a pacifier too frequently, she may have trouble latching on to your breast and nursing successfully, which will slow down your milk production. If you're giving your baby supplemental feedings (see page 66), she may be too full to nurse as often as is needed to keep up your milk supply.

If your baby is hungry fairly soon after a nursing session, nurse her again. Soon your breasts will produce enough milk to keep her full for a few hours. You'll know she's getting enough milk by tracking the number of wet and soiled diapers she produces each day, starting a few days after your milk comes in. (She should wet four to six disposables, or six to eight cloth diapers,

and soil three to four diapers per day). If keeping up your milk supply is an ongoing problem, ask your caregiver or a lactation consultant for help. He or she may recommend techniques that'll help build up and sustain your milk supply.

Demand Feeding

Nurse your baby on demand—that is, whenever she's hungry. Don't make a hungry baby wait until a specific time to nurse; doing so may upset both of you. Instead, look for her early hunger cues, like alertness or agitation, opening and closing the mouth, thrusting out the tongue, shaking the head, moving the head toward the breast when held, and sucking on a fist (or on anything!). Nurse your baby frequently, sometimes a dozen or more times a day. In the first days and weeks, a minimum of eight feedings a day will be necessary. (When discussing frequency of feedings, time references are from the start of one feeding to the start of the next, not end to start.) Frequent nursing tells your breasts to produce more milk and helps prevent the occurrence of potential problems, such as dehydration and the development of jaundice.

Some babies develop a predictable nursing pattern after two or three weeks. For example, they'll nurse once every two to three hours during the day, with longer stretches, every four to five hours, between feedings at night. This pattern is called "cluster feeding." Not all babies, however, feed at predictable times, and those who do may change patterns if they're having a growth spurt. A growth spurt often signals a baby to suck more frequently, resulting in more frequent nursing sessions, which encourage your breasts to meet her increasing needs. Typically, babies have growth spurts at two to three weeks, six weeks, three months, and six months. These spurts typically last only a few days. A growth spurt, however, is just one reason why a baby may change her feeding pattern. She may change for no obvious reason.

You don't need to wake your baby to nurse unless she's losing weight, has jaundice, or is not feeding frequently enough during the day. (If your baby has jaundice, she may sleep through a feeding time.) Remember: Pay attention to your baby's hunger cues, not the clock. The "right" schedule is the one that your baby dictates so she's kept happy and well fed.

How Long Should Each Feeding Last?

Let your baby nurse at each breast for as long as she wants, which can vary from five to ten to twenty to forty minutes or longer. She'll release the breast when she's full. The length of a feeding often depends on a baby's size and feeding style. Some babies suck vigorously and quickly, and have shorter feedings. Others suck a little, pause, and suck again. Other babies fall asleep at the breast, then wake up and nurse again.

Listen to your baby as she nurses; if she actively sucks and swallows throughout the feeding, she's getting the milk she needs. Also, if she wets four to six disposables, (six to eight cloth diapers) and soils three to four diapers each day, and she seems content after feedings, she's getting enough to eat. (If she's not, ask your caregiver or a lactation consultant for help.)

Taking Your Baby off the Breast

Although it's best not to interrupt a nursing session, you may have to remove your baby from the breast for some reason. To do so, gently slip a finger into the corner of your baby's mouth to break the suction.

Which Breast First?

Your baby nurses most vigorously at the first breast you offer, because she's most hungry when she starts. Strong sucking tells your body to produce more milk, so make sure both breasts receive the signal equally by alternating which breast you offer first. (Stick a safety pin on your nursing bra or use a nursing pad to remind you which breast to offer first at the next feeding.) Opinions vary on whether to feed your baby at one or both breasts per individual feeding. Completely emptying one breast fully at each feed is felt to be optimal to provide the "hindmilk" that is richer in fat than the thinner "foremilk" that comes out first, and important for the best growth and development in the baby. Whatever pattern you settle into over the first few weeks will likely be fine for you. Remember to expect your baby to lose 7 to 10 percent of her birth weight in the days after delivery. She is likely to regain her birth weight by two weeks of age.

Vitamin Supplements

Over the years, medical opinion has wavered on whether breastfed babies need vitamin supplements. Today, the American Academy of Pediatrics (AAP) recommends that parents give their baby a 400 IU supplement of vitamin D each day beginning soon after birth if she's breastfed exclusively (because she gets only small amounts of vitamin D in breast milk). Vitamin D helps build strong bones, strengthens the immune system, and decreases the risk of some chronic diseases such as diabetes. The AAP's recommendation stems from the fact that people produce vitamin D naturally after the skin is exposed to sunshine, and newborns aren't exposed to much sunshine, especially in the winter.

It's also important that nursing moms get adequate amounts of vitamins and minerals in their diets. It is recommended to take a prenatal vitamin or a multivitamin-mineral supplement to make sure your breast milk's nutrition is optimal. (For more about your diet, see page 68.)

Fluoride is a mineral that helps strengthen teeth, and it's recommended for all babies six months old and older. (See pages 132–33.) Talk with your baby's caregiver about fluoride and how your baby can get it (and how much she should get).

Supplemental Feedings

During the first few weeks, focus on getting your baby latching on to the breast and sucking effectively. (In individual circumstances of concern for dehydration, hypoglycemia, or an abnormal degree of jaundice, supplemental feeds via a supplemental nursing system/SNS or bottle of expressed breast milk or formula may be indicated.) After a few weeks, when she's nursing well, you can introduce her to a bottle (containing expressed milk or formula). Offering a bottle once or twice a week won't interfere with your milk production, and it'll let your baby feed well from either the breast or bottle. Remember: If your baby has trouble latching on and sucking, don't introduce her to an artificial nipple or pacifier until later. Sucking on these items will only interfere with her ability to nurse successfully.

Expressing Milk

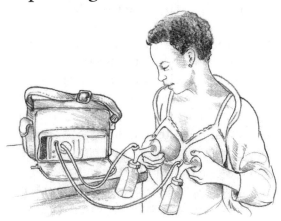

Expressing milk lets people other than nursing moms feed a baby breast milk, and it lets working women maintain breastfeeding. (Learn whether your state has laws about continuing to breastfeed in the workplace—it's crucial to know your legal rights if you encounter resistance from your employer. La Leche League has information on individual state laws.) Expressing milk also keeps up moms' milk production and can relieve breast fullness. Some women hand-express milk, but breast pumps—automatic, battery-powered, electric, or manual—are great ways to express milk more efficiently. They're available to buy or rent, or you may be lucky enough to borrow one. (See next page for more information on breast pumps.) You shouldn't feel any pain or discomfort when expressing milk, and make sure you can remove and clean all pump parts that touch the skin or milk. If using a breast pump, pump each breast until it's empty to help keep up your milk supply.

Store expressed milk in plastic bottles or cups with tight caps or in special plastic bags (three to four ounces in each). You can place the containers in the freezer or refrigerator. Fresh breast milk can be kept at room temperature for up to six hours, and it can be refrigerated for three to five days. Frozen breast milk can be kept in a deep freezer at 0°F for three to six months, and it can be kept in the back of an upright freezer for at least two weeks. Date all frozen milk, and use the oldest milk first.

Most babies prefer to drink milk warmed to at least room temperature. *Never* heat breast milk in a microwave; it can cause hot spots and degrades the milk's quality. Microwaved containers also may explode. Instead, warm the container in warm water.

Breast Pumps

If you're pumping constantly (perhaps because your baby is having trouble latching or you want to build up your milk supply), consider renting a dual-action, hospital-grade pump from a hospital, lactation consultant, or medical supply store. They're the fastest and most efficient type of pump, but also large, very expensive, and generally not available to purchase.

Otherwise, consider buying your own pump. There are three main types:

- Automatic, personal-use pumps have powerful motors and rapid suction, and can empty both breasts. They're the most expensive option (often costing around $300), but often come with carrying cases and other supplies included. These are a good choice for moms who plan to return to work full-time and pump often.

- Small electric or battery-operated pumps are lighter and cheaper (costing between $50 and $150) than automatic models, but also much slower and usually only capable of emptying one breast at a time. These work best for moms who only need to pump now and then.

- Manual pumps don't require electricity or batteries; moms squeeze a bulb or lever to create suction. This makes manual pumps convenient, but they're also the slowest option and may not completely empty a breast. Moms who rarely pump should choose this option. Manual pumps cost around $30 to $60.

Reverse-cycle Feeding

If you can't pump milk at work, another option to try is reverse-cycle feeding. This is when you feed your baby more in the evening and at night than during the day (with your baby receiving some daytime supplementation of expressed milk). Your baby will likely sleep more while you're away, and you'll probably want your baby to stay in your room at night, to make feeding easy and increase your bonding time. If you're worried she's not getting enough to eat, check her diapers and weight. (She should wet four to six disposables, or six to eight cloth diapers, and soil three to four diapers per day.)

Breast Care

- Wear a nursing bra, even up to twenty-four hours a day, while you're breastfeeding—the easy access to your breasts is very convenient. A cotton nursing bra lets your breasts "breathe," and make sure it fits well.

- Air-dry your nipples for fifteen minutes (if possible) after each feeding. To help prevent cracked nipples, leave a bit of colostrum, breast milk, or modified lanolin on the nipples.

- Shower daily to wash your breasts, but don't soap them. Soap removes natural oils and can lead to cracked nipples. Let them air-dry.

- If your nipples leak, line your bra with thin disposable cotton squares or washable, reusable breast pads to keep your clothes dry. Don't use waterproof liners; they won't let your skin breathe.

Engorgement

When your milk first comes in (usually between two to six days after giving birth), your breasts may feel exceptionally full. This uncomfortable and often painful feeling subsides within a few days, assuming your baby is latching on correctly. (You may also have this feeling later on when your baby goes too long between feedings). In the meantime, nurse frequently to help relieve breast fullness and tenderness. Engorged breasts often make the nipples flat and difficult for your baby to latch on. Squeeze a few drops of milk onto your nipple to soften it, making it easier for your baby. Wear a supportive bra, which will help push back on the breasts and decrease milk production. You can also take a warm shower or use warm compresses before nursing to help your milk begin dripping from your breasts and make the nipples softer. Once your baby is nursing, gently press on your breasts to encourage milk flow. Switching your baby's position during the feeding may also help milk flow. Let your baby nurse as long as she wants on the first breast. When she stops or falls asleep, offer her the other breast. If she isn't interested, pump or hand-express just enough milk from that breast to relieve the discomfort. If the warm shower or compresses are not of sufficient help, consider applying a cool cloth or ice pack to your breasts after or between feedings to reduce tenderness and swelling. Some caregivers suggest taking ibuprofen.

Sore Nipples

Lots of breastfeeding moms have sore nipples, even those who are nursing their second or third children. The soreness can last several days or even weeks. To prevent soreness, make sure your baby learns how to latch on to the nipple appropriately. (See pages 70-71.) Also, wash your nipples with water only and let them air-dry after washing or nursing. If you have a cracked, blistered, or sore nipple (particularly if the soreness gets worse as the baby nurses) try changing your baby's positions while nursing to move the pressure to an unaffected area. A small amount of expressed breast milk or creams, usually containing lanolin, may help soothe sore nipples. The temporary use of breast shields and hydrogel pads (available in pharmacies) may also help relieve pain. If nipple pain doesn't improve, have your caregiver or a lactation consultant examine your breasts.

Clogged Milk Ducts and Mastitis

When milk doesn't drain completely from the breast, sometimes the ducts become blocked, inflamed, and sore. A clogged duct may be a small, hard, sore lump or a tender spot in your breast. Sometimes it makes the breast red.

Several things can cause clogged milk ducts: an ill-fitted bra, shortened or skipped feedings, a bad breast pump, a cold, or stress. Sometimes there may seem to be no reason for them. To help clear a clogged duct, the best remedy is to nurse as often as you can and to rest as much as you can. You can also try massaging the sore area or applying warm compresses. Changing your baby's position during a feeding may help, and some affected women claim that positioning the baby so her chin is on the sore spot helps the healing. Some women use herbal remedies like echinacea, lecithin, and vitamin C, and others take ibuprofen sparingly to help relieve the pain and inflammation. Talk with your caregiver before taking any herbal remedy or medication.

Left untreated, a clogged duct can turn into a bacterial breast infection called mastitis. An infected breast becomes red and tender, and the infection can cause fever, aches, and nausea. Mastitis won't harm your baby. To treat it, continue nursing your baby, because removing the milk helps clear up the infection. If nursing is extremely painful, offer only the uninfected breast. Also, contact your caregiver; he or she will likely prescribe antibiotics to destroy the infection and may prescribe acidophilus to prevent you from getting a yeast infection.

Yeast Infection

A yeast infection of the breast often occurs following an antibiotic treatment or when you have a vaginal yeast infection. It can also occur when your baby has a yeast diaper rash or thrush (a yeast infection of the mouth). A yeast infection can make your nipples pinker and irritated, and it can make them very painful with tingling and burning during and between feedings. Sometimes, white patches appear on the breast. If either you or your baby has a yeast infection—with or without visible symptoms—you'll both need treatment. Talk with your caregiver for treatment suggestions, which may include an antifungal cream, oral medication, or liquid medication to apply to your nipples. (See Chapter 6 for more information.)

Hiccups

Your baby may get the hiccups often while nursing; this is normal. She can continue feeding, and the hiccups will stop on their own.

Biting

When your baby gets teeth, she may start biting your nipples as she nurses. Know that she's not being malicious, nor does her biting suggest she wants to be weaned. Rather, it's likely that her new teeth—or teeth that have yet to break through—are bothering her gums, and biting on anything makes them feel better.

This doesn't mean you should ignore it when your baby bites you—it can hurt! Biting typically occurs at the end of a feeding, when she's full and is simply playing. As soon as you feel a bite, gently but firmly say no to her and remove her from the breast. Using this approach consistently should teach her not to bite.

Premature Babies, Ill Babies, and Multiple Babies

Many premature or ill babies can breast-feed. In fact, breast milk often provides the best nutrition to help growth and prevent diseases (especially important for premature babies, who are at higher risk for infections). If you can't breastfeed your baby, you should express milk—preferably at least eight times a day—and give the milk to your baby through a feeding tube, cup, or bottle. Moms of multiples will have more than one mouth to feed, and many learn to nurse two babies simultaneously, one at each breast. It's important for nursing moms of multiples to have the support of lactation consultants and breastfeeding organizations like La Leche League to ensure that all their babies are getting the nutrition they need.

Support for Nursing Moms

Although breastfeeding your baby is natural, it still requires commitment and practice. Problems, like engorgement and infection, discourage some women. Working moms may feel uncomfortable expressing milk on the job or find it too time consuming. Some feel nursing chains them to their babies, as though they can't go anywhere because they must be ready for the next feeding.

Nursing moms need emotional support, as well as practical information. Breastfeeding organizations, like La Leche League (LLL), are designed to provide you with support and encouragement. Most communities have a local LLL chapter that holds regular meetings. Many communities also have lactation consultants who can help establish and support breastfeeding. More and more healthcare facilities have breastfeeding specialists on staff. Take advantage of the professional breastfeeding support you may have in your area.

Milk Banks

If you can't provide your baby with breast milk, you may want to use donor milk from a milk bank. Milk banks collect, screen, process, and distribute milk to those who need it, particularly babies who are premature or ill. There are currently eleven banks in the United States that follow the safety guidelines of the Human Milk Banking Association of North America (HMBANA). These banks carefully screen and pasteurize the donated milk before sending it out. (Giving your baby milk that hasn't been screened isn't safe.) For more information, see their website, http://www.hmbana.org/.

What Nursing Moms Need

Rest

Getting enough rest is essential to good milk production, especially during the first weeks of breastfeeding. Your body is still recovering from giving birth, and inadequate rest may make you feel more stress, which often interferes with milk production. Try to sleep when your baby naps and ignore all those tasks you'd like to get done. They'll get done eventually, but now is the time to focus on you and your baby.

Relaxation

Relax as much as you can, especially just before you nurse your baby. Emotional and physical tension can interfere with your letdown reflex and can keep your baby from getting the milk she needs. Try settling into a comfortable chair and turning on some soothing music before a feeding.

Liquids

Nursing mothers need to drink plenty of liquids (six to eight glasses a day). Get into the habit of drinking a glass of water or another liquid before or with each feeding. You may be more thirsty while nursing. Don't force yourself to drink, though. Just drink enough to quench your thirst. Pale yellow urine is a good sign you're drinking enough.

Medications

Many medications are safe to take while breastfeeding. But before taking any medication—prescribed or over-the-counter—talk first with your caregiver or lactation consultant.

Diet

When breastfeeding, your body will use nutrients to make breast milk first, then it'll nourish itself. Except when you're extremely deprived of nourishment, whatever you eat will usually provide good quality breast milk; however, your diet can affect *how much* milk you produce. A nursing mom needs to increase her caloric intake over her baseline by 25 percent (so if you usually eat two thousand calories a day, you'll need to add five hundred calories), and her diet, in addition to being well-rounded, should include about 65 grams of protein and plenty of calcium. (If you're worried about your weight, remember that breastfeeding burns five hundred calories a day, on average.) A guideline for your diet follows. (For a personalized daily food plan, see http://www.choosemyplate.gov.)

Food Groups	Daily Servings	Sources
Dairy	3 cups	Cheese, custard, milk, pudding, yogurt
Meat and Beans	6$\frac{1}{2}$ ounces	Fish, dried beans, lean beef or pork, lentils, poultry, eggs (Caution: The protein in nuts and peanut butter can appear in breast milk. If you have a family history of severe allergies or asthma, discuss this with your baby's caregiver.)
Fruits and Vegetables	5$\frac{1}{2}$ cups	Dark green leafy vegetables, orange and red vegetables, kiwi fruit, avocados, oranges
Grains	9 ounces	Bread, bulgur, cereals, pancakes, pasta, rice
Sweets and Fats	Moderate amounts	Chips, cookies, candy

A few things to keep in mind:

- Teen mothers who nurse will need more dairy and protein. Moms of multiples may need to add one thousand calories to this daily diet. If you're a teen or a mom of multiples, talk with your caregiver or a nutritionist about your nutritional needs for breastfeeding.

- If there is a strong family history of food allergies you may need to be more restrictive in your diet. (See page 164 for more on food allergies.)

- Some foods you eat may cause problems for your nursing baby.

    - Try limiting foods that cause gas (like cabbage, broccoli, garlic, and onions) if you notice she's fussy when you eat these foods.

    - Caffeine can also make your baby fussy. Many moms, however, are able to consume caffeine in moderate amounts (a serving or two) without problems.

    - Some babies are allergic to the protein in cow milk. If you think your baby is allergic, don't eat or drink anything containing cow milk for two weeks to see if the symptoms (eczema or skin rash, abdominal pain or cramps, vomiting, or diarrhea) disappear.

    - It's best if you don't regularly consume large amounts of alcohol or smoke cigarettes at any time in your life—but especially not while breastfeeding. (Contrary to earlier beliefs, beer consumption is not felt to increase milk supply.) Alcohol in your bloodstream crosses over into your milk, and large amounts of alcohol can harm your nursing baby as well as impair your caretaking abilities. However, drinking alcohol *in moderation* (an occasional single drink) is possible if you're careful. Alcohol that you consume reaches your milk in thirty to ninety minutes, so you may want to "pump and dump" if you're going to be nursing around this time. Also consider feeding your baby before having a drink, to give yourself time for the alcohol to leave your system before you must nurse her again. If you're exposed to cigarette smoke while nursing, so is your baby. If you just can't quit smoking, it's better to smoke and breastfeed than to smoke and not breastfeed, and you should smoke right after you nurse. (Make sure if anyone else smokes, he or she does so well away from you and your baby.) For more information, talk with your caregiver about using alcohol and tobacco while breastfeeding.

In rare instances, babies are weaned during the first year if their mothers have a serious medical condition that requires drugs incompatible with breastfeeding. If you're in this situation, do your own research on the condition and get a second opinion from another caregiver. Depending on the age of your baby and how often she nurses, certain drugs might not harm her.

Nursing Positions

Cradle Hold, Step-by-Step

Step 1: Sit with your baby in a comfortable chair. You may find using a footstool helpful, as well as pillows to help support your baby. (There are specially designed pillows to help bring your baby up to the level of the breast.) Lay the side of your baby's head in the crook of your arm. Support her body with your arm, and support her bottom with your hand. You and your baby should be belly to belly. Wrap her bottom arm around your side so it's not wedged between the two of you.

Another way to hold your baby is to rest her head in your hand and support her body with your arm, letting her bottom rest in the crook of your arm. This is called the alternate or cross cradle hold, and some nursing moms find it an easier position to master than the regular cradle hold.

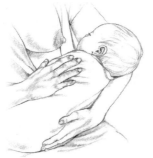

Step 2: Make a "breast sandwich" with your other hand by placing the fingers on one side of your breast and the thumb on the other side, at least two inches away from the areola.

Step 3: Pull your baby close to you. Tickle her upper lip with your nipple until her mouth opens wide.

Step 4: Center your nipple in front of your baby's nose so she'll latch on to it. When centering your nipple, after your baby has latched on you can change its position by pressing your thumb or fingers into the breast. But this method can move the nipple into an incorrect position, usually leading to a sore nipple. If the nipple isn't centered when your baby latches on, it's best to just take her off the breast (gently stick a finger in the corner of her mouth to break the suction) and try again.

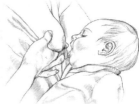

Step 5: When your baby has latched on properly, her bottom lip will flange out around the breast. If it's curled inward over her lower gum, pull gently on her chin until it flanges outward. Other signs of a good latch include your baby's cheek against your breast, audible swallowing, and overall comfort for you and your baby throughout the feeding.

Lying Down, Step-by-Step

(This method may be preferred if you've undergone a cesarean section, because it'll keep your baby off your belly.)

Step 1: Lie on your side on a bed or roomy couch with pillows around your head and shoulders.

Step 2: Curve your body slightly so your baby can fit comfortably next to you.

Step 3: Lay your baby on her side, slightly raising and supporting her head in the crook of your arm. Wrap your forearm around her and draw her feet close to you so she's angled into your body. This position will help keep her nose free to breathe while she's nursing.

Step 4: Be sure you're supported entirely by the furniture and pillows, not by your back muscles or elbow. Then follow steps 2 through 5 for the Cradle Hold to latch your baby onto the nipple.

Note: It's important that your baby does not sleep with your breast in her mouth. Pooled milk can cause dental decay in erupting teeth, due to milk sugar. Babies who feed lying down also have a greater chance of getting ear infections.

Football Hold, Step-by-Step

(This method may be preferred if you've undergone a cesarean section, because it'll keep your baby off your belly.)

Step 1: Use a comfortable, well-padded chair or rocker. You may want to place a pillow behind your back for support or under your baby so she's in a more convenient position to nurse.

Step 2: Avoid leaning forward while nursing. You'll end up with a backache.

Step 3: Support your baby in the football position (see page 20), turning her toward you at your side.

Step 4: Support your baby's head so it's higher than her stomach. This position lets her better burp up any swallowed air. Then follow steps 2 through 5 for the Cradle Hold to latch her onto the nipple.

Note: For further information on burping, see pages 81–82.

Weaning from the Breast

When?

There's no one specific time when your baby should be weaned; however, it's recommended that babies breastfeed for at least the first one to two years of life.

During the first year, your baby may suddenly stop breastfeeding. At this age, her refusal usually doesn't suggest she's ready to be weaned. More likely, she's on a "nursing strike." A change in the nursing routine or schedule, a change in your stress level, or even a change in the deodorant or soap you use may make your baby refuse to nurse. If your baby is six months or older, general distraction may be the reason for her loss of interest in nursing. With your patience and persistence, she should resume nursing. Talk with your caregiver or a lactation consultant for help getting your baby back on the breast.

Babies who self-wean usually do so gradually over a period of several weeks or months. Self-weaning is often the least traumatic and problem-free way of weaning. If, however, you decide to wean your baby, she may need extra attention, especially if you've been nursing for a long time. Try to give her all the cuddling and care you can.

How?

How you wean may be more important than *when* you wean. When it's time, do it gradually, gently, and with plenty of love and patience.

- Be as flexible as you can. Don't set strict goals or rigid schedules.

- Avoid sudden weaning for two reasons. It can dramatically decrease your hormonal flow, and it may trigger depression—and the loss of the nursing bond with your child may add to the depression. Sudden weaning can also traumatize your baby, who's learned to find comfort and solace, as well as nourishment, from nursing.

- Gradually cut back one feeding at a time. The lunchtime feeding is usually the first to go. Many babies cling the longest to the bedtime or first morning feeding. Offer your baby expressed breast milk, formula, or water from a cup or a bottle in addition to food (if she's started eating solids). If you wean to a bottle, choose a nipple with a slow flow. Every two to three days, substitute another bottle or cup feeding for the breastfeeding. Many babies can be weaned entirely in one to two weeks.

- If you're weaning from breast milk to formula or cow milk, and your baby doesn't like the taste, try a mixture of half breast milk and half formula or cow milk.

- If your baby weans early, she may miss sucking, especially at bedtime. Offer her a cup, pacifier, or bottle. (Don't offer a bottle to your baby in bed.)

- Except for very young infants, most babies often can be weaned directly to a cup. A weighted, two-handled cup with a valve-less spout works great for an inexperienced drinker.

- If you wean your baby gradually, you'll probably avoid engorged breasts. (See page 65.) If your breasts become uncomfortably full after a missed feeding, express some milk—but just until you're fairly comfortable again. (See pages 63–64.) Don't express too much, or you'll stimulate more milk production.

- If your baby is weaning well and suddenly suffers from teething or a cold, she'll probably want to nurse. Don't deny her this comfort while she's miserable. When she starts to feel better, you can resume weaning.

Formula-feeding Basics

This section focuses on how to feed your baby formula, but you can also follow the steps on pages 63–64 to learn how to feed expressed breast milk to your baby. It is not safe to give your baby homemade formulas or cow milk (in the first year) as a source of nutrition.

Kinds of Formula

Formula comes in several different forms and many different compositions. Formula companies are constantly changing and updating their products, usually striving to make them closer in constitution to breast milk. Formulas vary slightly among brands, and the cost of brands can vary more significantly. Most companies add vitamins to their formula, making vitamin supplements unnecessary. (It is recommended, however, to give additional vitamin D to formula-fed babies early on, before they are up to an intake of thirty-two ounces a day.) The American Academy of Pediatrics (AAP) recommends iron-fortified formula for all formula-fed babies for the first year to promote normal mental and physical development. Some parents worry that lots of iron will make their baby constipated. Actually, iron can cause either diarrhea or constipation, but it usually causes neither. If constipation becomes a problem, you can treat it while still giving your baby iron-fortified formula. (See page 150.) Most babies do well on the first formula they consume, and switching formulas should not be done without input from a care provider. Discuss with your baby's caregiver which formula he or she recommends for your baby.

There are three main kinds of commercially prepared formulas:

- *Milk-based* formula is made with cow milk that has been modified to be more like breast milk and fortified with vitamins, minerals, carbohydrates, and non-milk fats. Some milk-based formulas are "lactose free," but these generally aren't needed except in some post-diarrhea circumstances. When babies have milk intolerance, the problem is usually the protein, not the sugar (lactose), in milk.

- *Soy-based* formula is made from soybeans and is also fortified with vitamins, minerals, carbohydrates, and fats. It's usually consumed by babies who are allergic to the protein in cow milk, or are lactose intolerant. (It should be noted, however, that as many as 50 percent of babies who have milk protein allergy also have soy protein allergy.)

- *Hydrolyzed-protein* formula is cow-milk–based, but with the proteins broken down to various degrees to make them more digestible. Types may be listed as gentle, sensitive, or hypoallergenic. This formula is helpful for babies with severe protein sensitivity, but is about twice as expensive as regular cow milk or soy formula.

- Formulas may list other features, including added lipids, prebiotics (natural food substances that promote a healthy intestinal lining), probiotics ("friendly" bacteria), or organic ingredients. These features haven't proven to be worth the expense. Generics are an acceptable and less expensive option.

Infant formulas come packaged three ways:

- *Ready-to-feed* formula is premixed and ready to pour into a clean bottle. This is the most expensive formula, but also the most convenient.

- *Powdered* formula must be mixed with water. You can prepare one bottle of formula at a time.

- *Concentrated liquid* formula must be diluted with water before it's poured into a bottle.

If you use powdered or concentrated liquid formulas, your baby will get the fluoride her teeth need from the added water. If your water isn't fluoridated, your baby's caregiver may prescribe a supplement when your baby's about six months old. (See pages 132–33.)

Storing Formula

- Once you've opened a container of concentrated or ready-to-use formula and prepared bottles, cover and store the remaining formula in the refrigerator for up to forty-eight hours. After that time, throw it out.

- Once you've opened a can of powdered formula, cover the can and store it in a cool, dry place. The label will tell you how long you can use the formula.

- After you've prepared a bottle of formula, either use it immediately or refrigerate it. You can safely use prepared formula for twenty-four to forty-eight hours after it's been refrigerated.

- If you'll be away from your home for more than two hours, bring the supplies to prepare formula with you instead of preparing at home, to keep freshness longer.

- You can leave a prepared bottle at room temperature for up to two hours before bacteria starts to grow in the formula (a half-hour in very warm weather). After an hour, throw out the formula if your baby has eaten some of it. (Bacteria from her mouth will grow in the formula.) If she hasn't eaten any of it, you can safely refrigerate the bottle and use it up to forty-eight hours later.

Preparing Formula

Tips

- With common sense and good hygiene, there's no need to sterilize any of the feeding equipment or the water you use. Clean the equipment regularly and carefully wash your hands in hot soapy water before you prepare the formula.

- Prepare the formula exactly as your baby's caregiver prescribes or as the formula manufacturer recommends. Formula that's too concentrated or too diluted can make your baby sick. You do not need to use water with fluoride in it to mix the formula until your baby is six months old.

- Follow the steps on page 77 to prepare powdered or concentrated formula. A ready-to-use formula needs no preparation; simply pour it into a clean bottle.

Equipment

There are a number of bottle and nipple styles to choose from. Your baby may prefer a particular nipple, and you may find that some bottle systems are more convenient for you than others. The following list suggests how many bottles and nipples you'll need; it also outlines the advantages of various nipple and bottle features. You may want to buy a sample of each style in the beginning, then let your baby and your budget help you decide which to stock up on.

Bottles, 8–10 (plus 8–10 caps or covers and screw-on rings)

Feature	Description
Material	*Glass* bottles are durable, easy to clean, and don't contain harmful chemicals, but they're heavier than plastic bottles and can shatter if dropped or thrown.
	Plastic bottles are light and won't shatter, but they might not last as long as glass bottles. If you use plastic bottles, avoid purchasing hard plastics made of polycarbonate or bisphenol-A (which use the recycling symbols 3 or 7). They may leach chemicals and cause neurological problems for your baby. If you must use them, do not boil, microwave, or wash them in the dishwasher. Opaque bottles made of polyethylene or polypropylene (which use the symbols 1, 2, or 5) are best.
Shape	*Straight* bottles are cheap and easy to clean.
	Angled bottles have a forty-five—degree bend that keeps the nipple filled with liquid to reduce baby's air intake and makes it easier to hold a baby upright, which prevents liquid from washing into baby's middle ear (a cause of ear infections).
Usage	*Reusable* bottles are economical and environmentally sound because they can be used throughout your baby's bottle-feeding stage and create no waste. They also allow accurate measurement of the bottle's contents.
	Disposable bottles require less cleaning because the milk is drunk from a presterilized plastic liner, which is thrown away at the end of the feeding. This bottle type may minimize baby's air swallowing (and thus prevent gassiness) because you can squeeze air out of the liner before feeding; also, the liner collapses as baby feeds, which prevents additional air bubbles from entering.
Size	*Four-ounce* bottles are practical for newborns, who may drink only a small amount at each feeding. They're also handy for storing expressed breast milk.
	Eight- or nine-ounce bottles are practical for older babies with bigger appetites. However, they can be used for a baby of any age and are therefore more versatile and long-lasting.
Other features	*Bubble-free* bottles are ideal for gassy babies who don't like disposables. They let air in through the bottom of the bottle, which prevents it from mixing with the milk and being swallowed. Because both ends screw off, cleaning is easy.
	Chambered bottles are great for traveling with a formula-fed baby. They have separate compartments for premeasured powdered formula and water. At feeding time, you twist the top and the formula mixes with the water.
	Hands-free bottles have been used in the past, particularly for young multiples, but are now discouraged because they promote bottle-propping, which could cause a baby to choke, and gets in the way of the important bonding that takes place during breastfeeding.

Nipples	
Feature	Description
Material	*Latex* nipples are softer and more flexible than silicone nipples.
	Silicone nipples are firmer and hold their shape longer than latex ones. They're less porous than latex and thus less prone to bacteria. They typically last three to four times longer than latex. They're also heat-resistant and can withstand dishwashers.
Shape	*Bell-shaped* nipples are inexpensive and widely available.
	Flat-topped nipples mimic the shape of a mother's nipple.
	Orthodontic nipples are elongated, flat on one side, and indented in the center to encourage the tonguing action of breastfeeding. They may help reduce tongue thrusting and bite problems caused by standard nipples.
Flow	Nipples come with holes in varying numbers and sizes for varying flow speed. Here's a quick guide to choosing the right flow: Always use newborn nipples for a breastfed baby of any age. The following guidelines apply to exclusively bottle-fed babies. For a newborn, the nipple size is right if the milk drips steadily when you turn the bottle upside down. For older babies: If your baby is sucking hard, fussing, then sucking hard again, you probably need a faster-flow nipple. If your baby is sputtering and gulping, you may need a slower-flow nipple.

Other Basic Equipment

- Bottle brush
- Nipple brush
- Measuring pitcher in ounces (or milliliters), preferably one with a cover
- Funnel
- Large, long-handled spoon

Care of Equipment

- Thoroughly rinse the formula from each bottle immediately after it's used.
- Wash each bottle, ring, and nipple separately in hot soapy water, using the nipple and bottle brushes. Carefully squeeze water through the nipples to remove all residue. You can also wash everything in the dishwasher.
- Rinse everything in clean hot water and let air-dry.

Preparing Formula Step-by-Step

Step 1: Wash your hands thoroughly with hot soapy water. If you're opening a can of concentrated formula, clean the top of the can.

Step 2: Follow the directions on the can or bottle to prepare the formula. Again, be sure to prepare the formula exactly as recommended, to keep your baby from getting sick. Pour the formula into clean bottles. Using a funnel makes the job easier.

Step 3: Put the nipples, caps, and rings on the bottles. Store the bottles in the refrigerator. (See page 74 to learn how to store formula safely.)

How to Bottle-feed

How Much?

- Begin by offering your baby about one-half to one and one-half ounces (30 to 45 milliliters) at each feeding, in the first week. Work up to two to three ounces (57 to 90 milliliters) per feeding from two to three weeks. As soon as she starts emptying the bottle at two or three feedings each day, start adding half an ounce (15 milliliters) of formula to each bottle. Expect her to work up to twelve to twenty-four ounces a day, after the first week or so. Eventually, she'll drink eight ounces (240 millimeters) a feeding. You can follow these rough guidelines for the first year, but let your baby decide how much she food wants.

- Don't worry if your baby doesn't drink much formula at a feeding. Just as your appetite fluctuates, so does hers. If she's happy and thriving, it's usually okay if she doesn't drink much once in a while.

- Sometimes a baby will stop sucking during a feeding. Be patient; she's probably just resting. When she's ready, she'll start again. Don't force a bottle if it's clear she doesn't want any more, and don't pressure her to finish a bottle if she clearly isn't interested.

Demand Feeding

- Let your baby's hunger determine when she'll be fed. Feeding her whenever she seems hungry won't spoil her. (See hunger cues on page 61.) Bottle-fed babies usually feed every three to four hours. They eventually need fewer feedings at night.

- Don't wake your baby at night for a feeding. If she's hungry, she'll wake herself.

Age	Amount each day
Birth to 1 month	18–24 ounces
	(530–710 milliliters)
1 to 2 months	22–26 ounces
	(650–770 milliliters)
2 to 3 months	24–26 ounces
	(710–770 milliliters)
3 to 4 months	24–28 ounces
	(710–830 milliliters)
4 to 5 months	24–30 ounces
	(710–890 milliliters)
5 to 6 months	24–32 ounces
	(710–950 milliliters)
6 months to 1 year	24–32 ounces
	(710–950 milliliters)

Giving the Bottle to Your Baby

Tips

- Most babies prefer their formula or milk slightly warm, although some like it cooler. If you're using tap water to make a bottle, make sure it does not contain a significant amount of lead (more than 15 parts per billion or ppb). If there is lead in your water, it's better to use cold water than warm water. To warm a cold bottle, set it in a pan of warm water. Do *not* warm the bottle in the microwave. Using a microwave can cause hot spots that can scald the baby's mouth, and it can make the bottle break. Make sure the liquid isn't too hot by dripping a bit on the inside of your wrist.

- Check the flow of milk from the nipple. The milk should drip out steadily—initially about one drop per second. If it drips too slowly, your baby will tire of sucking before she's full and will probably swallow a lot of air instead. If the milk comes out too quickly, your baby will get full before she's sucked as much as she needs to. Plus, she may try to slow the flow by thrusting her tongue against the nipple, which can affect the development of her teeth. Throw away the nipple if the milk flows too quickly.

- Avoid propping a bottle or teaching your young baby to hold it herself before she learns to do it naturally. If left alone with a bottle, a baby could choke on the liquid. Avoid hands-free bottles, as they encourage bottle-propping, and get in the way of the important bonding that takes place during breastfeeding.

- Be attentive and remember that every baby needs the cuddling and love that comes while feeding.

- Avoid putting your baby to bed with a bottle. A baby who feeds lying down has a greater chance of getting an ear infection. Plus, falling asleep with a bottle in her mouth can lead to severe tooth decay, even if she hasn't yet cut her teeth.

Step-by-Step

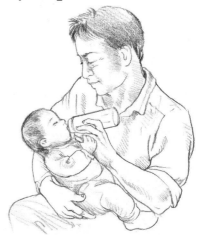

Step 1: Hold your baby on your lap, nestled in the crook of your arm. Gently touch her nearest cheek with the nipple to trigger her rooting reflex (see page 16). She'll turn toward you with an open mouth, searching for the nipple.

Step 2: Hold your baby with her head and upper body raised at a slight angle. She'll more easily swallow the formula or milk in this position than if she's lying on her back.

Step 3: Keep the neck of the bottle constantly filled with liquid by gradually lifting the bottom of the bottle as you feed your baby. She'll swallow more liquid and less air. When your baby's finished, burp her. (See pages 81–82 for instructions.)

Weaning from the Bottle

When?

There's no one specific time when your baby should be weaned; however, weaning can be easy when she's old enough to drink from a cup by herself (as early as five or six months old). Many bottle-fed babies who can drink from a cup are weaned completely by their first birthdays. Weaning to a cup earlier rather than later can prevent the bottle from becoming a security object. Plus, drinking from a cup improves hand-to-mouth coordination.

Signs that your baby may be ready to wean include: looking around while sucking on the bottle, mouthing the nipple instead of sucking on it, and putting down the bottle before she's finished it.

How?

How you wean may be more important than *when* you wean. When it's time, do it gradually, gently, and with plenty of love and patience.

- Occasionally offer your baby formula or water in a cup. A weighted, two-handled cup with a valve-less spout works great for an inexperienced drinker.

- If your baby loves her bottle and refuses to drink from a cup, continue offering the cup to her. When she eventually starts taking a sip or two, don't force her to drink more. She'll do so when she's ready.

- Once your baby is mobile, offer her a bottle only while she's on your lap.

- Gradually cut back one bottle-feeding at a time. The lunchtime feeding is usually the first to go. Many babies cling the longest to the bedtime or first morning feeding. Offer your baby formula or water from a cup in addition to food (if she's started eating solids).

- If your baby is weaning well and suddenly suffers from teething or a cold, she'll probably want a bottle. Don't deny her this comfort while she's miserable. When she starts to feel better, you can resume weaning.

Burping and Spitting Up

Tips

- Bottle-fed babies tend to swallow air as they feed, making them uncomfortable until they burp. (Breastfed babies might swallow air, too, if their mouths don't create a tight seal as they nurse or if they nurse while flat on their backs.)

- Unless your baby is very fussy, it's usually enough to burp her once during a feeding and once after. It may be helpful to burp a bottle-fed baby after she's eaten two or three ounces (or at least every three to five minutes) to help reduce the amount of any swallowed air.

- Don't interrupt your baby's feeding to burp her. Take advantage of her pauses in sucking and burp her then. If nursing, burp her before you offer your second breast.

- If your baby doesn't burp within a few minutes, resume feeding her and try again later if she's fussy.

- Before you burp your baby, drape a cloth diaper or towel over your shoulder or knees to catch any spit-up.

- Spitting up some formula or milk with a burp is normal. It happens when the stomach muscles gently dispel some formula or milk. (Vomiting, as a comparison, is when the stomach muscles vigorously contract and dispel most of the formula or milk.) Swallowing too much air or eating too much at a feeding often results in spit-up, especially for bottle-fed babies. Sometimes, though, it's due to relaxation of the muscles that control the passage between the stomach and the esophagus (or *reflux*—see pages 166–67 for more information). Your baby will spit up less often as she grows.

- Don't bounce or jiggle your baby after a feeding. Doing so may make her spit up.

- To help prevent spit-up, keep your baby upright for a half-hour after feeding. Also, elevate the head of her bed with blocks, or a folded blanket or towel under the head of the mattress. This setup will keep her head higher than her stomach. *Don't* use a pillow to elevate her head; it may suffocate her.

- If your baby spits up a lot of formula or milk, hold her in a more upright position when you feed her so any swallowed air isn't trapped below the formula or milk in her stomach.

Burping Methods

Option 1: Hold your baby with her head over your shoulder. Gently rub or pat her back until she burps.

Option 2: Set your baby upright and leaning slightly forward on your lap. Support her head and body. Gently rub or pat her back until she burps.

Option 3: Lay your baby face-down across your lap or on a mattress. Turn her head to one side and support it with your hand or arm. Gently rub or pat her back until she burps.

Introducing Solid Foods

When your baby is about four to six months old, she may be ready to start eating solids. Unlike when breast milk or formula was all your baby ate, you'll now be concerned that she's eating a well-balanced diet. Once she starts deciding what she will or won't eat, you realize that you don't have total control over her diet. (*You* may think she needs to eat strained peas, but *she* may think otherwise.) Your baby may be an easygoing eater, a vigorous masher, an energetic thrower, or a combination of all types, depending on the time of day, her mood, or who knows what!

When?

For your baby's health, the American Academy of Pediatrics (AAP) recommends waiting to introduce solids to her until she's at least four and preferably six months old. At that age, her body may be ready for the additional calories and nutrients that solid foods offer. When your baby's ready to try solid foods, her usual intake of breast milk or formula may no longer satisfy her. Make sure, however, that her demand for more feedings isn't due to a growth spurt. (Growth spurts usually occur at two to three weeks, six weeks, three months, and six months—but the demand for more food lasts only two or three days for each spurt.) Your baby may also give you some of the following cues to show she's ready to eat solid foods:

- She sits well with minimal support.

- She can support and control her head well.

- She tries to take food off your plate or grab your fork.

- She turns her head away when she's done drinking or eating.

- She has lost the tongue thrust reflex. (See page 16.)

- She opens her mouth when she sees the spoon approaching.

- She has new teeth that she wants to use to chew food.

Why Wait?

Before they're four to six months old, most babies' digestive systems aren't developed enough to process solids effectively and safely. Many babies can't control their tongue and mouth muscles well enough to swallow solid foods safely.

Plus, if you're nursing your baby, breast milk is designed to provide all the nutrition she needs until she's ready to eat solid foods. Feeding her solids too soon only fills her with nutritionally inferior foods.

Here are a few more reasons to delay introducing solids to your baby:

- Delaying the introduction of solid foods may help avoid food allergies and allergic conditions like eczema and asthma. If your baby's digestive tract isn't mature enough, the large proteins found in solid foods can sometimes get through the lining of her intestinal wall. If this happens, her immune system kicks in and produces antibodies, resulting in an allergic reaction.

- Introducing solid foods too early may contribute to obesity later on. A 2011 study by the AAP found that among formula-fed infants, introducing solid foods before age four months was related to a higher risk of obesity.

- Contrary to popular belief, it's never been clearly demonstrated that mixing cereal in a baby's bedtime bottle will help her sleep through the night. In fact, the practice may do your baby more harm than good.

How to Introduce Solids

Keep in mind the following suggestions when your baby is ready to try a solid food:

- Introduce solid foods while your baby is still getting most of her nourishment from breast milk or formula. Offer solids at anytime of the day you prefer and either before or after she's nursed or had a bottle. Solids should supplement, not replace, breast milk or formula.

  Offer solids on a small spoon, not in a bottle, unless specifically instructed to do so for gastroesophageal reflux disease.

- Offer your baby solids when she's active and calm.

- Don't force your baby to eat solids. She'll eat when her body needs them. Introducing solid foods should be an enjoyable, stress-free activity.

- Respect your baby's preferences. Even at six months old, she'll have likes and dislikes. With this said, however, it can take ten to fifteen tries (maybe even more) for a baby to accept a new food. Don't give up on a food just because your baby spits it out for the first, fifth, or twelfth time!

- At first, introduce solids one at a time. Wait at least two to four days after each new food to make sure it doesn't cause an allergic reaction. If your family has a history of allergies, wait a full week before offering the food again. Avoid stews, soups, or multigrain cereals; if any of these causes an allergic reaction in your baby, you won't know exactly which ingredient caused it.

Food Intolerance and Allergic Reactions

If your baby begins wheezing or develops rashes, a sore bottom, or diarrhea after you've introduced a new food to her, she may have a food intolerance or be experiencing an allergic reaction. Most food-allergy reactions are mild and no reason for concern, but if your baby's reaction is severe or if you're unsure whether it's mild or severe, contact your baby's caregiver or a healthcare professional immediately. If your baby has a mild reaction after eating a food, make sure you don't give her that food for several months. Then reintroduce it at first in very small amounts. (See Chapter 6 for more on food allergies.)

Common Sources of Food Allergies

Here's a list of the most common sources of food allergies in babies:

- Cow milk
- Soy
- Egg whites
- Wheat
- Fish (such as tuna, salmon, and cod)
- Shellfish (such as shrimp, crab, and lobster)
- Nuts, especially tree nuts and peanuts (and peanut butter)

If you have a family history of allergies to any of these foods, talk with your baby's caregiver before introducing them to your baby.

Other Foods to Avoid

Avoid introducing the following foods to your baby for at least the first year of her life:

- Honey—this food is associated with infant botulism, a potentially deadly disease.

- Popcorn or any other food that she could choke on. These foods are best delayed until age three or four, as they are particularly likely to cause choking.

- Heavily sweetened foods, like soda, lemonade, or baby food desserts.

- Juices—giving babies plain water is a much healthier option than fruit juice, which offers no nutritional benefits over whole fruit and can contain added sugars.

Feeding Schedules

- At first, offer your baby a solid food once a day. Some parents find midmorning or midafternoon a better time than family mealtimes because there's less distraction. Note: If your baby nurses but also eats lots of solids, she might not nurse as often or as long, which could consequently decrease your milk supply.

- After a couple of weeks, offer her solids twice a day.

- After about a month, start regularly offering her solids between nursing sessions or bottle-feedings. At those times, your baby will have an appetite for solids but not be ravenous. Observe her appetite and satisfaction with what you're offering.

- Let your baby set the pace. She'll know when she's had enough food, just as she knows when she's had enough breast milk or formula. If you patiently let her set the pace, she'll gradually wean herself from the bottle or breast to solids. Also, try not to make your baby finish a portion. If you praise her for "cleaning her plate," she may polish off her food because she wants your approval, not because she's hungry.

Age	Amounts of Food Per Day
6 to 7 months	Breast milk or iron-fortified formula
	Iron-fortified rice cereal mixed with breast milk or formula (up to 8 tablespoons)
	Strained fruits, meats, or cooked vegetables (up to 8 tablespoons)
8 to 9 months	Breast milk or iron-fortified formula
	Iron-fortified rice cereal mixed with breast milk or formula (8 tablespoons)
	Strained or finely chopped fruits and cooked vegetables; bite-size pieces when ready (6–8 tablespoons)
	Strained meats and puréed egg yolks (4 tablespoons—no egg whites until one year old if any family history of food allergy)
10 months to 1 year	Breast milk or iron-fortified formula
	Iron-fortified cereal mixed with breast milk or formula (6–8 tablespoons)
	Mashed or bite-size fruits and cooked vegetables (6–8 tablespoons)
	Ground or chopped meat and other protein foods, like egg yolks (1–2 ounces)
	Potato and whole-grain or enriched-grain products

This is just one example of a food plan. Many parents start with other foods or introduce foods in a different order.

How Much Food?

- At first, give your baby one to two teaspoons (5 to 10 milliliters) of food. Dilute the food with breast milk or formula.

- As her appetite grows and she becomes a more accomplished eater, gradually increase the amount to four to six tablespoons (59 to 89 milliliters). (A small jar of commercial baby food typically contains eight tablespoons—118 milliliters—of food.) Use the chart on the previous page as a guideline for your baby's first year.

- Again, never force your baby to eat and don't make her eat "one last bite" when it's clear she's full.

- Your baby's behavior will tell you when she's full. She'll turn her head away from the spoon or close her lips tightly and refuse to take anything more into her mouth. Crying, gagging, or spitting out food may suggest your baby doesn't want more food, but these signs may also suggest that she hasn't learned how to eat solids—or they may mean you need to improve how you spoon-feed her.

How to Spoon-feed

From the time she was born, your baby knew how to eat only by sucking, so she may need time to learn how to eat from a spoon. To introduce spoon-feeding, make sure your baby is sitting up, then place a small dab of food on the tip of a baby spoon or demitasse spoon. Place the spoon just between your baby's lips and let her suck the food off it. Eventually, she'll take food from the spoon directly into her mouth.

Messes

Babies learn about food by touching it, tasting it, and smelling it. This means, of course, that babies are messy eaters. The more you try to fight this fact, the more stressful mealtimes will be for you and your baby. Instead, relax and try to make mealtimes enjoyable, whatever the mess. If you want to make cleanup easier, place newspapers on the floor around where your baby eats. Wear an apron or clothes you don't mind getting stained, and put a bib on your baby.

What Kinds of Foods?

Your baby's first solid food will likely be a little iron-fortified rice cereal mixed with breast milk or formula. As your baby grows, her menu will expand. Remember: If your family has a history of allergies, see pages 84–85 to learn what foods to delay introducing to your baby.

A Few Words about Juices

Contrary to popular belief, juice is *not* necessary to a baby's diet. In fact, drinking too much juice can lead to tooth decay, diarrhea, and diaper rash, and can make your baby gain excess weight. If you do give your baby juice, make sure she's old enough to drink it from a cup and offer no more than four ounces a day. (You can water down juices, but still don't offer your baby more than four ounces of juice.) Make juice part of a snack, not part of a meal.

Vitamin Supplements

Making sure your baby eats a balanced diet best ensures that she's getting necessary vitamins. Once your baby starts eating a variety of solid foods, you might not need to give her any vitamin supplements, unless her caregiver instructs otherwise. Check, in particular, about iron and vitamin D. When your baby is six months old, make sure she's getting fluoride (see pages 132–33).

Commercially Prepared Baby Foods

Commercially prepared baby foods are convenient and have been sterilized, and many contain vitamin and mineral supplements. Some manufacturers use organic foods. Most manufacturers have removed unnecessary additives, but still check the labels to make sure there's no added salt, sugar, or other preservatives or fillers (flour or modified starch).

Here's a summary of the different commercially prepared baby foods:

- First Foods—4–6 months: Puréed, strained single-ingredient foods available in 2.5-ounce portions.

- Second Foods—6–8 months: Puréed combination food available in 4-ounce jars.

- Third Foods—8–10 months: Combination foods that often include milk and wheat and may contain spices; available in 6-ounce jars.

Safe Feeding

Take all the precautions possible to keep your baby's food safe. Her immune system will need a couple of years to fully develop, so she'll be susceptible to bacterial growth. Here a few things to remember when feeding your baby:

- Make sure your hands and all utensils used to prepare and serve your baby's food are clean.

- Don't feed your baby straight from a baby food jar. Instead, spoon what you think she'll eat into a separate bowl and feed her from it. This will keep the bacteria in her mouth from transferring to the jar and multiplying in the remaining food until she eats it later.

- Keep warm foods warm and cold foods cold. You should take the same precautions with your baby's food as you do with your own. Don't leave food out for more than one hour at room temperature. Refrigerate opened jars of food (as well as formula and breast milk) promptly.

- When your baby starts eating regular food or homemade baby food, make sure you cook it—especially meats—thoroughly.

Warming Baby Food

You don't need to warm your baby's food. In fact, she may prefer it at room temperature. If you warm the food, heat a jar of it in a pan of water on the stove or heat the food in a microwave set on low. Be very careful not to overheat it, and test the temperature of the food yourself before feeding it to your baby. Commercial baby food warmers are also available.

Finger Food

When your baby is between eight and twelve months old, she'll probably want to start feeding herself. At this age, she's grown a few teeth and developed better hand coordination. Make sure that any finger foods you give her are soft, easy to swallow (or dissolve quickly in the mouth), and cut into bite-size pieces. Here's a list of nutritious finger foods that can be cut into small pieces and are appropriate for stomachs just getting used to solid foods.

- Shredded chicken pieces
- Cooked egg yolks
- Hamburger pieces
- Diced beef, veal, and lamb
- Bananas
- Cooked pieces of apples, pears, and peaches
- Ripe avocado
- Mashed potatoes
- Rice
- Macaroni, cooked very soft
- Lima beans
- Tofu (soybean curd)
- Sugarless dry cereal

Preparing Homemade Baby Foods

Many parents agree that homemade baby foods are often better than commercially prepared foods. For example, if you make your baby's food, you can…

- Control more of what's in your baby's food.

- Save money.

- Protect the environment—no packaging to throw away.

- Use organic produce and natural meats and poultry.

- Provide more variety than what's available in commercially prepared baby foods.

- Make foods that fit with your family's diet.

You can quickly turn almost any of the foods you eat into something your baby will enjoy. All you need is something to grind the food, such as:

- Manual grinder: baby, small, or large food mill; fork; potato ricer; purée sieve; food chopper

- Electric grinder: blender; electric food mill; electric food chopper; electric mixer with attachments

You also need something to store the baby food. Here are some inexpensive options:

- Ice cube trays: perfect for freezing baby food in small, individual portions.

- Small freezer zipper bags: great for storing ice cubes of baby food and finger foods.

- Small food storage containers (less than three inches deep): can store baby food from the freezer to microwave.

- Baking sheet: drop one- to two-tablespoon portions on a baking sheet and freeze. When frozen, place portions in freezer zipper bags.

Tips for Preserving the Vitamins and Preparing Baby Food Safely

- Buy fresh produce no earlier than the day before you plan to prepare it.

- Keep produce at room temperature until peak ripeness.

- Don't wash the food until you're ready to prepare it.

- Wash produce well, preferably with a produce rinse product to help remove pesticides.

- Chop a food before cooking it to speed up cooking time.

- Steam or cook food in the microwave with just a tablespoon of water.

- Don't add sugar, salt, or other seasonings while making baby food.

- Cook foods in small portions to prevent overcooking. Once cooked, refrigerate or freeze the portions after letting them cool briefly.

- Test the temperature of cooking meats with a food thermometer to make sure they're cooked properly.

- Wash your hands in hot soapy water before preparing food.

- Use plastic or nonporous cutting boards. Wash them in hot soapy water after preparing each food item.

- Keep utensils and cutting boards used for raw meats, poultry, and fish separate from those used for raw fruit or vegetables.

- Wash knives, utensils, and countertops in hot soapy water after preparing each food item.

- Never place cooked food on a plate that held raw meat, poultry, or seafood. Avoid leaving any of these foods at room temperature.

- Make sure storage containers for baby food are clean.

- Use paper towels to clean up kitchen surfaces. If you must use cloth towels, wash them often in the hot cycle. If using sponges, wash them in the dishwasher and replace them often.

Homemade Baby Food Storage Guide		
Food	Refrigerator (40°F or 4°C)	Freezer (0°F or -18°C)
Cooked fruits and vegetables	2 days	1 month
Cooked meat, poultry, fish	24 hours	1 month
Frozen fruits and vegetables that are thawed	2 days	Do not refreeze.
Cooked meat, poultry or fish that has been thawed	24 hours	Do not refreeze.

Preparing Baby Foods Step-by-Step

Step 1: Cook the meats, fruits, or vegetables you plan to offer your baby. You can use canned fruits and vegetables, but they're not as nutritious as fresh or frozen foods.

Step 2: Purée, grind, mash, or finely chop the cooked foods. At first, make sure the food's texture is quite smooth. (Beginning eaters can choke on lumpy or coarse food.) The more experienced your baby becomes at eating, the less smooth her food's texture will need to be.

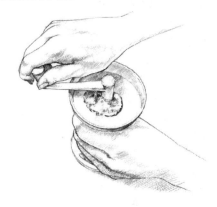

Step 3: Spoon the prepared food into an ice cube tray or onto a baking sheet and freeze it. (Do not refreeze thawed foods.) When frozen, store the cubes or portions in freezer zipper bags. Heat whatever amount you need in a pan on the stove or in the microwave

Pediatric Obesity

Almost one-third of children in the United States over two years of age are over-weight. Issues such as genetic susceptibility, socioeconomic class, and geographic location have an impact on one's chances of being overweight, and researchers are still studying the specifics of what parents can do in the first year to prevent obesity, but here are a few logical steps you can take to start your child on a healthy path:

- Don't smoke during pregnancy. A recent study suggests that intrauterine exposure to smoke can be a risk for childhood obesity.
- Gain a healthy amount of weight during pregnancy. Women who gain too much may deliver babies with high birth weights, which could increase the risk for later obesity.
- Breastfeed, if possible. A breastfed baby is 20 to 30 percent less likely to be obese through at least early adolescence.
- Wait to introduce solid foods until your baby is at least four to six months.
- Allow your infant to stop eating at the earliest signs of being satisfied. Your role is to provide healthy, safe, and nutritious foods; your infant's role is to choose when and how much to eat.
- As your baby gets older, set a pattern of regular family mealtimes and snacks in a happy setting (with the TV and computer off).
- Don't regularly serve foods and drinks that are high in sugar, sodium, and calories, and low in nutrients, such as chips, cookies, carbonated soda, and fruit drinks. A treat every once in a while is okay.
- Don't put your infant on a diet. Fat, particularly, should not be restricted in the first two years due to the brain still growing.
- Bring your baby to her care provider for regular checkups. She or he will monitor growth rates of length, weight, and head size, while factoring in familial patterns. You can work together to set the stage for proper and good nutrition that will bode well for the following years.

Chapter Four

Your Baby's Safety

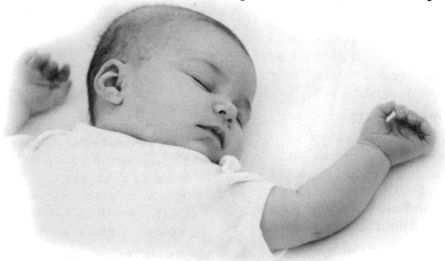

Today's better healthcare has largely eliminated or controlled many diseases that once killed babies. In fact, vehicle accidents kill or injure more children under age four than any disease. As a parent, your job is to provide a safe environment that your baby can explore. Anticipate his development so you can childproof your home before he enters a new stage. And, of course, make sure he's properly secured in an approved car seat that is correctly installed in your car, when you travel.

Babies are naturally curious and active, but their sense of balance and wariness of dangerous situations don't develop until they're older. Once your baby begins to wiggle, roll over, grasp objects, creep, and eventually crawl and walk, he'll need your supervision to explore his environment safely.

The following pages offer a guide to childproofing your home, plus information on buying safe baby equipment. Every six months, childproof your home again. Focus on eliminating dangerous situations that your baby's drawn to. Also, consider the season—winter is an especially dangerous time for fires, and spring and summer often require water and bicycle safety precautions.

Here's a general outline of a baby's typical development during the first year. (See Chapter 5 for details.)

Age	Baby's Abilities
Birth–2 mo	Your baby will wiggle and may start to roll over (though this is uncommon).
3–5 mo	Your baby may begin to rock and roll over, grasp things, sit up, and put things into his mouth.
6–9 mo	Your baby may begin to creep, crawl, pull himself up, and pull everything else down.
10–12 mo	Your baby may begin to stand, climb, and even walk.

Childproofing Your Home

General Safety Guidelines

Here's a list of general home childproofing tips. Following them are tips for childproofing specific rooms and areas in your home.

- Cover unused outlets with safety caps. Use safety covers over outlets with electric plugs in them. Don't overload outlets. Make sure no electrical cords are frayed or damaged.

- Put bulbs in all empty light sockets.

- Don't let your baby near electrical appliances when they're in use, and always turn them off when you're done. Also, keep all cords to small appliances, equipment, and lamps out of his reach so he can't pull the objects onto himself.

- Keep any objects that can fit inside a cardboard toilet paper tube out of your baby's reach (pins, buttons, screws, beads, coins, marbles, small toys, and other small or sharp objects). It takes only a minute for a baby to put a small object in his mouth and choke. This warning also applies to any small, hard foods, like nuts or popcorn.

- Check your floors often for small objects, especially if you have older children who play with small toys or if you have a hobby that uses tiny materials.

- Keep scissors, knives, razorblades, tools, and all breakable or broken objects out of your baby's reach.

- Keep purses, briefcases, and bags out of your baby's reach. They often contain coins, sharp objects, medications, and other hazards.

- Keep all plastic bags and sheets of thin plastic out of your baby's reach. Dry cleaning bags are especially dangerous—tie them in a knot before throwing them away. Never cover a crib mattress with thin plastic.

- Never leave a baby alone with a balloon. Remove all popped-balloon pieces immediately so your baby doesn't choke on them.

- Appliance cords, telephone cords, cords from blinds, and other cords or straps can strangle babies. Keep them out of your baby's reach. Any cords on toys should be shorter than seven inches, but watch your baby carefully when he's playing with any toy with a cord.

- Never put necklaces, cords attached to pacifiers, or cords of any kind around your baby's neck.

- Keep your baby away from used ashtrays, glasses containing alcohol or hot liquids, lit candles, matches, or cigarette lighters—these last two items are the most common cause of fatal fires.

- Don't smoke while caring for your baby. Cigarettes can burn him, and the smoke can irritate his lungs and make him more susceptible to diseases. *Never* smoke in bed.

- Install smoke and carbon monoxide detectors in your basement and in the hallways near bedrooms. Make sure you have at least one smoke detector on each floor of your home. If they are not lifelong detectors, test them monthly and replace batteries yearly. Vacuum or dust them regularly.

- Have a fire escape plan and practice it monthly. Make sure windows and doors can open easily.

- Place guards in front of open fireplaces, heaters, steam radiators, hot air registers, floor furnaces, and riser pumps. Have your furnace, fireplaces, and chimney cleaned and inspected yearly. Avoid using electric space heaters or kerosene heaters. If you must use them, keep them away from bedding, clothing, and curtains. Unplug them at night.

- Always keep firearms and ammunition locked up separately.

- Remove furniture with sharp edges from rooms where your baby crawls around. Soft, plastic safety edges are great for covering sharp corners on coffee tables and other low furniture. You can also use foam tape to cover the edges of glass tables.

- If you have hardwood floors, don't allow your child to walk or run on them in socks or booties without slip-resistant soles.

- Some large-screen TVs, bookcases, and computer monitors are front heavy and can fall over, seriously harming or even killing those crushed. Consider installing wall tethers to front-heavy TVs.

- If your home's walls, windows, or doors were last painted before 1977, consider repainting. Old paint contains lead that can harm your baby, especially if he eats any paint chips. You can find devices to check for lead at some paint stores or home improvement centers. If repainting, follow the Environmental Protection Agency's guidelines for safely removing lead-based paint (see http://www.epa.gov/lead/pubs/reno-vaterightbrochure.pdf).

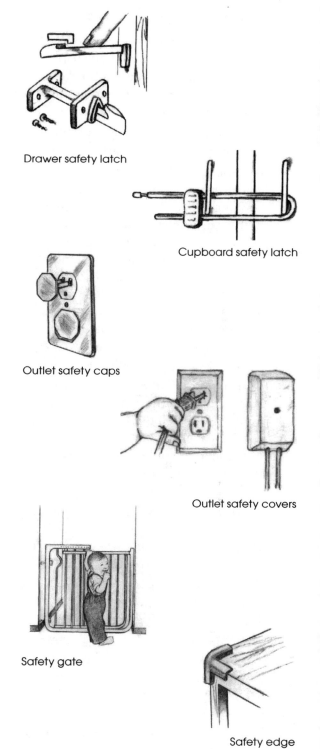

Drawer safety latch

Cupboard safety latch

Outlet safety caps

Outlet safety covers

Safety gate

Safety edge

Kitchen or Dining Room

- Keep toxic materials (see pages XXX–XX) locked up or out of your baby's reach. Use drawer and cupboard safety latches to prevent him from getting into potentially dangerous items.

- Make sure your baby can't get into any garbage pails or wastebaskets.

- If possible, have someone else care for your baby in another room while you're cooking and serving meals, or use a high chair or play yard to keep your child away from danger. Hot grease and food can splatter a baby sitting nearby in a baby carrier, and a mobile baby can get into lots of danger. If these options aren't possible, be extremely careful transporting hot food and liquids around your baby, and make sure he's well away from cooking food at all times.

- Turn all pot handles inward so your baby can't pull them off the stove. Simmer foods on the front burners and boil foods on the back burners. Keep anything that could catch fire away from the stove and oven.

- Never leave the oven door open, and keep your baby away from oven doors that are hot to the touch. If possible, keep your infant out of the kitchen entirely when the oven is on.

- Don't let your baby play with knobs on a gas stove. If necessary, remove the knobs when you're not using them.

- Don't drink hot liquids while your baby's in your lap. When carrying hot liquids, make sure you don't trip over your baby or anything that could cause a spill onto your child.

- Keep all objects away from the edges of counters and tables, out of your baby's reach.

- Unplug appliances when not in use.

- Sharp knives and appliances such as food processors should be kept in latched drawers or cupboards.

- Avoid putting small magnets on the outside of your refrigerator. They're a choking hazard.

- Keep matches out of sight and reach.

- Don't warm bottles in a microwave oven as heating can be uneven (causing hot spots) and bottles can explode if overheated.

- Avoid using tablecloths. Babies love to pull on the edges, and can pull objects onto themselves.

- Install a multipurpose, dry chemical, portable fire extinguisher in the kitchen. Know when and how you should use it.

Bathroom

- Never leave your baby alone in the bathtub—not even for a second.

- Before bathing your baby, always make sure the bath water isn't too hot. Turn off the faucets tightly so your baby can't turn them on. Set your hot water heater to 120°F (48.9°C) so your baby won't be unintentionally scalded.

- Always keep the bathroom door closed, and don't let your baby play in the bathroom. A bathroom contains too many hard objects and slippery surfaces, and a curious child could drown in a toilet bowl. Consider installing a lock on the toilet seat cover.

- Keep hot curling irons and electric razors well away from your baby. Unplug and put away hairdryers when they're not in use, especially if they're near any source of water, and store them in another room if possible.

- Put away medicines and other potentially hazardous materials—cleansers, cosmetics, and soaps (see pages 96–97)—immediately after use. Store them in a locked, high cabinet out of reach.

- Buy medicine in childproof containers and store them in locked cabinets.

- Always check medicine labels in a well-lit room for proper dosages before administering medications to your baby. Don't give medications prescribed for one baby to another.

- Don't save leftover medications; safely discard them.

- Don't call medicine and supplements "candy." Many poisonings are overdoses of good-tasting medicine and supplements, like candy-flavored vitamins.

Nursery

- Never leave your baby alone on a changing table, bed, couch, or other elevated surface. While changing your baby, use a safety strap or keep one hand on him at all times. If you must leave the room in the middle of a diaper change, take him with you or lay him in a crib or other safe place.

- Buy only flame-retardant clothing for your baby. If you must use clothing that isn't flame retardant, make sure it fits snugly so there's little air between the fabric and your baby's skin. (Air feeds a flame if the fabric is on fire.)

- When your baby can sit up by himself, lower the crib mattress. Set it at its lowest point before he can stand.

- Don't leave large toys in a crib, and if you're using bumper pads (not recommended), remove them when your baby begins pulling up. Toys and bumper pads can be used as steps to climb out.

- Place humidifiers, vaporizers, and portable heaters out of your child's reach, and keep them away from his bedding and anything else flammable.

- Contact your local fire department to learn whether it recommends sticking a "tot finder" decal on the window of your baby's nursery. Find out what

other fire safety measures it recommends. If the nursery isn't on the ground floor, make sure you've got a fire escape plan that provides a safe way to reach the ground. Buy a non-combustible escape ladder, if necessary.

- Install window guards to prevent falls.

Stairs

- To prevent falls while carrying your baby as you walk up and down a staircase, keep all objects off the stairs. Remove extension cords and throw rugs near or on the staircase. Hold the handrail while climbing up or down. Carpet your stairs if possible. Don't wax uncarpeted stairs.

- When your baby is mobile, barricade the tops and bottoms of staircases with safety gates. Babies learn to climb up before they learn to climb down. Don't use accordion-style gates with V-shaped openings (these can pose strangulation hazards); do use gates that are mounted to the wall. (Gates kept in place by pressure aren't as sturdy.) Any gaps should be less than 1½ inches (3.8 centimeters) wide.

- If you have a basement door, install a self-latching lock to prevent falls down the stairs.

Laundry

- Store all laundry detergents and cleaning products out of your child's reach.

- Clean your dryer vent after every use to avoid lint buildup that can catch fire.

- Don't let your baby near your iron or ironing board; an ironing board is easily tipped over, and an iron is hot, heavy, and easily pulled down by tugging on the cord. Always turn the iron off when you're done.

- Tie dry cleaning bags in a knot before throwing them away.

Outdoors

- Don't bring your baby—or any child—in the yard when you're using lawnmowers, snowblowers, or any power equipment. Never ride with or carry your baby when you're operating this equipment.

- Never leave your baby alone outside.

- Make sure your baby doesn't pick up dangerous objects or put them in his mouth.

- Your baby needs some sun exposure to stimulate the production of vitamin D, which is necessary for building strong bones. Two to three times a week during the warmer months, expose some of your baby's skin (hands, arms, and face) to sunlight for five to fifteen minutes. If your baby has darker skin, have him sunbathe slightly longer. To prevent burning at other times, place a wide-brimmed hat on your baby's head and, until he's six months old, dress him in as much clothing as is comfortable and lightly apply a PABA-free sunblock (at least SPF 15) on his hands and face. Once he's six months old, slather sunblock on any exposed skin. Midday sunlight is the strongest, so expose your baby to the sun before 10 A.M. and after 3 P.M.

- Use and store barbecue grills away from anything flammable. Use grills outside only, and don't place them against the wall of your home. Make sure your child can't touch the grill. Charcoal should be cold before it is dumped.

- Always place barriers around fire pits or campfires. Constantly supervise your child around an outdoor fire. Make sure the fire's completely out before leaving it.

- Store gasoline, kerosene, and propane away from your home and only in approved safety containers.

- If pesticides or herbicides are applied to your yard, keep your child away from the yard for at least forty-eight hours.

Toxic Substances

- Post the phone number of the national poison control center (800-222-1222) near every telephone and program it into your cell phone(s). Consider also posting and programming the phone number of your local poison control center.

- If your baby has swallowed a substance, call the poison control center. Get to a medical facility as soon as possible, if recommended. (See page 179.) Do *not* give your baby syrup of Ipecac.

- If your baby has a substance in his eye, hold his eyelid open and pour a steady stream of lukewarm water into the inner corner of the eye. If a substance is on his skin, remove clothing and rinse the skin with lukewarm water.

- Keep all toxic substances in a locked container and stored in a drawer or cupboard, out of your baby's reach. Keep the drawer or cupboard closed and use safety latches or strapping tape to prevent your baby from opening it.

- Keep all toxic substances in their original containers with their original labels.

- Discard containers that have held hazardous substances into a garbage pail with a locked lid, or remove them from your home.

- Don't let your baby chew on newspaper, magazine, or book pages. Some inks may be toxic.

- Don't let your baby chew on gift-wrap ribbons. The dye in some ribbons may be toxic.

- Don't let your child chew on windowsills, porch steps, bars on iron gates, or any other surfaces. They may have been painted with lead-based paint.

- Don't take medication or supplements in front of your baby. If he wants to put everything into his mouth that you put into yours, he may find your medications and supplements attractive.

Environmental Concerns

The list of potentially toxic materials in the environment is growing. These include substances like radon, asbestos, mercury, molds, lead, water contaminants, and many more chemicals. Keep a diligent watch for updated information on these types of substances. (The Environmental Protection Agency's website is a helpful resource: http://www.epa.gov/.)

Following is a general list of household products and other potentially poisonous substances. Many others may be poisonous as well. If you question whether a substance is poisonous, ask your baby's caregiver or call the poison control center.

• Alcoholic beverages	• Lighter fluid
• Ammonia	• Lye and alkalies for cleaning drains, toilet bowls, and ovens
• Antifreeze	
• Aspirin, vitamins containing iron, and other drugs and medicines	
	• Metal polish
• Bleach	• Mothballs
• Borax	• Mouthwash
• Car cleaner	• Nail products
• Cleaning fluids and powders	• Oil of wintergreen
	• Paint thinner
• Cosmetics	• Perfumes
• Detergents	• Perm solutions
• Hair relaxer	• Pesticides
• Insect and rat poisons	• Plant sprays and weed killers
	• Rust remover
• Kerosene, gasoline, and benzene	• Shoe polish
	• Turpentine
• Lamp oil	• Washing soda
• Lead-based paint	• Wax remover
• Liquid furniture and car polish	• Windshield washer fluid

Poisonous Plants

Many household and garden plants are poisonous—you might not want to keep plants in your home. Otherwise, know the names of all your plants, and keep them out of your baby's reach. Never let him eat or suck on any part of a plant. Nibbling on leaves, sucking on plant stalks, or drinking water where plants have been may poison him.

Following is a partial list of poisonous plants; there are many more. There are also many plants that are mildly toxic. Contact the national poison control center (800-222-1222) or your local poison control center for a more complete list of toxic plants.

• Azalea	• Mistletoe
• Crocus (autumn)	• Morning glory
• Delphinium	• Nightshade
• Elderberry	• Oleander
• Holly	• Poison ivy
• Hydrangea	• Poison oak
• Japanese yew	• Poison sumac
• Larkspur	• Rhododendron
• Lily of the valley	• Toadstools
• Marijuana	• Wisteria

Baby Gear

This section reviews the most common, helpful baby gear. (See pages 31–33 for information on bath gear.) It also includes information on what to look for when buying products and how to use them properly. Here are a few general safety tips to remember about baby gear:

- Mail all completed product registration and warranty cards so you're notified of manufacturer recalls.

- Check that all new baby gear has a certification safety seal from the Juvenile Products Manufacturers Association (JPMA).

- Don't place any gear directly under ceiling fans or by heating elements or windows.

For more information on product safety and quality, read a current product ratings guide, like *Consumer Reports*. (Available online at http://www.consumerreports.org.)

Car Seat

 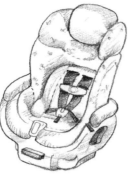

As mentioned previously, vehicle accidents injure or kill more children younger than age four than any other kind of accident or disease. For this reason, it's illegal for children to ride in vehicles without being strapped into car seats, although state laws vary on what age children must be before they can travel without them, and car seat weight and height limits differ by model. Most crashes occur within five miles (8 kilometers) of home at speeds of less than twenty-five miles (40 kilometers) per hour, so always use the car seat no matter how short your ride.

Car seats reduce the chance (by well over 95 percent) that your baby will be harmed or killed in a vehicle accident. When a vehicle hits an object or stops suddenly, everyone inside continues to move forward at the same speed at which the vehicle was traveling—and restraints prevent them from becoming flying projectiles. You can't protect your baby while traveling in a vehicle by holding him snugly in your arms. Even if you're wearing a seat belt, the force of a crash will tear your baby from your arms. And if you strap your baby in with you, a crash will slam your own weight into his body, causing serious or fatal injuries. Car seats are designed to spread the force of a crash evenly over a baby's body.

Most hospitals and birth centers won't let you drive your baby home if you don't have a federally approved car seat that's properly installed. For guidelines on buying a car seat, check the American Academy of Pediatrics (AAP) website at http://www.aap.org under "Car Safety Seats: A Guide for Families." This source is updated annually. To make sure the car seat is safely installed, have a certified child passenger safety (CPS) technician check it. These experts can be located by entering your state and zip code at http://www.seatcheck.org. The National Highway Traffic Safety Administration is another resource, and can be accessed via telephone at 888-DASH-2-DOT (888-327-4236) from 8 A.M. to 10 P.M. (Eastern Standard Time) Monday through Friday or online at http://www.nhtsa.dot.gov/people/injury/childps/CPSFitting/Index.cfm.

Car seats for infants come in different types: infant-only seats and convertible infant-toddler seats. Infant-only seats are rear-facing and meant for babies weighing up to twenty-two or thirty-five pounds, depending on the model. Many have a detachable seat that can snap into and out of a base that remains in the car, allowing parents to transfer the seat without moving the baby. Some seats can snap into stroller frames. Infant-only seats are convenient, but babies outgrow them, requiring parents to buy a larger car seat, usually within the first year.

Convertible infant-toddler seats can be used in rear- and forward-facing positions, and are meant for babies weighing up to forty pounds. They come with one of three restraint options: a five-point harness, T-bar shield, or overhead/tray shield. For newborn use, be sure to purchase one with a five-point harness. Experts believe they're the safest choice. (Shields may not keep a baby's upper body properly positioned, and could hit a small baby's head in a crash.) Convertible seats are heavier than infant-only seats and may be more difficult to transport, but are cost-effective. If you buy one of these seats for your infant, make sure he is well supported.

Whichever seat you choose, it is extremely important that you keep it rear-facing until your baby reaches the highest weight or height allowed by the manufacturer, or age two years (the current recommendation by safety experts).

All new car seats on the market must meet the federal government's standards, but a car seat can still present safety problems if it's installed incorrectly or doesn't fit your baby. Avoid buying a used car seat if you can, and consider more than price when making a decision. Look for a new seat with easy installation, adequate restraints, belt adjustments, tethers, washability, and a well-padded seat with plenty of head and back support. Here are some other tips on buying and using car seats:

- Read the manufacturer's instructions and always keep them with the seat. Send in any registration cards so you'll be notified of recalls.

- Read your vehicle owner's manual for important information on how to install a car seat correctly in your vehicle. For individual help installing a specific car seat in a specific car, consult a certified child passenger safety (CPS) technician.

- Install the car seat in the back seat, preferably in the center. Never place a child younger than thirteen years old in the front seat of a vehicle.

- Never put a rear-facing car seat in the front seat of a car with an airbag.

- Properly attach the car seat to the vehicle's seat belt or Lower Anchors and Tethers for Children (LATCH) system. (All passenger vehicles and car safety seats made after September 2002 come with the LATCH system. Unless both the vehicle and the car seat have this system, you'll need seat belts to secure the seat.) Check the manufacturer's instructions to route the seat belt or LATCH through the correct path on the car seat. The seat shouldn't move more than an inch side to side or front to back. Buckle or attach it, and pull it tight.

- If using the seat belt, check the buckle to make sure it doesn't lie just at the point where the belt bends around the car seat. (If it does, you won't get the belt tight enough.) Check your vehicle owner's manual to see if you can lock the seat belts into position or if you'll need to use a locking clip. Locking clips come with most new car seats. (Some have them built in.) Read the instructions for information on how to use the locking clip.

- Use the correct harness slots for your baby's size.

- Place the plastic harness clip, if provided, at or below your baby's shoulder level to hold shoulder straps in place.

- Make sure the straps lie flat and aren't twisted. Adjust the straps to accommodate the thickness of your baby's clothes, checking that the harness still holds him snugly.

- If your baby's head slumps forward, the seat might not be reclined enough. Tilt the car seat until it's reclined as close as possible to a forty-five–degree angle (according to manufacturer's instructions). You can place a rolled towel or other firm padding such as a pool noodle under the base of the seat near the point where the back and bottom of the vehicle seat meet.

- Dress your baby in clothes that allow the car seat straps between his legs.

- In cold weather, tuck blankets around your baby *after* securing and adjusting the harness straps. Don't place blankets under or behind him.

- Pad the sides and crotch of the seat with rolled-up receiving blankets or a small diaper to keep your newborn from slouching.

- Don't attach anything to a car seat. Attached items could pose a danger in an accident.

- If using built-in car seats, make sure you follow the manufacturer's weight and height recommendations. All built-ins are for children at least a year old and who weigh at least twenty pounds.

- If you're transporting a premature or very small infant, be sure to use a car seat without a shield. While still in the hospital, your baby should be observed in the car seat to make sure the semi-reclined position doesn't lower his heart rate or oxygen level or cause other breathing problems. If your child has special needs, he may need a car seat that's custom-designed for his situation. Check with the Automotive Safety Program at 800-543-6227 or http://www.preventinjury.org/index.asp.

- You should buy a new car seat, if possible. If you can't, here are tips for buying or borrowing used seats:

  - Don't use a seat that's more than ten years old. Check with the manufacturer to find out how long it recommends using the seat. Some manufacturers recommend that consumers use seats for only five or six years.

  - Don't use a seat if you don't know its entire history. Never use a seat that's been in a crash.

  - Don't use a seat that doesn't have a label stating the manufacture date and seat name or model number.

  - Don't use a seat that doesn't come with manufacturer's instructions.

  - Don't use a seat that has cracks in its frame.

  - Don't use a seat that's missing parts. If you want to use the seat, check first with the manufacturer to make sure you can replace the missing parts.

  - Don't use a seat in a boat. They don't float.

- Don't transport unsecured heavy or loose objects while traveling with your baby in a vehicle.

- Never leave your baby alone in a vehicle—not even for a minute.

- At about nine to twelve months, your baby may protest being in his car seat and try to get out. Insist that he stay in his seat and inform him that the car cannot move unless he's safely buckled in.

General Car Safety

When your baby is old enough to be mobile, keep him away from driveways or streets where he may be hit by a vehicle. Drivers should always walk around and behind their vehicles before getting in to make sure no one is in the blind spot.

Crib

A crib can be your child's bed until age two or older. Here are some guidelines when looking for a crib and some safety tips for using it.

- Thousands of babies are injured in falls from cribs each year. A recent study found that crib injuries increase when babies become more mobile, so make sure to lower the mattress when your baby can sit up, and put the mattress in the lowest position before he can stand.

- Don't buy a crib with a detachable drop-side rail. They've been associated with infant suffocation and strangulation, and will no longer be manufactured. If you already own a crib with a detachable drop-side rail, seriously consider buying a new crib with four fixed sides. Otherwise, be sure that there are no gaps in the sides or corners that could trap your child. Make sure that the latches for the side rail and mattress support are too difficult for your baby to release. Always leave the side rails up when your baby is in the crib.

- Purchase a new crib, if possible. Older cribs might not meet current safety standards. If you must use an older or secondhand crib, check it carefully for potential hazards and replace the mattress.

- Check that the space between slats is no more than $2\frac{3}{8}$ inches (6 centimeters) wide to prevent your baby's head from becoming trapped.

- Make sure there are no missing, loose, cracked, or splintered slats.

- Make sure the crib has no sharp or jagged edges.

- Check that the mattress fits snugly in the crib. (No more than two fingers fit between the edge of the mattress and the side of the crib.) Remove any plastic covering the mattress.

- Securely attach the mattress support to the headboard and footboard.

- Make sure the screws or bolts holding crib parts together are tight and none are missing, to prevent the crib from coming apart. Recheck often that parts are tight-fitting, and only replace parts with ones from the manufacturer.

- Check that corner posts (finials) are no higher than $\frac{1}{16}$ inch (1.5 millimeters). Loose clothing can become snagged on them if they are higher.

- Check that the headboard or footboard has no cutouts that could trap your baby's head.

- Cover the mattress with a well-fitted crib sheet.

- Don't place any pillows, comforters, sheepskins, stuffed animals, or other soft items in the crib.

- If using bumper pads (not recommended because they can suffocate a baby), remove them once your baby can move around the crib or stand. Make sure the bumper pads go all the way around the crib and are secured with at least six straps or ties that are less than six inches long. Avoid soft, pillow-like bumpers. Your baby could become trapped between the bumper and the side of the crib. Once he can stand, he can use the bumper as a step to get out of the crib.

- Use sleep sacks to keep your baby warm. If you use a blanket (not recommended), tuck it tightly into the mattress and have it cover your baby only up to his chest.

- Make sure that mobiles are securely attached to the side rails and the hanging items on mobiles aren't long enough to strangle your baby. Check that there are no cords from window coverings within his reach.

- Don't place the crib near a window, to prevent falls.

- Once your baby is five months, remove crib gyms and hanging mobiles from the crib.

- When the height of the side rail is less than three-quarters of your baby's height, or once his height reaches thirty-five inches (89 centimeters), move him to a bed.

Changing Table

A changing table can be a convenient place to dress and change your baby's diaper. You must take care to prevent falls, however.

- A guardrail with a minimum two-inch (5-centimeter) height should surround the entire changing surface.

- Make sure the center of the surface is concave, so your baby won't slide to the edge.

- Always use safety straps and never leave your baby unattended.

- Keep supplies out of your baby's reach.

- Be wary of flip-open changing areas that extend beyond the main table. The table may topple when a baby is placed near the edge of the overhang.

Bassinet or Cradle

Here are some guidelines when looking for a bassinet or cradle and some safety tips for using it.

- Purchase a new bassinet, if possible. Older bassinets may not meet safety standards. If you must purchase an older or secondhand bassinet, check it carefully for potential hazards. In 2008, almost a million Simplicity 3-in-1 and 4-in-1 bedside sleeper bassinets were recalled, due to a strangulation hazard; these bassinets still may be sold in secondhand shops or online.

- Make sure the bassinet or cradle has a sturdy bottom and a wide, stable base so that it can't collapse.

- Follow the manufacturer's guidelines on the appropriate weight and size of babies that can use the bassinet or cradle safely. Bassinets and cradles are usually outgrown quickly. Babies about one month or ten pounds will usually need a crib.

- Check that the spaces between spindles are no more than $2\frac{3}{8}$ inches (6 centimeters) wide.

- Make sure the screws and bolts are tight.

- Make sure foldable legs have secure locks or latches.

- If the model has wheels, make sure they have secure locks.

- Check that the mattress is firm and smooth and fits snugly. (No more than two fingers fit between the edge of the mattress and the side of the bassinet or cradle).

- Check that trim and decorative bows and ribbons are stitched securely.

- Make sure there's sufficient wall clearance for swinging or rocking cradles.

- Make sure a swinging or rocking cradle can be immobilized.

- If the model has a hood, make sure it folds back, or it'll get in the way when putting your baby inside.

- Don't place any pillows, comforters, sheepskins, stuffed animals, or other soft items in the bassinet or cradle.

- Bassinets and cradles can be toppled, so they might not be safe if you have other children or pets in the home.

- Don't transport a bassinet or cradle while your baby is inside it.

Bedside Co-sleeper

A co-sleeper is a three-sided bassinet that can be attached directly to the parents' bed. Some bedside co-sleepers can convert into freestanding bassinets, changing tables, and play yards. They're designed to keep a baby close to his parents for bonding and breastfeeding, and are meant to meet the American Academy of Pediatrics (AAP) guidelines for sudden infant death (SIDS) prevention, which suggest it's best for a baby to sleep in the same room but not the same bed as his parents. The Consumer Product Safety Commission (CPSC) has not yet set safety standards for co-sleepers. See the bassinet section above for some general guidelines, and be advised that almost a million Simplicity 3-in-1 and 4-in-1 bedside sleeper bassinets were recalled in 2008, due to a strangulation hazard; these bassinets still may be sold in secondhand shops or online. (See http://www.armsreach.com for more information on bedside co-sleepers.)

Play Yard

A play yard (or playpen) is a great, safe place to put your baby when you need some "hands free" time. Don't overuse it, though. Your baby needs to explore his environment, so don't substitute a play yard for a properly childproofed home. Here are some guidelines when looking for a play yard and some safety tips for using it.

- A play yard is designed for a baby who can't yet climb. Choose one that matches the height and weight of your baby. Fully assemble the play yard, including the side rails, before you put your baby inside it.

- Place the play yard on a firm floor to prevent the legs from collapsing.

- Keep the play yard away from potentially dangerous objects—for example, lamps, blinds, stoves, and heaters.

- Don't put padding or other objects (large toys, boxes) that your baby can climb on in the play yard.

- Never leave your baby in a mesh play yard if its side rail is down. He could get caught between the pad and loose mesh and suffocate.

- Look for a play yard with mesh holes no larger than ¼ inch (6.4 millimeters). The mesh needs to be firmly attached to the top rail and the floor plate. If you choose a wooden play yard, make sure the slats are no more than 2⅜ inches (6 centimeters) apart. Never use accordion-style, fence-type enclosures.

- Make sure any metal catches are outside the mesh or railing, and check that the hinges and latches on folding models lock tightly.

- Frequently check the vinyl or fabric that covers side rails for holes or tears.

- Don't tie toys to the play yard once your infant is five months. Your baby could become entangled in them and strangle himself.

- Never leave your baby unsupervised in a play yard.

- Don't move the play yard while your baby is inside it.

- If the play yard has an attachable raised changing table, make sure to remove the table when your baby is in the play yard.

Stroller

Choosing the right stroller depends on your lifestyle. In general, look for a stroller with buckles and belts that are easy to fasten and adjust, an adjustable seat and canopy, washable fabric, an adjustable handle, an easy folding mechanism with a safety catch, brakes, wide wheel base, and swivel wheels. Adjust the stroller without your baby in it to avoid getting his fingers pinched in the hinges. Make sure your baby's fingers can't reach the wheels.

If using a secondhand stroller, check with either *Consumer Reports* (http://www.consumerreports.org) or the Consumer Product Safety Commission (http://www.cpsc.gov/) to make sure the model hasn't been recalled. Make sure the used stroller is sturdy with smooth-rolling wheels and secure safety belts. Check for cracks or splits or sharp edges. Don't hang bags on stroller handles. They could make the stroller tip over. Never leave your baby unattended in the stroller.

Here are brief descriptions of the different kinds of strollers:

- Lightweight (or umbrella): Convenient and portable, but not designed for newborns.

- Standard: Sturdy and has a reclining seat and storage room, but can be cumbersome and expensive.

- Convertible (stroller with removable car seat): Very convenient, but many models are pricey.

- Jogging: Can travel on all terrains, but aren't designed for newborns and can't fold up as compactly as standard strollers.

- Carriage: Have large wheels for smooth rides and can be quite fancy but also heavy, difficult to store, and very expensive.

Baby Carriers (Backpacks and Front Packs)

A carrier is great way to transport your baby, either outside or in the house. Your baby will enjoy the warm containment it provides, and you'll like the freedom it gives you to move about. Choose a style that suits your setting. (For example, a carrier made of corduroy or heavy-gauge nylon may be too warm for the dog days of summer.) To be safe, pick a carrier that fits your baby's height, weight, and age. (Check the manufacturer's specifications.) Here are other safety guidelines to follow when considering the different kinds of carriers.

- Front packs:
Look for one that'll support your baby securely and allow a choice of positions. Make sure all straps, buckles, snaps, and belts are durable. Look for wide, padded, adjustable shoulder straps; a padded waist/hip belt; a sturdy padded headrest; and leg holes banded with elastic or padded fabric. Make sure you can easily slip the carrier on and off. Check that the fabric suits the season. Keep in mind that front packs are outgrown fairly quickly, usually around three months.

- Sling:
Make sure that the fabric won't smother your baby. A cotton sling is warm, soft, breathable, and machine washable.

- Backpacks (for a baby five to six months old or older, when his neck is strong enough to withstand jolts):
A backpack or other upright positioner should not be used for premature babies or babies with respiratory problems because it may make it hard for them to breathe. Look for one with wide, padded, adjustable, nonslip shoulder straps and hip belt. The lighter the pack is without the baby, the lighter it'll be with the baby. Look for a roomy, adjustable inside seat with an adjustable safety harness that clasps across the chest and shoulders. Check that the leg openings aren't too big or small for your baby and that the pack supports his back. Make sure the metal frame is well padded. Check that there are no rips, sharp edges, rough surfaces, or joints that can pinch or cut your baby. Choose a model with easily accessible compartments. Consider one with a protective canopy. Look for a model with a support stand that locks firmly. As babies get older they may become restless in the backpack, so make sure the straps are used correctly and your baby is secure. When using the backpack, bend with your knees, not from your waist, so your baby doesn't fall out. Never set the backpack on the ground with your baby in it—the pack can tip easily and injure him.

Bouncer Seat (Infant Seat)

A bouncer seat can soothe a fussy baby or occupy him while you take a few "hands off" minutes. Here are some guidelines when looking for a bouncer seat and some safety tips for using it.

- Make sure the seat has secure safety straps and nonskid material on the bottom. Always use the straps and never leave your baby unattended.

- Choose a seat with a wide base and outside frame so your infant sits deep inside and won't tip.

- Never place your baby in the bouncer seat on an elevated surface like a table. His bouncing may cause the seat to move, perhaps off the edge of the surface. The most common injuries occur when a baby falls out of the seat from a high surface. (In 2007, a million Bumbo seats were recalled after parents placed them on elevated surfaces and babies were injured.)

- Stop using the seat when your baby exceeds the manufacturer's recommended weight or development level. His movements could tip over the seat.

- The American Academy of Pediatrics (AAP) states that babies who spend too much time in bouncers may develop positional plagiocephaly (or flattened head syndrome), so don't keep your baby in the seat for longer than thirty minutes at a time. (For more on plagiocephaly, see page 163.)

High Chair

Once your baby starts to eat solid foods and can sit up on his own—usually between six and eight months—he'll need a place to sit so you can feed him easily. Some parents use a baby chair that attaches to a table. These chairs work well in tight quarters, are portable, and cost less than most high chairs. (If you choose to do this, the chair should lock onto a table and the table should be heavy enough to support the weight.) But most parents use a high chair to feed their baby and to let him feed himself. Here are some guidelines when looking for a high chair and some safety tips for using it.

- Falls are the most common and serious cause of high chair-related injuries. Look for a chair with a stable, wide base to avoid tipping.

- Make sure the seat is well padded. (Buy a cushion if the chair is wooden.)

- Check that the front seams don't have sharp edges that can scratch your baby's legs. Check the bottom of the tray for holes or sharp edges that could hurt his fingers. Make sure a wooden chair is free of splinters.

- Check the seat, harness, tray, and frame for hard-to-clean areas. Any fabrics should be plastic or vinyl that can be easily wiped clean.

- Look for a tray you can easily move. Some trays even release with one hand.

- Check the restraint system. The safety straps should be adjustable and secure your baby firmly across the hips and between the legs. Make sure your baby can't unlatch the safety buckle. Never allow standing in the high chair. If the high chair has wheels, make sure they lock.

- Look for a chair with adjustable parts that lock securely. Make sure locks are secure with each use. A chair with height adjustments works well for tables—and adults—of varying heights. An adjustable tray won't pinch your baby's belly. An adjustable footrest will keep your growing baby's legs from dangling.

- Closely supervise your baby while he's in the chair. Don't let other children pull on the chair or climb on it.

- Set the chair away from doorways, refrigerators, counters, ranges, and other equipment. Don't place the chair so close to the table that your baby can use his legs to push off it and possibly tip over.

- Make sure any caps or plugs on the high chair are securely attached so they can't become a choking hazard.

Baby Monitor

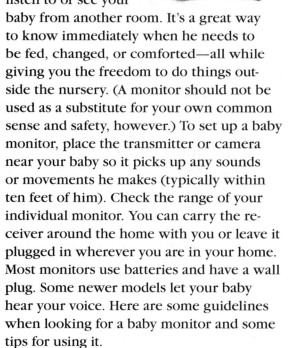

A baby monitor (really, a radio or video transmitter and receiver) lets you listen to or see your baby from another room. It's a great way to know immediately when he needs to be fed, changed, or comforted—all while giving you the freedom to do things outside the nursery. (A monitor should not be used as a substitute for your own common sense and safety, however.) To set up a baby monitor, place the transmitter or camera near your baby so it picks up any sounds or movements he makes (typically within ten feet of him). Check the range of your individual monitor. You can carry the receiver around the home with you or leave it plugged in wherever you are in your home. Most monitors use batteries and have a wall plug. Some newer models let your baby hear your voice. Here are some guidelines when looking for a baby monitor and some tips for using it.

- Look for a compact model. The smaller the receiver, the more easily you can carry it with you.

- Choose a monitor that alerts you when the batteries are low.

- Consider choosing a model that has a sound-activated light. If you're busy doing something that won't let you hear sounds coming from the receiver, a glance at it will tell you whether your baby's making noise.

- Consider choosing a model that comes with two receivers. They're handy if you want to leave one in one room and carry the other with you around the home.

- If you choose an analog model, try not to discuss anything private when the monitor is on. Interference from concrete walls, cordless phones, cell phones, or other baby monitors can broadcast your conversations to another family's monitor or any receiver. If you live in an apartment or close to others, a digital model (which will encode the sounds) is likely smarter. Also, choose a model with the right bandwidth for your area. Some high-end models offer a bandwidth up to 900 megahertz for better clarity. But if you live in an area with lots of potential interference, a low bandwith (40 megahertz) may be more appropriate.

- To prevent electrical shocks, never place a monitor in or around water.

Baby Swing and Jumper

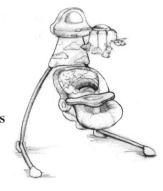

A baby swing or jumper can be just what frazzled parents and babies need. A swing's gentle and rhythmic movements can soothe a newborn, and a jumper can help an older baby burn some energy while entertaining himself. Don't rely on either too much, though. Use a swing or jumper sparingly and for short times. To your baby, nothing can replace your loving touch.

Most swings are battery-operated, and they come in both traditional and portable models. Most swing front to back, but some models have a cradle-style option that swings side to side. Here are some guidelines when looking for a swing and some tips for using it.

- Look for a swing that's sturdy without any loose screws or bolts. Make sure the seat and crossbar are strong and well constructed to keep your baby from falling forward. Check for potentially dangerous springs that might injure his fingers.

- A swing is designed to rock a small infant. Most manufacturers recommend that parents stop using a swing when their baby weighs between fifteen and twenty-five pounds (check manufacturer's instructions for specific weight limit).

- Make sure the swing has secure restraining straps to keep your baby from sliding out.

- Look for a swing with a removable, washable seat cover. Check that strong stitching and heavy-duty snaps secure the seat. Also check that the seat cushion is adequately padded (you can add padding).

- Consider choosing a swing with a reclining seat, which can work well for very young or sleepy babies.

- If you'll use the swing outside, look for one with a canopy to help protect your baby from sun and wind.

- Consider choosing a swing that plays music and has an activity tray to help keep your baby entertained.

- Keep an eye on your baby at all times while he's in the swing.

Baby jumpers come in different styles and formats. Jumpers that hang from doorways are considered less safe: The doorframe might not be sturdy enough to hold the jumper, babies can bump into walls, and the straps may break. Babies also tend to get motion-sick more often in doorway jumpers.

Here are some guidelines when looking for a baby jumper and some tips for using it.

- Choose a jumper that fits your baby's height, weight, and age. (Check the manufacturer's specifications.) Make

sure he can't slip through the leg and side openings.

- Assemble, install, and use the jumper according to the manufacturer's instructions.

- If using a secondhand jumper, make sure it has all its parts, comes with the manufacturer's instructions, and hasn't been recalled.

- Before putting your baby in the jumper, pull down on it to make sure the clamps and straps are properly secured.

- Limit your baby's time in a jumper to ten or fifteen minutes. If he jumps longer, he can harm his hips and delay his crawling and walking skills.

- Never use a jumper as a swing or carrier. To prevent accidental bumping, teach older children not to push or pull the baby while in the jumper.

- Keep an eye on your baby at all times while he's in the jumper.

Stationary Walkers and Play Centers

Once common for many babies, baby walkers are no longer recommended. These devices have not only injured and killed babies by letting them roll down staircases, into hot stoves, and near other hazards, but they may also impede the development of crawling and walking skills. For these reasons, the American Academy of Pediatrics (AAP) has recommended a ban on baby walkers since 1995, and Canada has officially banned them.

As an alternative to a baby walker, many parents use a stationary play center. A stationary play center has a sturdy, round base with an elevated seat. It's shaped like a walker, but your baby's feet rest on the base and don't touch the ground. It lets your baby remain upright to practice standing but doesn't let him move around the room, making it safer than a baby walker. Look for one that can't be easily tipped over and supports your baby well. Many models come with attached toys to entertain your baby. As with baby jumpers and swings, limit the amount of time your baby spends in a stationary play center; he needs lots of unrestricted playtime to best promote his developing motor and balance skills.

Other Safety Issues

Bicycle Seats

Bicycle seats aren't recommended for babies during the first year. It's also not safe to ride a bicycle with your baby in a front pack or backpack. Even a ride in a bicycle-towed trailer before one year of age can jar your baby's body too much. Trailers can be dangerous to use on roadways as they are low and motorists might not see them. Once your baby's a year old and his neck can support a bicycle helmet, a bicycle trailer is still a safer way than a bicycle seat to take him for a ride.

Boating and Life Jackets

If you include your baby in your family's water activities, make sure he wears an appropriate personal floatation device (PFD) that's been approved by the United States Coast Guard. Follow the weight guidelines for the PFD, and make sure your baby will float in an upright position if he gets into the water. For a younger baby, it must have a floatation collar. The PFD must fit properly and you should not be able to lift it over your baby's head. *Never* use inflatable toys and rings as life preservers. Make sure you and everyone else on a watercraft wear life preservers; in case of an accident, you'll need to be able to assist your baby.

Shopping Carts

Every year, falls from shopping carts seriously injure children. To keep your baby safe, use all the safety straps for built-in seats. If using your own seat, place it completely in the cart. Don't balance it on the edges. Never let your baby ride unrestrained, and constantly keep an eye on him while he's in the cart.

Before you place your baby into a cart, use a sanitizing wipe on the handles and seat to protect him from germs. Many stores now provide wipes, but consider keeping a small supply in your purse or diaper bag.

Pet Safety

- Before your new baby arrives, think about spaying or neutering your pets; this makes them calmer and less likely to bite. You should also address any behavior problems they may have and clip their nails or claws.

- Once your baby is born, have your partner or a family member take something with your baby's scent (a blanket, for example) home, to familiarize your pet with it.

- Always supervise your baby when he's in a room with animals. Watch your pet for any aggressive or defensive behaviors.

- Once your baby is crawling, make sure to keep pet food and pet toys out of his reach.

- If you plan to get a new dog, do research beforehand. Certain breeds (Rottweilers, German shepherds, and pitbulls) are less family-friendly.

- Reptiles can cause salmonella infections in children. Your child should not have contact with any lizards, turtles, or snakes until he is five years.

Babysitters

Whether you're planning to stay at home with your baby or you're returning to work and arranging for daycare, it's vital to have an evening out alone every now and then. When you're ready to leave your baby in a babysitter's care, follow these steps to find the perfect one for your family.

Search Early

If possible, start searching for a babysitter before your baby arrives. Ask friends, neighbors, relatives, other parents, and caregivers whether they know of any good candidates. Call the student employment service at a local college or high school and post fliers at gyms, youth centers, or places of worship. A baby-sitting agency is a good source for finding prescreened sitters (check your yellow pages for more information). You'll have to pay the agency for its services, but agency employees are usually older and more experienced than average teenage babysitters.

Interview candidates. Once you have a list of candidates, look for someone you feel is old enough to do the job well. That person may be as young as age eleven, if he or she seems confident and knowledgeable about childcare. Most parents feel comfortable with a babysitter who's older (usually no younger than age fourteen), but you're the best judge of a babysitter's ability to care for your child.

Ask each baby-sitting candidate the following questions. During the interview, trust your instincts and pay attention to how the candidate answers the questions. After the interview, if the candidate seems promising, introduce him or her to your baby. Watch how they interact and record your observations and impressions.

Babysitter Interview

- How long have you been baby-sitting?
- Do you have experience caring for infants? Are you trained to perform CPR and first aid (including infant training)?
- Why do you like working with children?
- What do you like best about baby-sitting? What do you like the least?
- What other childcare experience do you have?
- Do you still baby-sit for your prior clients?
- What are the ages of other children you've watched?
- What activities do you enjoy doing with children?
- How do you soothe a crying baby?
- What's the best way to put a baby down to sleep?
- Have you ever given a baby a bath?
- If the babysitter will be transporting your baby:
  - What kind of car do you have?
  - What's your driving record?
  - Do you know how to install and use a car seat?
- If the babysitter will be feeding your baby:
  - How do you prepare a bottle (breast milk or formula)?
- If you have pets:
  - Are you allergic to any animals?
  - Are you comfortable around pets?
- What do you do in your spare time? Any hobbies? Other jobs?
- Do your parents support your baby-sitting jobs (if the babysitter is under age eighteen)? Will your parents be home while you're baby-sitting?
- Tell me about your school life. Sports? Activities? Grades? Do you like school?
- Will you need a ride to and from your house?
- How much per hour do you charge?
- May I have a list of families I can call for references?

Call References

After you've selected a few promising candidates, it's important to call their references. Don't ask former employers whether they simply *liked* the babysitter; ask them the following specific questions and note their answers in detail:

- When and for how long did the baby-sitter work for you? How did you hire him or her?

- How many children did you have when the babysitter started? Any infants? What gender and how old were they?

- What was your general impression of the babysitter? What did he or she do especially well? What tasks could he or she have done better? Anything you would change about him or her?

- How would you describe the babysitter's personality? Was he or she caring and warm? Patient? Respectful? Creative? Prompt and reliable? Did he or she have a positive attitude? Lots of energy? Sound judgment? Initiative?

- Did your children get along well with the babysitter?

- How did the babysitter handle emergencies? What's an example?

- How did the babysitter discipline your children? Did you ever suspect child abuse? Did you conduct any background checks?

- Was the babysitter clean and well-groomed?

- Did the babysitter follow your rules and respect your home? Any problems with drinking, smoking, or unauthorized visitors?

- Would you use this babysitter again?

- Would you mind sharing pay information?

- Any advice on ways to develop a good working relationship with this person? Anything else I should know about him or her? May I contact you again if I have additional questions?

Prepare for Your Babysitter

Before leaving your baby in a babysitter's care for the first time, arrange for the baby-sitter to visit your home so he or she can get to know you, your home, and your baby. You can ask him or her to arrive a half-hour or so before your scheduled departure. Or if you feel your babysitter doesn't have a lot of experience caring for infants, you may want to pay him or her to drop by and care for your baby a few times while you're home. You can use the time to take care of other tasks, knowing that if problems arise, you're nearby.

Give the babysitter as much information as you can, from emergency phone numbers (including the phone number of the place you'll be) to your baby's sleeping, feeding, and bathing schedules—even include what food is off limits. If your baby needs medication, show the babysitter how and when to give it to him. If you're going someplace where you can't be contacted, call home periodically and leave the phone number of someone the babysitter could contact in case of an emergency. (Make sure ahead of time that person will be home.) Have a flashlight and first-aid chart and supplies handy, and review your fire escape plan with the babysitter.

Maintain the Relationship

Once you've established a good relationship with a babysitter, it's important to maintain it. Trusting a babysitter with your baby should tell him or her a lot about how you feel about the relationship. The responsibility should make him or her want to do the best job possible. Tell your babysitter specifically what you've noticed that he or she does well. And always remember to treat your babysitter with respect. This may be his or her first real job, and he or she wants to be considered mature and capable.

Traveling

Traveling with your baby usually takes some planning (sometimes a *lot* of planning), but it can be done and often with minimal fuss. The key is to plan ahead while staying flexible. To keep your baby calm and content during any trip, dress him appropriately and bring along toys, snacks (if he's eating solid foods), and plenty of diapers. On a road trip, know that you'll need to stop more often than you otherwise would, for feedings and diaper changes.

Before a trip, especially a lengthy one, talk with your baby's caregiver about where you'll be traveling and for how long. It's important that your baby keeps to his vaccination schedule, and you may need to work the trip around the schedule (or vice versa). Check what medical facilities are available at your destination in case your baby requires medical attention. Bring along a first-aid kit, any medications your baby may need to take, and your baby's caregiver's contact information.

Air Travel

According to the Federal Aviation Administration (FAA), parents don't have to buy seats for children younger than age two. Instead, parents can carry their babies on their laps. This less expensive option may sound tempting, but it's much safer for your baby to travel in his own seat while sitting in his car seat.

Any currently manufactured car seat approved for use on an airplane must have an FAA approval label. If you plan to fly on a smaller commercial plane, check with the airline to make sure your baby's car seat will fit in the airplane seat. Typically, a seat whose base is less than sixteen inches (40.6 centimeters) wide will fit in most coach seats. Properly secure the car seat to the airline seat and strap your baby in correctly. Make sure his height and weight don't exceed the car seat's recommended limit for airplane travel.

If you use a car seat on an airplane, book adjacent seats ahead of time for you and your baby. A car seat must be placed in a window seat that's not in an emergency exit row—this is so it won't block your (or another passenger's) movement in an emergency.

If you want to save money but also want to try to have your baby ride in his car seat, take the seat with you to the gate. Your flight might not be full, and you can ask to be assigned next to one of the unassigned seats and use it to secure your baby's car seat (if, of course, either seat is next to a window and neither is in an emergency exit row). Try to book a flight at an off-peak time to increase your chances of getting an empty seat. If you learn at the gate that the flight is full, check the car seat. Make sure you and your baby aren't assigned to a row with another "lap baby." In an emergency, there'll be only one extra oxygen mask for each row. Don't strap your baby into the seat belt with you; instead, strap yourself in and hold on to him.

Here are some other tips for air travel with your baby:

- An umbrella stroller works well for air travel. You can use it in airports, and it can fold up and fit in an overhead compartment.

- Nurse your baby (or give him a bottle or pacifier) during takeoff and landing. Sucking and swallowing will equalize the air pressure in his ears.

- Consider beforehand your baby's feeding schedule during the flight and pack any necessary equipment (for example,

a blanket for privacy during breastfeeding or extra water-filled bottles and powdered formula). If your child is eating solid foods, choose foods that aren't messy or can be easily cleaned up. Keep in mind that flights are often delayed and you may need to prepare for extra feedings.

- Pack a change of clothes for your baby in your carry-on luggage. If he spits up or his diaper leaks, you'll be ready with a fresh outfit.

- Remember to bring small toys to entertain your baby. Make sure, however, that the toys won't annoy other passengers, especially if they're trying to sleep.

- In general, try to pack anything in your carry-on luggage that you wouldn't want to be left without during the flight: baby wipes, diapers, a favorite toy, and so on.

- Some airplane restrooms have changing tables, but many don't. If you need to change your baby's diaper at your seat, put the soiled diaper into an airsickness bag and toss it into the restroom trash.

Other Safety Tips

- If you're staying in a hotel, find out whether babyproofing equipment will be available. If not, bring your own (including electrical outlet covers, door latches for bathrooms and minibars, covers for sharp-edged furniture, and safety gates if you're staying in a room with a balcony). Check the hotel floor to be sure there are no small objects your baby could put into his mouth. Reserve a crib beforehand and look it over carefully before placing your baby in it.

- If you're traveling in a car, always use a car seat in the correct position. Place a wide-brimmed hat on your baby or use shade screens on the windows to keep him cool and safe from sun exposure. Never leave your baby alone in a car.

- If traveling by bus or train, bring along your baby's car seat. There might not be safety belts to secure the seat, but your baby will be more protected in his seat than in your lap.

Chapter Five

Your Baby's Development

A baby's first year is an exciting time for parents. During this period, your baby changes from a helpless newborn to an active toddler who explores, communicates, solves problems, and begins to assert her independence in many ways. This transformation brings new experiences to you and your baby and lets you both develop new skills.

Although children usually develop skills in the same sequence, each child learns them on her own schedule. For example, your baby may learn to crawl earlier than other babies, but she may learn to hold a spoon later. She'll eventually learn all the skills she's supposed to, and she'll spend the first year practicing and perfecting the skills she's already learned.

All children have an instinctual urge to learn, explore, and grow. Provide your baby a safe, interesting environment for her to discover, and limit her activity as little as possible (while still keeping her safe, of course). You probably won't need to formally teach her skills at this age, but interact with her as much as possible. She'll learn from the games she'll naturally play with you and from your actions that she'll eventually imitate. Observe her preferences and attempts to initiate interaction. Learn her cues and respond to them. As your baby grows, she'll try new ways to learn more complex skills.

This chapter presents a baby's typical milestones of development during the first year. Keep in mind that skills don't develop according to a strict timeline. In most cases, there's no reason to worry if your baby strays from the schedule during the first year.

Note: If you have a premature baby, she might need more time to reach certain milestones. Her caregiver will likely use her adjusted age (her age based on her due date, rather than her birth date) to assess her development. Don't worry; she'll probably catch up to other children by two to three years.

Developmental Warning Signs

There's a wide range of normal development in the first year, but sometimes when a baby misses milestones, it's due to an underlying problem. Here are signs to watch for:

- If your baby is slow to hold her head up, roll over, sit, and reach for or exchange objects, she may be showing signs of cerebral palsy. Cerebral palsy is a disorder that involves brain and nervous system functions such as muscle tone, movement, and motor skills. It's caused by brain damage or malformation that happens during pregnancy, birth, or after birth until age two years. There's no cure for cerebral palsy, but treatment will help control symptoms.

- If your baby doesn't smile, make eye contact, or coo and babble, she may be showing early signs of autism. Autism is a disorder that hinders the brain's development of communication skills. Nobody knows exactly what causes autism, though it's believed to be genetic. It's difficult to diagnose the disease before age twenty-four months, but talk to your caregiver so you can both keep an eye out for further warning signs. Researchers believe the earlier a child receives treatment, the better she'll fare.

- If your baby doesn't react to sound, or coo or babble by the end of the first year, she may be showing signs of hearing loss. See pages 168–69 for more on this issue.

If you ever suspect something's wrong with your baby, consult with her caregiver. She or he can give your baby a developmental assessment test to look for motor skills, language skills, and cognitive ability, and refer you to specialists, if necessary. (For further information on cerebral palsy and autism, see the recommended resources in the appendix.)

Birth through Two Months

During the first two months, it may seem as though your baby only eats and sleeps. Most of her movements are reflexes, whether she's awake or asleep (see pages 16–17). During her brief alert periods, she begins to use basic senses, one at a time, to learn about herself and her surroundings. Her inability to control her movements, however, severely limits her exploration.

At this age, your baby doesn't realize that there are objects or people separate from herself. Everything is part of her world. Her future confidence and trust in relationships and even her independence are now developing. By caring for her consistently, you teach her that her world is a safe, secure, fairly predictable place where her needs are met regularly and lovingly. This sense of security will eventually let her try new things, feel comfortable in an unfamiliar place, and continue to grow and develop.

During the first month, your baby may...

- make reflex movements—for example, grasping or stepping. (See pages 16-17.)
- lift her head briefly when having some "tummy time" (lying on her stomach); otherwise, she can't hold it up without support.
- make eye-to-eye contact at close range, usually eight to twelve inches (20.3 to 30.5 centimeters) away from you.
- stare at objects (without reaching for them) and prefer looking at faces and patterns. Babies respond well to sharply contrasting colors (for example, black and white).

- sleep a lot and be alert for only brief times each day.
- comfort herself by mouthing and sucking her fist and fingers.
- show enjoyment by quieting down and possibly smiling briefly.
- distinguish one or two people by their voices.

During the second month, your baby may...

- roll from side to side. Make sure you watch her at all times; she could roll off a bed or table.
- lie with one arm straight out, her head turned to that side, and the other arm flexed up (the "fencing" position).
- have better head control. While sitting, your baby may unsteadily hold her head up; while lying on her stomach, she may hold it up for a few minutes.
- prefer looking to or sleeping on one particular side. (However, always put your baby on her back to sleep.)
- begin to control her grasp and hold an object for a few minutes.
- use only one sense at a time (for example, sucking in bursts, then looking around during pauses).
- prefer looking at faces or moving objects, but focus only on close objects.
- begin to follow some movements with her eyes.
- begin to seek and respond to attention by smiling, making sounds, and actively moving her arms and legs.
- cry at predictable intervals, make cooing sounds, and generally respond to sounds.
- recognize her primary caregiver's voice and touch.
- connect some positions and people with certain events—for instance, her mother with feeding.

Three through Five Months

As your baby's periods of alertness become longer and more frequent, she becomes dramatically more active. During this time, she gradually learns to grasp objects and bring them to her face for a look and a taste. She uses her body—especially her mouth—to discover each object's characteristics. She's developing the ability to sit when supported, which frees her hands and increases her field of vision and lets her investigate her surroundings more fully.

Your baby's social awareness is blossoming. She seeks and acknowledges attention by smiling, making noises, and moving her whole body. The people and objects around her interest her, and she enjoys her own activity as well as others' activities.

During the third month, your baby may...

- rest on her forearms when lying on her stomach and holding her head up.
- sit supported for a few minutes.
- begin to reach for an object with both hands, bat at things, and kick with force.
- explore a room for light colors, shapes, and patterns, and search for a sound source.
- smile spontaneously.
- look and suck at the same time.
- be attentive for up to forty-five minutes at a time.
- begin to show memory of sequences, effects, and people.
- use various movements and expressions to show her moods and needs.
- make sounds in response to talking and singing.

During the fourth month, your baby may...

- roll from back to side or from stomach to side or back.
- sit supported, with her head steady, for ten to fifteen minutes.
- push herself straight up from her stomach.
- look at and play with her hands.
- reach for (and possibly miss), grasp, hold, and release objects.
- put everything in her mouth.
- splash in the bath.
- turn her head and eyes to look in all directions, watch moving people, or locate a sound source.
- begin babbling and practicing sounds.
- laugh.
- become attached to an object or toy.
- discriminate among faces and know her primary caregiver.
- be alert for at least one hour at a time and have sustained interest in details.
- anticipate a feeding by increasing her activity and enjoy eating as a social and play time; she might not need a night feeding.

During the fifth month, your baby may...

- move by rocking, rolling (from stomach to back or back to side), twisting, and kicking.
- sit with a firm back while propped up for up to a half-hour.
- be easily pulled to standing.
- reach for and grasp an object easily.
- wave and raise arms in anticipation of being picked up, and cling when held.
- bring her feet to her mouth and suck on her toes.
- babble to get attention and make sounds to herself, her toys, or her image in a mirror.
- show fear, disgust, or anger by making sounds.
- awaken at dawn, ready and eager to play.
- be alert for one or two hours at a time and resist interruptions in play.

Six through Nine Months

Your baby's world grows significantly when she can roll, creep, and eventually crawl. (Note: Some perfectly healthy babies *never* learn to crawl.) Few objects will escape her insatiable curiosity, and she's beginning to examine things within her reach by squeezing, poking, and tasting them.

More and more, your baby is learning by watching and imitating others. She's starting to understand that you still exist when you're out of sight. She's also beginning to perceive and respond to others' moods.

Your baby is starting to make her likes and dislikes known. She may also at times prefer exploring to cuddling on your lap. If she's eating solid foods, she may feed herself.

During the sixth month, your baby may...

- roll from back to stomach.
- sit up by herself for a short time, with her head balanced and her hands free.
- love to stand (with lots of support) and bounce.
- begin to drop things from her high chair, look for them, and cry for others to pick them up.
- transfer toys from hand to hand and rotate wrists to turn and manipulate toys.
- want to handle all food and utensils.
- repeat combinations of sounds ("da-da-da"), watch mouths closely, and try to imitate inflections.
- show enjoyment of music by humming, swaying, or bouncing.
- babble while varying pitch, volume, and speed.
- watch and play with a sibling or another child.
- remember that her primary caregiver exists even when out of sight.
- show her uniqueness. She lets you know how much activity is enough, the amount of sleep she needs, and what foods she prefers.

During the seventh month, your baby may...

- creep on her stomach—first backward, then forward—and try to crawl.
- explore her body.
- carry a toy a lot of the time.
- love objects that make noise or love to bang or shake objects to make noise.
- say several syllables and use different ones in the same breath, like "Ma, mu, da, bah."
- want to be included socially.
- show increasing dependence on you and fear of separation. She may also fear strangers.
- show tension and irritability before a big developmental step like sitting or crawling.
- dislike having a familiar toy removed and resist pressure to do something she doesn't want to do.
- want to help with feeding. She may explore foods with her hands, smear them into her mouth, close her lips on a spoon to remove food, and hold a cup and spoon.

During the eighth month, your baby may...

- crawl.

- learn to pull herself to standing and discover what furniture is stable in the process.

- use her hands to get herself into a sitting position.

- empty cabinets, drawers, and bookshelves.

- push away unwanted objects.

- put an object into a container and shake it.

- pick up a small object with her thumb and two forefingers.

- hold a bottle to drink.

- babble with various sounds, inflections, and two-syllable utterances. She may shout for attention.

- listen selectively to familiar words and begin to recognize some.

- repeat sounds or movements she's already made.

- respond to cues of upcoming events. For example, she may blink before a cup hits the floor or cry when you put on your coat to leave.

- solve simple problems, like push a button on a toy so it makes a sound.

- resist bedtimes and naps.

During the ninth month, your baby may...

- stand briefly, while you hold her hand.

- sit up steadily by herself and pivot a quarter of the way around.

- grasp a small object with her thumb and forefinger.

- put her fingers into holes.

- pass an object from one hand to the other.

- finger-feed herself bits of food and drink from a cup with help.

- understand and respond to one or two words other than her name, and respond to simple commands, like "no-no," "wave," or "clap."

- look with interest at pictures in a book.

- perform for familiar audiences and repeat actions if she gets applause or laughs.

- prefer watching children to watching adults.

- begin to show persistence.

- enjoy nursery games like pat-a-cake and peekaboo, respond to them, and remember a game played earlier.

- fear bathing, heights, and separation from you in a strange place.

- begin to evaluate and respond to others' moods.

Ten through Twelve Months

During these months, your baby begins to change from an infant to a toddler—and from a babbler to a talker. She's just learning the rules of acceptable, safe behavior and is seeking social approval. She's also gradually refining the use of her hands so she can use other objects as tools.

Your baby may begin imitating the words she hears, and she's beginning to understand the meaning of more of the words that she can say. As she learns to help herself, her self-confidence and assertiveness grow. She's becoming a fully functioning, competent, self-assured person.

During the tenth month, your baby may...

- stand with little support (for a few moments).
- walk while holding on to furniture.
- climb on chairs.
- walk without holding on to furniture (with help from you).
- lift her leg to help get dressed.
- carry an object in each hand.
- hold and bite a cookie. She may even finger-feed herself an entire meal.
- say "dada" and "mama," though she might not understand them as specific names.
- understand and obey some simple commands.
- imitate nonspeech sounds, like coughs, kisses, and tongue clicks.

- imitate actions, remember them, and repeat them later.
- remember where unseen toys are.
- become self-conscious and sensitive to social approval or disapproval.
- develop a sense of identity and possession and show tenderness toward toys.

During the eleventh month, your baby may...

- walk, holding on to one or two hands.
- stand without help much of the time.
- climb up stairs, but have trouble climbing down.
- use two hands at the same time for different functions. For example, she may support herself while picking up a toy.
- experiment with dropping and picking up objects.
- try the same activity with each hand or with each side of her body.
- help get dressed more actively—for example, pulling off a sock or putting her foot in a shoe.
- hold a cup with both hands and bring a spoon to her mouth.
- explore containers by lifting their lids and putting objects in and taking them out while looking inside.
- understand much more than she can say.
- mix a word into her babbling or use one word to express a whole thought.
- be very dependent on you, imitate family members constantly, and play actively with a caregiver other than her mother.
- be shy with strangers and play alongside, but not with, another child.
- resist and test limits and seek approval.

During the twelfth month, your baby may...

- walk with legs wide, but may prefer crawling.

- stand from a squat, pivot a quarter of the way around, and lower herself to sit.

- use one hand more than the other to reach, suck her thumb, and finger-feed. She may use a spoon and spill often.

- hold a crayon to make marks.

- push toy cars and balls and give a toy to someone on request.

- bang toys or objects together.

- stack blocks.

- cooperate in getting dressed.

- use trial and error to solve problems.

- turn into a very picky eater and become resistant, especially at mealtime and naptime.

- show affection to people and objects.

- have renewed fear of strangers and strange situations.

Toys for the First Year

To your baby, everything is a toy—fingers, toes, buttons, strings on clothing, people and pets, household objects, and even pieces of lint. During the first year, she'll play with anything she thinks is a toy to learn about herself and her world. For this reason, make sure her environment is as safe as possible. (See Chapter 4 to learn more about keeping your baby safe.)

Provide new challenges for your baby by offering her toys that aren't too difficult or frustrating and aren't too limited or simple. (See the following pages to help you find toys that fit your baby's developmental abilities.) You don't need to buy lots of expensive toys. Your baby will be perfectly happy playing with homemade toys or with common household objects. For example, you can…

- suspend some colorful pictures from a clothes hanger to make a mobile. (Make sure any strings or cords are secured tightly and out of your baby's reach.)

- give your baby a set of plastic mixing bowls or containers. She can drop things into and dump things out of them.

- string two or three empty thread spools together to make a simple "clacking" toy.

Keep in mind the following considerations when buying or making toys for your baby.

Safety

Look for toys that don't have sharp edges or points. Make sure your baby can't break or chew off pieces from them. To make sure your baby won't choke on a toy, choose one that can't fit into a cardboard toilet paper tube (also make sure none of its parts can fit inside). Any cords on toys should be shorter than seven inches, but watch your baby carefully when she's playing with any toy with a cord.

Check that all parts of the toy are nontoxic.

Durability

Make sure any toy you choose can stand up to any abuse your baby will give it.

Versatility

A good toy stimulates more than one sense. It also has many uses for babies of different ages and developmental levels. For example, some clutch toys are brightly colored, provide faces to look at, are easy to hold, have different textures to touch and mouth, and feature a bell inside to stimulate hearing and encourage shaking or turning.

Toy	Age	Developmental Activity
Pictures	From birth on	Pictures help develop your baby's visual perception (including focus, distance, detail, color, and image recognition). Attach brightly colored or sharply contrasting decals, posters, or other pictures (especially pictures of faces) to your baby's crib, the wall, or a mobile. Make sure the items are out of her reach. At first, your baby can focus on objects only eight to twelve inches (20.3 to 30.5 centimeters) away; by four to six months, she can focus on objects across the room.
Books	From birth on	At first, your baby might not show much interest in books, but they play an enormous role in her language development. Read to her as often as you can. Choose books with brightly colored, interesting illustrations. Young babies especially like to look at pictures of faces. Name and describe objects as you point to them on the page. Make animal sounds or tell stories. When she's nine or ten months old, your baby will love handling a book, turning pages back and forth, mouthing it, and dropping it. Make sure the board books you choose are sturdy or expendable—or both.
Mobile	Birth to 2 months	A mobile with bright colors and shapes will pique your baby's interest. Choose one that you think will best engage your baby from her perspective. Place it close to her face but out of her reach.
	3 to 6 months	At this age, your baby will reach for her mobile as she learns to coordinate her hand movements by grasping at a target. Move the mobile so your baby will also use her feet to try and reach the target. A mobile that makes noise when your baby moves it or kicks the mattress will pique her interest even more. Remember to remove a mobile once your baby can stand.
Mirror	2 to 6 months and beyond	A mirror helps your baby develop an interest in faces and understand the idea that faces are part of people and that she's an individual. Hang a small, unbreakable mirror on the inside of her crib, above her face as she lies in the crib, or next to the changing table. Your baby will enjoy watching herself and will eventually look into any mirror.
Stuffed animals	2 months and beyond	Stuffed animals stimulate lots of activities—an interest in faces (two months), reaching and grasping (three to six months), and early manipulation of objects and interest in textures (six to eighteen months). A stuffed animal's face may attract your baby, but primarily it's something soft to reach for, grasp, and mouth. *Never* leave stuffed animals in your baby's crib. If your baby breathes near one too closely while sleeping, she may not get enough oxygen and inhale too much carbon dioxide.
	4 months and beyond	Your baby may show affection to one particular stuffed animal. She may see that other children around her often hug, talk to, and pay more attention to a stuffed animal than to other toys. So she may follow suit and become more attached to a stuffed animal than to another toy.
Rattle/ squeak toy	2 to 4 months	Rattles, squeak toys, or anything with bells attached let your baby watch a moving object and look for the sound source. Move a brightly colored, shiny rattle or squeak toy slowly in front of your baby's eyes. At first, she'll move only her eyes; eventually, she'll move her head, too. Gently shake the rattle or squeak the toy in front of her, then to each side. She'll learn to look for the sound source.
	3 to 7 months	As she gets older, rattles or squeak toys can help your baby develop her ability to reach, grasp, and release. She'll learn to handle, shake, and bang toys. Hold or suspend the toy within your baby's reach. Put it in front of her, then to each side.

Toy	Age	Developmental Activity
Crib gym or exerciser	3 to 6 months	This product provides various objects to look at, pull, push, kick at, and grasp. Set it across the top of your baby's crib or above your baby when she's lying on her back on the floor. Remove a crib gym once your baby can stand.
Ball	3 to 4 months	A brightly colored ball with a noise-making object inside lets your baby watch a moving object and look and reach for a sound source. Turn or roll the ball slowly in front of your baby.
	4 months and beyond	When your baby can roll over, creep, crawl, and finally walk, she'll love a brightly colored, noise-making ball that she can hold in one hand. She can turn, shake, bang, drop, roll, and chase after it.
Stacking rings	3 to 6 months	The brightly colored stacking pieces are easy to grasp, durable, and smooth. They're perfect objects for your baby to reach for, handle, and mouth.
	9 months and beyond	At this age, your baby will learn to control her hand movements so she can stack the objects. At first, your baby will simply stack the objects off the post. When this task no longer challenges her, show her how to put one object on its post and then take it off. Your baby's curiosity and need to imitate will prompt her to stack all the objects on the post.
Small blocks	5 to 6 months and beyond	Blocks are versatile and long lasting toys. Small, brightly colored blocks are easy to handle and see. Your baby will learn to coordinate her hand movements and pick up and drop blocks into containers. She'll bang blocks together to make noise. Even when she's a preschooler, she can use blocks for building, dramatic play, and learning about size, shape, color, and numbers.
Nesting toys	5 to 10 months and beyond	Nesting toys are objects of the same shape but different sizes that help your baby develop hand coordination and learn that objects exist even when she can't see them. Another way to help your baby learn object permanence is to cover a small toy with a cup, then uncover it. She'll soon play the game herself.
Activity box or cube	6 to 18 months	This toy provides objects that your baby can manipulate, turn, push, poke, or hit. It has various gadgets, like doors to open, balls to spin, and telephone dials to turn.
Pull toys	8 months to 2 ½ years	Pull toys will give your crawling or walking baby a sense of power over objects as well as enjoyment. Many pull toys tip over easily, which will frustrate your baby. Choose a pull toy that's sturdy and stable. Look for one that's brightly colored and makes noise when pulled.
TV	Birth to 2 years	The American Academy of Pediatrics (AAP) recommends that children younger than age two shouldn't watch TV at all. Your baby's first year is a critical time for growth and development. Her language and social skills will develop far more by talking and interacting with you and others than by watching any program, DVD, or video on TV.
Teething toys	4 months and beyond	When babies begin to teeth, they may chew on objects to ease the pain. It's a good idea to purchase a few teething toys to give your baby something safe to mouth. Look for toys that are nontoxic, unbreakable, and big enough that your baby won't swallow them. They may come in animal shapes or look like key rings. (See http://www.sophiegiraffe usa.com/ for one popular teether.)

Baby Exercises

Although your baby will likely move her body a lot on her own, the following exercises will work her muscles and test her reflexes as well as provide you some playtime with her. Do these exercises on a firm surface and when your baby is alert and content. (Cranky or tired babies will find these exercises annoying, not fun.) Remember to use discretion. Make sure your baby is developmentally ready, for example, when trying the Inchworm.

The Grasp: This exercise tests your baby's grasp reflex. Place one index finger in each of your baby's palms. She'll grasp them. Gently pull her hands toward you; she'll pull back on your fingers. (Don't raise her head and shoulders.) If her hands are closed into fists, pat and bounce her hands to open them.

Arm Cross: This exercise relaxes your baby's chest and upper back muscles. Place one thumb in each of your baby's palms. She'll grasp them. Open her arms to the sides and then cross them over her chest. Repeat slowly, gently, and rhythmically.

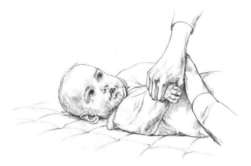

Arm Raising: This exercise improves the flexibility of your baby's shoulders. Grasp your baby's forearms near the elbows. Raise them above her head, then lower them to the sides. Repeat slowly, gently, and rhythmically. Then alternate arms so one rises while the other lowers.

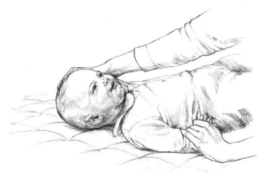

Leg Bending: This exercise improves the flexibility of your baby's hips. It may also help her pass gas. With your baby on her back, grasp her lower legs and gently bend her knees toward her abdomen and chest. Then gently lower her legs until they're straight. Repeat this exercise several times using both legs, or alternate legs, bending one while straightening the other.

Baby Bounce: This exercise relaxes your baby's whole body. Place your baby on her back or belly on a very large, slightly deflated beach ball, a foam pad, a bed, or any soft, bouncy surface. Slowly, gently, and rhythmically press on the area around your baby so she rocks up and down. She'll relax as she feels the movement. Also try patting her rhythmically on her stomach, chest, back, arms, and legs.

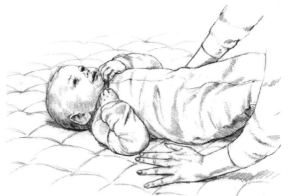

Inchworm: When your baby has some head control, this exercise helps her extend her legs and strengthen her lower back muscles. With your baby on her belly, bend her knees underneath her body and tuck her feet close to her bottom. Press your thumbs against her soles. The pressure will make your baby's legs straighten, which will move her body forward like an inchworm.

Chapter Six

Medical Care for Your Baby

Making sure your baby is healthy during the first year will help him become a physically, emotionally healthy child and adult. Your baby's well-child checkups are very important. They'll help reduce the number of visits needed for illness or injury. Furthermore, regular checkups will let your baby's caregiver catch any abnormal changes in your baby's growth, development, or behavior. These visits will also give you the opportunity to share with a healthcare professional what you've experienced, what you've found challenging, and what puzzles you about parenting.

On the following pages, you'll learn more about the well-child checkups and vaccinations recommended for the first year. There's also a section on the development of your child's teeth, a general discussion of how to handle common medical problems, and information on how to treat fever. The chapter concludes with step-by-step treatments for the illnesses and emergencies that your baby may face during his first year.

Well-child Checkups

Because your baby will undergo many developmental changes during the first year, he should have several routine examinations during those months. Your health insurance plan as well as your baby's needs and vaccination schedule will determine when he'll have well-child checkups. (Of course, if he develops health problems that require further attention, his caregiver or other healthcare professionals will see him more frequently.)

With hospitals and birth centers discharging babies earlier than in years past, today's babies generally need a checkup sooner than they did just a decade ago. Typically, a baby will have his first checkup sometime before he's a week old (a breast-fed baby's first checkup may be as early as one to three days). He'll have more checkups at two, four, six, nine, and twelve months old. At nearly all of these checkups, a caregiver will...

- create a medical record and take a medical history or health profile, including a family history.

- measure your baby's height, weight, and head circumference.

- ask screening questions for vision, hearing, anemia (by doing a hemoglobin test when your baby's about nine months old) and lead poisoning, if applicable.

- assess developmental and behavioral progress.

- discuss what to expect in your baby's development from one checkup to the next—topics could include nutrition, sleep, and safety.

During the checkup, your baby's caregiver will use a stethoscope to listen to your baby's heart and lungs, an otoscope to look into the ears, and a light source (ophthalmoscope and/or penlight) to check the eyes and mouth. The caregiver should also check the abdomen, genitals, hips, and legs.

Well-child checkups are an ideal time to ask questions and share concerns about your baby. If possible, try to use only one or two caregivers. This way, you can build a relationship with him or her, and you can discuss your baby's development with someone who's been monitoring it from the beginning.

Vaccinations

Vaccinations are part of most babies' well-child checkups. During the first year, your baby's caregiver will recommend that your baby receive vaccinations to protect him against major diseases, including hepatitis B, polio, diphtheria, pertussis (whooping cough), tetanus, haemophilus (Hib) influenzae, rotavirus, influenza, and some strains of pneumococcal disease. Your baby may also be tested for tuberculosis, if there's any risk of exposure to this disease.

A vaccination is a preparation of dead or weakened organisms that's injected into your baby (usually, his upper thigh). A vaccination helps produce immunity to a specific disease by making the body build antibodies to resist the organisms and provide protection to future exposure to the disease.

Some babies have mild reactions to certain vaccines. For example, usually within twenty-four hours after the vaccination, your baby may become fussy or develop a slight fever or soreness and swelling at the site of the injection. See pages 134–37 to learn how to treat a fever. Take care when moving a sore leg and apply warm washcloths to the swollen area. Limiting the number of vaccinations can help reduce local reactions. Today, more vaccines can be combined, with as many as five vaccines in one injection, which means your baby could receive fewer injections.

In rare cases, reactions are more severe, and some parents question the safety of vaccines and worry about their potential side effects. The Food and Drug Administration (FDA) recommends that parents get the facts about the benefits and risks of vaccines as well as the potential consequences of not vaccinating their children against certain diseases. Here's a list of things you can do to learn about vaccinations and prepare you and your baby for them.

- Your baby's caregiver is required by law to provide you information that explains the potential risks of each vaccine. Review the information carefully—and do your own research—then talk with the caregiver about any concerns. Some trustworthy sources include the Centers for Disease Control (http://www.cdc.gov) and the National Vaccine Center (http://www.nvic.org). See appendix for further resources.

- In recent years, parents have been concerned about a rumored connection between autism and preservatives found in vaccines, particularly thimerosal (mercury). Evidence from several studies has concluded that there is no such connection, and significant amounts of thimerosal are no longer included in childhood vaccines (with the exception of some preparations of the influenza vaccine). For more information on this and other common concerns, see the Vaccine Safety section of the CDC's website at http://www.cdc.gov/vaccine safety/Concerns/Index.html.

- Talk to the caregiver about whether you can control certain reactions to vaccines (for example, giving your baby infant acetaminophen before or after vaccination to prevent or reduce a fever).

- Make sure to tell the caregiver if you, your baby, or another child of yours reacted badly to a vaccine.

- Ask the caregiver whether there are any reasons why your baby shouldn't be vaccinated. For example, your baby's immunity may be compromised by illness with fever, or there's a family history of allergic reactions to previous vaccinations or their components (like allergies to eggs, which are used to grow influenza vaccines).

- Report unexpected reactions to the caregiver. He or she will report serious reactions to the Vaccine Adverse Event Reporting System (VAERS), a national program for monitoring vaccine safety. You can also contact them yourself at http://vaers.hhs.gov/index or 800-822-7967.

- Record the dates and types of vaccinations your baby receives. You'll need this information when you fill out school forms and the like in the future.

Recommended Vaccination Schedule for the First Year*				
The following schedule may vary slightly among individual clinics and practices.				
Vaccine	1st Dose	2nd Dose	3rd Dose	4th Dose
Hepatitis B**	Birth	1–2 mo	6–18 mo	
Rotavirus	2 mo	4 mo	6 mo	
DTaP	2 mo	4 mo	6 mo	
Hib	2 mo	4 mo	6 mo	12–15 mo
Pneumococcal Conjugate	2 mo	4 mo	6 mo	12–15 mo
Inactivated Poliovirus	2 mo	4 mo	6–18 mo	
Influenza***	No sooner than 6 months, during influenza season annually			

* After the first year, your baby will also receive vaccinations to protect against varicella (chicken pox), measles, mumps, rubella (German measles), and hepatitis A. He'll also receive additional ("booster") doses of the vaccines given in the first year.

** If the mother is a hepatitis B carrier, an additional vaccination should be given.

*** Two doses given at least four weeks apart are recommended for children getting their first influenza vaccination. If your baby only gets one dose in his first year of vaccination, he should get two doses the following year.

Dental Care

On average, a baby's first tooth appears when he's six to seven months old. Your baby's first tooth, however, could appear any time from birth to eighteen months. The tooth may simply pop through without warning, or your baby may signal its arrival by drooling, fussing, chewing on everything in sight, waking frequently at night, and generally seeming bothered by sore, throbbing gums. Some babies want to nurse or bottle-feed more than usual when suffering from teething; others might not. Each baby responds differently to teething. (See page 182 for more on teething.)

A few more teeth are likely to appear during the first year, and your baby will probably grow a full set of primary (baby) teeth by the time he's two or three. The following diagram shows the average time each primary tooth appears. Don't worry, though, if your baby's teeth come in earlier or later.

Start caring for your baby's primary teeth even before they're visible. Healthy baby teeth are essential to the development of your baby's jaw and permanent teeth.

- Feed your baby a nutritious diet. Take him out in the sunshine so his body can produce vitamin D, which strengthens teeth and bones (see page 63). Your caregiver may also recommend a vitamin D supplement.

- Your baby should not have supplemental fluoride during his first six months. After six months, he'll need it only if the fluoride concentration in your household drinking water is less than 0.3 parts per million (ppm). To find out how much fluoride is in your drinking water: Call your local water department if you drink from a municipal water supply; call the bottling company if you drink bottled water; or ask your local water department about fluoride testing if you drink well water.

- When your baby's weaned, offer him plenty of foods rich in calcium, like milk, cheese, and yogurt. Calcium is the primary mineral in teeth.

- Don't let your baby use a bottle as a pacifier, and don't put him to bed with a bottle. If he does use a bottle as a pacifier, he may demand several refills of milk or juice, especially at night. This habit encourages decay because it constantly bathes his teeth in sugary liquids (milk contains lactose, a form of sugar). If you must give him a bottle in bed, make sure it contains only water.

- The American Dental Association (ADA) recommends that you start cleaning your baby's teeth as soon as they appear. To remove plaque, use a sterile gauze pad or a clean washcloth to wipe the teeth, or gently brush them with a soft, infant-sized toothbrush. No toothpaste is necessary, but if you choose to use some, make sure it's only a pea-sized amount.

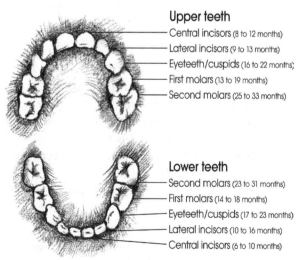

Upper teeth

Central incisors (8 to 12 months)
Lateral incisors (9 to 13 months)
Eyeteeth/cuspids (16 to 22 months)
First molars (13 to 19 months)
Second molars (25 to 33 months)

Lower teeth

Second molars (23 to 31 months)
First molars (14 to 18 months)
Eyeteeth/cuspids (17 to 23 months)
Lateral incisors (10 to 16 months)
Central incisors (6 to 10 months)

- The ADA, American Academy of Pediatric Dentistry (AAPD), and American Academy of Pediatrics (AAP) all suggest that a dentist examine your child within six months after his first tooth comes in and no later than his first birthday. (Local practice may differ—consult with your dentist.) The dentist will check for tooth decay and other problems, and show you how to properly clean your baby's teeth.

Handling Common Medical Problems

When your baby is sick or hurt, you want to know quickly what's best to do. The step-by-step treatments on pages 139–85 will help you care for your baby and tell you when professional help is necessary. These treatments cover common injuries, illnesses, and emergencies that your baby may face during that first year.

The treatments in this section are medically based, but they don't replace professional medical care. An illness's symptoms can vary, and it can affect different children in different ways. Your baby's caregiver may need more than one visit to diagnose an illness accurately. He or she may also recommend treatments other than those listed here.

If you have any questions about your baby's health or the best way to handle an illness or injury, contact his caregiver. Also, depending on the urgency of the situation, call 911, your health insurance's nurse line, or your baby's caregiver if you see any of the following symptoms:

1. Any clearly life-threatening injury or accident

2. Fever (see pages 134–37)

3. Serious diarrhea

4. Blood in the urine or stools

5. Sudden loss of appetite that lasts four days or longer

6. Unusual crying

7. Difficulty breathing

8. Unusual vomiting

9. Off-color appearance, listlessness, or behavioral change

10. Convulsions or seizures

11. Eye or ear injuries or infections

12. Falls or blows to the head that cause unconsciousness (even if brief) or have effects that last longer than fifteen minutes

13. Burns with blisters

14. Unusual rashes

15. Indications of pain (wincing if a spot is touched)

16. Suspected poisoning—call national poison control center first (800-222-1222)

17. Swallowing a foreign object

Basic Supplies

Here's a list of first-aid and home healthcare supplies to keep on hand—safely out of your baby's reach.

- Infant acetaminophen or ibuprofen (see next page for dosage information)

- Adhesive bandages (assorted sizes)

- Adhesive tape ½ to 1 inch wide

- Cool mist humidifier or vaporizer

- Cotton balls

- Cotton safety swabs (designed for children)

- Diaper rash cream or ointment

- Baby nail clippers

- Heating pad

- Hot-water bottle

- Nasal aspirator (bulb syringe)

- Rubbing alcohol

- Sunblock (at least SPF 15 and PABA-free)

- Digital thermometer (For a newborn, use a rectal or axillary thermometer. An ear thermometer is appropriate after your baby is three months old.)

- Tweezers

Fever Guide

Many parents think a fever is their sick baby's number one enemy. They'll battle fever with all the medication and sponge baths they can give their little one. These parents mistakenly believe that a fever is a disease that can harm their baby. In reality, a fever is a symptom of the body's fight against a disease or infection. When fighting a disease or infection, the body generates excess heat that spreads to the head and limbs, where it radiates off the skin.

In general, don't try to bring down a fever that's lower than 101°F (38.3°C) taken rectally or by ear (for babies older than three months only), and don't consider a fever as a threat to your baby's well-being. You should, however, watch your baby especially closely if he has any fever and he's younger than three months.

Here are some facts about fevers:

Fever Levels

- Rectal temperatures are more accurate than underarm temperatures. The normal rectal temperature is 99.6°F (37.6°C), while the normal underarm temperature can range from 96.6°F to 97.6°F (35.9°C to 36.4°C). Normal temperatures vary among ear thermometers; check the manufacturers' specifications. (Remember, ear thermometers don't measure accurate temperatures in babies younger than three months.)

- If your baby's underarm temperature is 99°F (37.2°C) or higher, he may have a fever. Take a rectal temperature to be sure. He has a fever if his rectal temperature is 100.4°F (38°C) or higher.

- A high peak temperature for a fever doesn't necessarily mean the disease or infection is comparably severe.

- Unless your baby feels warm to the touch (for example, he feels warmer than your neck) or is acting sick (not eating or sleeping well, increased fussiness, and so on), you don't need to take his temperature.

- A high fever is 104°F (40°C) and higher, no matter which method you use to take a temperature. A fever won't harm a person until it reaches 106°F to 107°F (41.1 to 41.7°C), and fevers of this temperature occur with heatstroke, not common illnesses.

- A person's temperature fluctuates with activity and the time of day. A normal temperature is usually highest in the late afternoon and early evening.

Fever Treatment

- Until your baby's three months old, don't give him any medication until you've called his caregiver. Also, never give him aspirin or products that contain aspirin. Aspirin has been linked to Reye's syndrome, a serious condition of progressive vomiting and decreasing consciousness. For more accurate doses that are easier to give to your baby, use infant acetaminophen in liquid form. Infant acetaminophen also comes as rectal suppositories that work well when your baby's vomiting prevents the medicine from staying in his system. Don't use infant ibuprofen until your baby is at least six months old.

- A fever makes a body lose more fluid than is normal. To prevent dehydration while he has a fever, encourage your baby to nurse more often or drink more bottles.

- Don't treat a fever with medication until your baby's rectal temperature is higher than 101°F (38.3°C)—and only then if he seems uncomfortable. Light clothing, extra fluids, and a pleasant, cool room are often better treatments for fevers than medications.

- Don't give your baby cold sponge baths or tub baths, including alcohol baths, to treat a fever. Only sponge bathe with tepid water if instructed to do so by your provider.

- Dress your baby lightly and make sure the environment is not too warm.

Recommended Infant Acetaminophen and Ibuprofen Doses for Fever

Infant acetaminophen and ibuprofen come in various forms and concentrations. A dropper made by one manufacturer might not give the same amount of medication as another manufacturer's product. Also, most health caregivers determine dosages based on a baby's weight, not his age. See the charts on the next page for rough guidelines. If you have questions about dosages, contact your baby's caregiver or a pharmacist. Here are more guidelines for giving your baby acetaminophen and ibuprofen:

- Always use a medicinal product's dropper or cup to measure dosages.

- Never give ibuprofen to a baby younger than six months, and don't alternate giving your baby acetaminophen and ibuprofen to treat a fever unless your baby's caregiver instructs you to do so.

- Carefully measure and time the doses of acetaminophen or ibuprofen you give your baby. An overdose of fever medication can cause nausea, vomiting, and excessive sweating—it can even be life threatening. If you suspect that your baby has had an overdose, call the national poison control center (800-222-1222) or his caregiver immediately.

- Never give your baby more than one dose of acetaminophen in any four-hour period or ibuprofen in any six-hour period. The medication takes effect in about thirty minutes.

- Take your baby's temperature before giving another dose of medication. Taking his temperature can track a rising fever or keep you from giving unnecessary medication.

- Don't awaken your baby to give him medicine or take his temperature—sleep is more important than either.

Recommended Infant Acetaminophen Doses

Weight	Age	Dosage	Infant Drops	Children's Liquid/Elixir
6-11 lbs. (2.7-5 kg)	0-3 mo.	40 mg	0.4 mg	N/A
12-17 lbs. (5.5-7.7 kg)	4-11 mo.	80 mg	0.8 mg	½ tsp. (2.5 ml)
18-23 lbs. 8.2-10.5kg)	12-23 mo.	120 mg	1.2 ml	¾ tsp. (3.75 ml)

Recommended Infant Ibuprofen Doses

Weight	Age	Dosage	Infant Drops	Children's Liquid/Oral Suspension
12-17 lbs. (5.5-7.7 kg)	6-11 mo.	50 mg	1.25 ml	½ tsp. (2.5 ml)
18-23 lbs. (8.2-10.5kg)	12-23 mo.	75 mg	1.875 ml	¾ tsp. (3.75 ml)

Contact your baby's care provider if...

- your baby is younger than three months old and has a rectal temperature of 100.4° F (38° C) or higher. He could have a serious infection, even without other symptoms.

- your baby is three to six months old with a fever higher than 101°F (38.3°C).

- your baby is any age with a fever higher than 103°F (39.4°C).

- your baby has a serious disease and has any fever.

Note: If your baby has had a convulsion with a fever (febrile convulsion), his caregiver may prescribe a slightly different treatment when he has another fever. Febrile convulsions are rare, and a child almost always outgrows them by the time he's six years old. (See page 151.)

How to Take Your Baby's Temperature

For safety's sake, use a digital thermometer and never leave your baby alone while taking his temperature. Glass thermometers can break, and some may contain mercury, a dangerous toxin. The American Academy of Pediatrics (AAP) encourages parents to properly discard mercury thermometers. (Contact your baby's caregiver to learn how to discard a mercury thermometer safely.)

Rectal digital thermometers provide the most accurate readings for babies and toddlers. Follow these steps to take your baby's rectal temperature:

1. Clean the bulb with rubbing alcohol or soap and water. Rinse with cool water.

2. Put a small amount of lubricant on the bulb. Turn on the thermometer.

3. Place your baby on his stomach across your lap or on a firm surface. Or put him on his back and hold his ankles in one hand and bend his knees toward his chest.

4. Gently insert the thermometer until the bulb disappears (about ½ to 1 inch or 1.3 to 2.5 centimeters) into the rectum.

5. Hold the thermometer in place loosely with two fingers while keeping your hand cupped around your baby's bottom. When the thermometer beeps, remove it and check the reading. A rectal temperature of 100.4°F (38°C) may mean your baby has a fever.

Although less accurate than a rectal temperature, you can use a digital axillary (underarm) thermometer. Put the thermometer in your baby's armpit. Bring his arm down and hold it against his body. Wait until the thermometer beeps and then read it.

You can use an ear thermometer for a baby who's at least three months old. Some parents prefer this thermometer because it's fast and easy to use. You must, however, place it correctly in your baby's ear. Too much earwax may make the reading inaccurate. Gently insert the end of the thermometer in your baby's ear canal, and press the start button. You'll get a reading within seconds.

Don't bother taking your baby's temperature with an oral thermometer; he's simply not mature enough to keep the thermometer in place long enough to get an accurate reading.

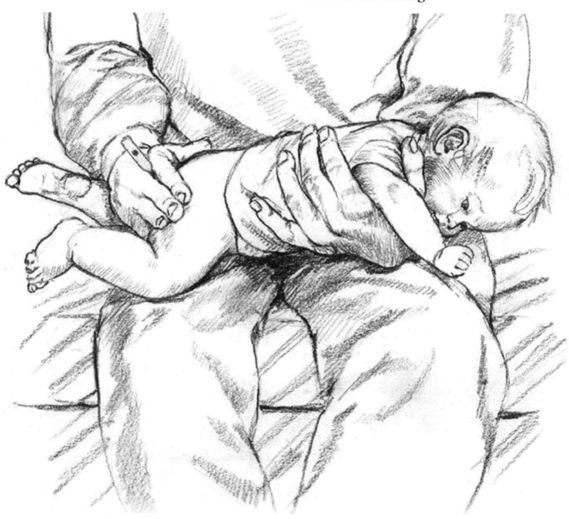

Symptoms Index

If you're perplexed by what illness your baby may have, look up the symptoms you've noticed in this index. See what other symptoms match (or don't match) your baby's. Then make an educated guess about what illness your child has. Don't use this index to play doctor, and don't assume that every baby with bronchiolitis, for example, has every symptom listed under that entry. Work closely with your baby's caregiver if you have any doubts about your baby's symptoms.

Appetite, loss of 143,146,176,178,180
Bites.. 140, 174
Blackheads.. 139
Body movement, jerking 151
Bowel movements
    frequent... 158
    liquid 158, 182
    hard.. 150
Breathing problems.............140, 141, 143, 144, 146,
    .... 155, 164, 171, 178, 179
Chest pain 166
Chewing fingers or other objects..................... 182
Chills 160, 173, 178
Choking.. 144, 179
Congestion...146, 160
Constipation... 150
Convulsions 151, 179, 180
Coordination, loss of 149
Cough 143, 146, 152, 155, 166, 173, 178
Coughing blood 179
Crying.. 147, 149, 182
Diarrhea 158, 164, 179
Dizziness 140, 171
Drooling... 151, 156, 179, 182
Drowsiness 156, 185
Ear
    discharge from.. 160
    sore... 160
Eyes
    crossed 154
    discharge from 160, 177
    red 146, 177
    sunken 155
    swollen.. 177
    watery.. 146
Fever.............................. 143, 146, 147, 151, 152, 155,
    .... 156, 158, 160, 170, 171, 173,
    ....176, 178, 180, 182, 184, 185

Headache.. 149, 160
Hearing loss 160, 168
Heart failure.. 141
Hoarseness 146
Irritability.................................. 146, 160, 166, 176, 182
Itching 162, 174
Listlessness 146, 173, 176, 185
Mouth, dry 156, 170, 171, 185
Muscle spasms... 151
Nausea.. 140, 179, 184
Neck, stiffness in 151, 163, 176
Pimples... 139, 157
Rash... 162, 170, 179, 180
Runny nose 143, 146, 147, 160, 173
Seizures.. 151, 176, 179
Skin
    bluish.................................... 140, 144, 151
    discoloration.......... 153, 162, 164, 170, 171, 172
    dry 156, 171
    scaling of.............................. 153, 162, 172
Sleeplessness.. 160
Sneezing... 146, 164
Speech development, slow 168
Stomach pain 147, 150, 166, 178
Unconsciousness 140, 141, 149, 171, 179
Urine
    bloody 184
    discolored 172
    foul smelling.. 184
    frequent... 184
    infrequent.. 156
    painful.. 184
Vomiting.....................140, 149, 151, 156, 158, 164,
    .... 166, 171, 176, 178, 179, 185
Whiteheads 139, 157
White patches on tongue and/or inside
    the mouth 183

Acne (Newborn)

Description

A condition that causes a newborn's skin to break out in pimples. Many experts believe it results from maternal hormones crossing through the placenta to the baby during pregnancy.

What You Need to Know

- Newborn acne is common and usually clears up on its own. It often appears when a baby is three to six weeks old and disappears or improves significantly without treatment, usually in days or weeks.

- Oily areas produce the most pimples: around the nose, on the back, or near the scalp.

- If your baby has small red bumps in the folds of his skin, he probably has heat rash, not acne. See page 170 for more on heat rash.

Supplies

Washcloth, soap, and water

Symptoms

- Blackheads (pimples with dark centers)

- Whiteheads (pimples with white centers)

Get Professional Help If...

Your baby's skin seems especially dry, irritated, weepy, or possibly infected.

What to Check

Does your baby's acne seem to be spreading rapidly and causing discomfort?

Treatment

- Wash the affected skin gently with a wet washcloth, then pat the area dry. The clogged pores should open and heal by themselves without further treatment.

- Make sure your baby sleeps on clean sheets that are washed with gentle detergents.

- Don't use over-the-counter acne medication or creams. In rare, severe cases, your baby's caregiver may prescribe a medication.

Anaphylaxis

Description

Anaphylaxis (also called anaphylactic shock) is a sudden, severe, potentially fatal, allergic reaction to insect bites or to certain foods (like nuts), materials (like latex), and medications (like penicillin). Though rare, true anaphylaxis is always an emergency.

What You Need to Know

- Symptoms may begin in as little as five minutes to two hours after exposure to the allergen, but life-threatening reactions may progress over hours.

- Some people have a reaction, and the symptoms go away only to return two to three hours later. Often the symptoms occur in the respiratory tract and take the person by surprise.

- Anyone with a history of anaphylactic reactions is at risk for another severe reaction. Those with food allergies and asthma may be at increased risk for having a life-threatening anaphylactic reaction.

Supplies

- Epinephrine (EpiPen), antihistamines, if prescribed by a medical professional

Symptoms

- Hives, and swelling of the throat, tongue, neck, or face

- Wheezing or severe breathing problems

- Rapid pulse and decreased blood pressure

- Sweating

- Dizziness, fainting, loss of consciousness

- Nausea, vomiting, abdominal cramps, diarrhea

- Extremely pale skin or skin turning blue

Get Professional Help If...

Your baby has difficulty breathing, becomes unconscious, or has a combination of the above symptoms.

What to Check

If your baby has had previous reactions, learn to recognize the symptoms and call for professional help or follow prescribed treatment.

Treatment

- The best treatment is to avoid the allergens that cause reactions.

- If your baby is at risk for anaphylaxis, his caregiver should prescribe an epinephrine injection device (EpiPen) for emergency use and train you to use it. During an emergency, administer the prescribed medicine and call 911.

- Your baby may need to wear a medical identification bracelet.

Breathing Emergency/Cardiac Arrest

Description

A life-threatening situation when your baby's breathing or heartbeat stops. In infants, most cardiac arrests are caused by lack of oxygen such as from respiratory failure, drowning, or choking. In 2010, the American Heart Association updated its guidelines to recommend everyone begin cardiopulmonary resuscitation (CPR) with chest compressions to keep blood circulating to the brain. Remember the new acronym, C-A-B (circulation, airway, breathing).

What You Need to Know

- Time is critical. Act quickly while someone calls for help.

- If your baby isn't breathing due to choking and he's still conscious but unable to vocalize, follow the procedures on page 145 to try to dislodge the object, then begin CPR if needed (see page 142).

- If your baby isn't breathing due to electric shock, don't touch him directly if he's still touching the electrical source. Turn off the electric current, remove the fuse (or trip the circuit breaker), or stand on a nonconducting mat, like a rubber doormat, and push him away from the source with a nonconducting object, like a dry board. Never use a wet or metal object.

- If your baby isn't breathing due to anaphylaxis (see page 140), administer any prescribed medication and call 911.

- If you don't know why your baby isn't breathing and you're trained in CPR, use the techniques on page 142. If you're not trained, you should still do continuous chest compressions (about one hundred a minute, one-and-a-half inches down the chest) to keep blood flowing to the brain and body.

- Don't tilt your baby's head if you suspect a head or neck injury. Many falls result in a head or neck injury. Instead, a trained professional should use the jaw thrust technique. If no professional is with you and you're losing time, then you should perform the head-tilt/chin-lift method (see page 142), as getting oxygen to the brain takes priority.

Supplies

None

Get Professional Help If...

Your baby's heartbeat or breathing stops and he's unconscious. Have someone else call 911 and follow the steps for CPR while waiting for help. If you're alone, begin CPR for at least two minutes or five cycles before you call 911. Don't stop CPR for longer than a minute. Continue until help arrives or your baby has a pulse and is breathing on his own.

Treatment

If your baby is choking, see page 145 for procedures. Otherwise, see the following instructions for infant CPR. CPR for babies younger than one year differs from the technique used for older children. A CPR course prepares you best for this emergency, but you should try chest compressions even if you're untrained.

CPR Step-by-Step

Step 1: Gently touch your baby to see whether he's unconscious. If conscious, he'll respond and breathe. (If he responds, but does not breathe, he may be choking. See page 145 for procedures.) Don't take more than ten seconds to try to determine if he's breathing and don't check for a pulse unless you are a trained health professional. If you don't get a response, lay him on his back and begin CPR, starting with compressions.

Step 2: Place two fingers on the breastbone at or just below an imaginary line connecting the nipples. Gently press your fingers about one-and-a-half inches into the chest (or at least one-third of the thickness of the chest). Let the chest come all the way up after a compression. Do this thirty times at a rate of about two compressions per second, or at least one hundred compressions per minute. If you're not trained in CPR, continue to do compressions until help arrives. If you are trained, continue to step 3.

Step 3: After thirty compressions, clear the airway. Tilt your baby's head by lifting his chin with one hand and pushing down on his forehead with the other. (If you suspect a head or neck injury, and a trained professional is with you, he or she should do the jaw thrust technique instead. If a trained professional is not present, then use the head-tilt/chin-lift method, as getting oxygen to the brain takes priority.) Quickly (no more than ten seconds) check for breathing. Listen for breaths and look for chest movement.

Step 4: Cover your baby's entire mouth and nose with your mouth and gently blow until you see his chest rise. Let air escape, as his chest goes down. Give two breaths over about two seconds. If no air goes in, adjust his head and try one more time.

Step 5: Go back to compressions. Continue to alternate thirty compressions with two rescue breaths until help arrives. Do not check for a pulse unless you are a trained health professional, as this may delay important resuscitation. If two people are available to do CPR, the rate of compression to rescue breaths can be fifteen to two.

Note: According to the American Academy of Pediatrics (AAP), it is now acceptable to use an AED (automated external defibrillator) on infants less than one year of age in cardiac arrest. Pediatric pads are recommended but adult pads can be used if necessary. Have someone bring an AED if one is available and follow the instructions to use it.

Bronchiolitis
(Typical Cause of Wheezing in Babies)

Description

Inflammation and swelling of the smallest air passages (bronchioles), caused by viral infection, often respiratory syncytial virus (RSV).

What You Need to Know

- Bronchiolitis occurs mostly in babies. Bronchitis is the infection of larger airways, and it's rare in babies.

- Bronchiolitis has many of the same symptoms as pneumonia.

- It usually lasts several days or even weeks, but will disappear on its own.

- RSV infections are most common between October and March.

- Ear infections can accompany bronchiolitis.

- It may put some children at risk for developing asthma.

- The virus that causes bronchiolitis is highly contagious. Careful hand washing and use of hand sanitizers helps prevent spread.

Supplies

Thermometer, prescribed medication, clear liquids, cool-mist humidifier or nebulizers

Symptoms

- Runny nose
- Rapid, shallow breathing
- Labored breathing:
- Periods of apnea (breathing may stop temporarily for more than ten seconds)
  - Nostrils widen and move more often
  - Muscles between the ribs move in and out (increased work to breathe)
  - Grunting sounds with exhalation
  - Wheezing (a high-pitched noise, especially when exhaling)
- Fever (See pages 134–37.)
- Cough, often raspy
- Loss of appetite

Get Professional Help If...

- Your baby has the above symptoms, especially if his breathing is rapid or labored.

- His lips, skin, or fingertips appear bluish, or breathing seems to tire him.

- He refuses fluids because he is working too hard to breathe. Dehydration may occur.

- He has another medical condition, like heart disease or prematurity, while having bronchiolitis symptoms.

What to Check

- Note temperature daily.
- Monitor symptoms.

Treatment

Follow the treatment recommended by your baby's caregiver. It may include:

- Frequent breast milk or other clear liquids, or formula

- Humidifying the air

- Prescribed nebulizer treatments (a special machine gives medication in mist form). The medication may help open the breathing tubes in some patients.

- Using a nasal aspirator with saline drops

Choking

Description

A life-threatening obstruction of the airway caused by an object, food, or croup.

What You Need to Know

- Choking signals include bluish lips, nails, and skin; the inability to vocalize, breathe, or cry; high-pitched cries; and ineffective coughs.

- If your baby can still vocalize, cry, cough, breathe, sputter, or move air at all, don't interfere with him or call for help. His normal reflexes will best clear and open his airway. Let him cough to try to remove the object. If this doesn't work and you can see the object, you can try to sweep it out but be careful not to push it farther into his mouth.

- If your baby has stopped breathing and he's unconscious, call for help, then try to restore his breathing. See page 142.

Supplies

None

Get Professional Help If...

Your baby can't vocalize, cry, cough, or breathe and he's turned blue or if he is unconscious. Have someone call for help while you begin emergency procedures.

Treatment

Note: The following instructions are for babies younger than age one. Techniques for older children are different. After performing the following procedures for one minute, call 911 if your baby's not breathing and the object hasn't been dislodged.

Choking Step-by-Step

If your child is still conscious but unable to vocalize or cry, follow these steps. If your baby becomes unconscious, begin infant CPR. See page 142.

Step 1: Place your baby face-down on your forearm, keeping his head lower than his body. Support his jaw and chest with your hand. Rest the arm holding him on your thigh, pressing the upper arm against your body for further support. Use the heel of your free hand to give five quick blows (backslaps) between his shoulder blades.

Step 2: If the object doesn't dislodge, place your free arm along his spine and cradle his head in your hand. Then carefully turn your arm so it rests on your thigh and your baby is face-up (his head still lower than his body). Use two fingers to give five quick thrusts (one inch deep) into the breastbone between the nipples and one finger-width below them.

Step 3: Repeat steps 1 and 2 until the object is dislodged or your baby becomes unconscious. If he becomes unconscious, begin CPR. See page 142.

If your baby coughs up the object and starts to breathe, still call 911. If you can see the object, but your baby has not coughed it out, you can try to sweep it out but be careful not to push it farther into the mouth.

Cold
(Upper Respiratory Infection)

Description

A common, contagious viral infection of the nasal and throat membranes, sometimes also affecting the ears and chest.

What You Need to Know

- Newborns and young babies often sneeze mucus that's left over from birth. This is not a signal of a cold.
- Most babies have eight to ten colds in the first two years.
- Colds are most contagious in the first three to four days; symptoms usually subside after the third day without treatment. Colds spread most commonly through coughing, sneezing, and hand contact.
- Antibiotics don't cure colds (because colds are caused by viruses, not bacteria) and may worsen them or upset a baby's stomach.
- Ear infections are the most common complication of colds.
- Most colds don't require any treatment.

Supplies

Thermometer, liquids, nasal aspirator, infant acetaminophen or ibuprofen, saline drops (available over the counter)

Symptoms

- Congested, runny nose, with thin and clear mucus early on but often thick and colored as the cold progresses
- Red, watery eyes
- Sneezing
- Cough/hoarseness
- Difficulty breathing
- Listlessness or irritability
- Decreased appetite
- Fever (See pages 134–37.)
- Sore throat or difficulty swallowing
- Mild swelling of the lymph nodes

Get Professional Help If...

- Your baby's younger than six months old and has cold symptoms.
- He has a cough that persists for more than a week.
- His breathing seems labored.
- His lips or fingernails are bluish.
- He becomes particularly irritable or listless.
- He seems to have pain in one or both ears.
- He has a fever of 101°F (38.3°C) or higher. (See pages 134–37.)
- He is refusing feedings.

What to Check

Take your baby's temperature if he seems warm or sick. (See pages 136–37.)

Treatment

- Encourage your baby to nurse more often or to drink more bottles.
- If your baby's younger than six months old, use a nasal aspirator to gently clear mucus from his nose before feedings and naps. If this procedure causes discomfort or irritation, try using normal saline drops.
- To help mucus drain from your baby's head, elevate the head of his bed with blocks, or place a folded blanket or towel under the head of the mattress.
- Talk to your baby's caregiver about giving your baby infant acetaminophen or ibuprofen or any over-the-counter medications. Ibuprofen should not be used before six months of age. (Over-the-counter medications can thicken mucus and have other side effects.)
- A cool-mist humidifier may help thin the mucus. Make sure you clean the humidifier according to the manufacturer's instructions.

Colic

Description

Prolonged periods of daily intense and excessive crying in babies. One definition of colic is "a baby who cries more than three hours a day, more than three days a week, for more than three weeks." Although there isn't a full medical explanation, a colicky baby may have an immature nervous system, causing him to be sensitive to stimulation and unable to be consoled.

What You Need to Know

- One in five babies gets colic, usually beginning between the ages of two and four weeks and lasting about three months.

- Because there's no definite or obvious reason for the crying—which may continue for hours—colic can frustrate parents.

- Some evidence suggests that a nursing mother's consumption of cow milk or other potentially irritating foods can cause some cases of colic.

- Babies who are fed cow milk-based formula may become less colicky if offered a hydrolyzed-protein formula. You should be able to tell in a few days if this makes a difference.

- Almost all babies are fussy in the evening during the first few months; this fussy period is not colic.

- Some babies are fussy because of gastroesophageal reflux disease (see pages 166–67).

Supplies

Thermometer, pacifier, hot-water bottle or heating pad

Symptoms

- Inconsolable crying that persists around the clock but is usually worse in the early evening

- Acting hungry, but then crying halfway through feeding

- Drawing up the legs to the body; clenching fists

- Distended stomach (caused by gas)

Get Professional Help If...

- You suspect colic but want reassurance that there's no other medical problem.

- Your baby cries persistently for more than four hours.

- There is a fever (see pages 134–37), runny nose, cough, vomiting, or other signs of illness.

- Symptoms don't significantly improve by the time your baby's four months old.

- You need support to help you cope.

What to Check

- Possible causes of discomfort, like illness, diaper rash, or constipation (hard stools).

- If formula-feeding, make sure you prepare the formula properly. Also make sure the formula flows from the nipple at about one drop per second.

Treatment

- There's no surefire treatment, so try various methods to soothe your baby. It's possible no method will work. Be patient as you try these methods:

    - cuddling, swaddling (see page 22), rocking, walking your baby

    - taking him on a trip in a car or a baby carrier

    - using a pacifier or "white noise," such as a vacuum cleaner, hairdryer, washing machine, or clothes dryer. (Don't place your baby in any type of carrier on top of a dryer.)

    - laying him face-down across your knees and rubbing his back

    - burping him frequently

    - applying mild heat to his abdomen

- Don't overstimulate your baby by jiggling or moving him too much.

- No matter how distraught you're feeling, *never* shake your baby. This can cause blindness, brain damage, or death.

- If you're nursing your baby, eliminate cow milk from your diet for two weeks to see whether that reduces your baby's symptoms. Occasionally, eliminating onions, cabbage, or caffeine can make a difference.

- Don't overfeed your baby as this may make him more uncomfortable. You shouldn't need to feed him more often than every two hours (from the start of one feeding to the start of the next).

- Remember: Colic is temporary and will disappear when your baby's older (usually when he's around three months old).

- Arrange for someone else to care for your baby, even if only for a few hours. It's critical that you get a break every now and then.

- Discuss your frustration with others.

Concussion/Head Injury

Description

Concussion generally refers to a brief, temporary loss of consciousness following a hard knock or blow to the head. Technically, concussion is defined as confusion or behavior change with or without loss of consciousness.

What You Need to Know

- Minor head injuries are common and inevitable but rarely a cause for concern.

- Serious injuries can cause internal bleeding that puts pressure on the brain. Symptoms can appear even one to two days following the injury.

- If you suspect your infant's neck is seriously injured, do not move him unless absolutely necessary. Moving him could make the injury worse.

- Although a loss of consciousness means there was a brief disturbance in the brain, most often it doesn't cause serious damage.

- A good rule: If your baby acts fine, he usually is fine.

Supplies

Ice, soap, and water

Symptoms

These symptoms will vary according to the severity and location of the injury.

- Some scalp bleeding, a "goose egg," crying up to ten minutes. These signs are common after a minor bump.

- Odd behavior, giving a high-pitched cry, or loss of alertness. These are signs of a more serious injury.

- Vomiting

Get Professional Help If...

- Your baby loses consciousness.

- After hitting his head, he cries and is inconsolable for more than ten minutes.

- He vomits more than twice.

- One of his pupils becomes larger than the other.

- He behaves abnormally, experiences a loss of coordination, shows any seizure activity, or is persistently irritable.

- He suffers a cut that's deep or bleeds a lot (it might need stitches).

- He has a large bump on his head.

What to Check

- How does your baby act? If the injury is serious, he'll most likely act abnormally.

- Watch him closely for twenty-four to forty-eight hours after the injury. If the blow was hard, your baby's caregiver may advise that you wake your baby a few times during the night to check his behavior.

Treatment

- Watch your baby for abnormal behavior.

- Apply ice or cold compresses to the injured area to relieve pain and reduce swelling.

- Apply ice and pressure to blows that cause bruising or bleeding and swelling. Keep in mind that head cuts bleed easily. Wash cuts with soap and water.

Constipation

Description

Hard (possibly large and dry or small and pebbly) bowel movements that are difficult to pass.

What You Need to Know

- Constipation is often overdiagnosed. Diet or illness may cause hard bowel movements; more rarely, a congenital defect of the nerve cells of the anus (Hirschsprung's disease) causes them. Breastfed babies are rarely constipated.

- It's normal for babies to strain and turn quite red while passing a normal bowel movement. This alone does not mean a baby is constipated.

- Constipation tendency may run in families, which can put an individual baby at higher risk.

- Constipation refers to stool consistency only, not frequency. Babies differ greatly in their bowel habits. After one to two months of exclusive nursing, breastfed babies may have very infrequent bowel movements.

- When you start your baby on solid foods, his stools will often change. Rice cereal and bananas tend to cause constipation, so balance these foods with high-fiber ones, like peas and beans.

Supplies

Prune juice, water

Symptoms

- Hard stools
- Painful bowel movements
- Abdominal pain relieved after having a bowel movement

Get Professional Help If...

- Your baby's bowel movements seem painful, with the pain lessening afterward.

- His stools are bloody either on the inside or outside.

- His stools are pellet-like, firm, and dry.

- He's constipated frequently.

- His constipation doesn't improve with home treatment.

What to Check

Is your baby drinking fewer fluids than usual or eating more solid foods that cause constipation?

Treatment

- Try giving your baby one to two teaspoons (5 to 10 milliliters) of prune juice. Use one part water to one part prune juice. You may need to adjust the amounts for more effectiveness.

- If your baby's eating solid foods, consider giving him more high-fiber solids, like peas, beans, broccoli, apricots, plums, and prunes.

- Give your baby more water.

- Before giving your baby laxatives, enemas, suppositories, or mineral oil, first call your baby's caregiver. Don't try to stimulate a bowel movement with a rectal thermometer unless the caregiver has instructed you to do so.

Convulsion
(Fit, Spell, Seizure)

Description

Convulsions or seizures are caused by abnormal electrical impulses in the brain that result in a temporary change in movement or behavior. A series of involuntary muscle spasms may make the body stiffen. Convulsions sometimes cause temporary unconsciousness or confusion. In babies, convulsions may be more subtle.

What You Need to Know

- A convulsion is usually not life-threatening. Most appear with fever (especially in children up to age three years but rarely after age six). Fever-related convulsions (febrile convulsions) usually end within five minutes and don't cause permanent damage.

- Fever-related convulsions usually occur when there is a family history of this condition and can recur in the early years. Even diligent anti-fever measures might not prevent them.

- Most convulsions will stop on their own.

- Other less common causes of convulsions include poisoning, severe infection, and epilepsy. In epilepsy, seizures recur usually without the presence of fever or injury. If epilepsy is diagnosed, antiseizure (anticonvulsant) medication may be prescribed.

Supplies

To treat a fever: Thermometer, cool water and washcloth, infant acetaminophen suppository

Symptoms

- Bluish face and lips
- Uncontrolled, jerking body movements; rigidity or stiffness
- Vomiting/drooling
- Rolling eyes
- Fever might be present.

Get Professional Help If...

- This is your baby's first convulsion. It's okay to call 911 for any convulsion, but it usually will have stopped by the time help arrives.

- A convulsion lasts more than two or three minutes or is especially severe. Call 911 for any convulsion lasting more than fifteen minutes.

What to Check

- How does your baby act before and after convulsions?

- How long did the convulsion last?

- Did the convulsion affect one or both sides of his body?

- Is there a fever (see pages 134–37), or are there symptoms of infection or poisoning (see page 179)? Has there been any recent head injury?

Treatment

- Place your baby on the floor or on a bed. Remove objects that may injure him.

- Turn him on his side with his hips higher than his head to prevent him from choking on vomit or saliva.

- Loosen any tight clothing he's wearing.

- Don't place anything in his mouth, like tongue depressors, fingers, liquids, or medication, while he's convulsing. He will not swallow his tongue.

- Once the convulsion is over, treat a fever as you normally would, or give your baby an infant acetaminophen suppository.

- Get medical help. If fever is present, your baby will need to be examined to determine the cause, including the possibility of meningitis.

Cough

Description

A reflexive spasm in response to an irritation or infection of the respiratory system.

What You Need to Know

- Various conditions can cause coughing, including viral or bacterial infections (such as colds, croup, bronchiolitis, and pneumonia), asthma, allergy, or respiratory blockage.

- Coughing helps clear the respiratory system of irritants and foreign objects.

- If coughing is forceful enough, it can trigger vomiting

Supplies

Thermometer; liquids; cool-mist humidifier (optional); blocks or folded blankets or towels

Symptoms

- Coughing is a symptom of another condition. (See page 138 for cross references.) If accompanied by fever, irritability, or difficulty breathing, it is likely triggered by an infection.

- Coughs can be characterized by such terms as wet (productive, congested), dry, barky, irritative, harsh, raspy.

Get Professional Help If...

- Your baby is younger than two months old and has a persistent cough.

- His breathing is rapid, labored, or wheezy.

- His fever (see pages 134–37) is persistent.

- His cough lasts more than one week.

- He's swallowed a foreign object or choked on food.

What to Check

- Try to identify the cause of your baby's cough to decide what treatment to use.

- Take his temperature every four to six hours.

- Note whether the cough is worse during the day, night, or both.

Treatment

Treatment will depend on the type of cough.

- Give your baby plenty of liquids to soothe the throat and loosen the mucus.

- A cool-mist humidifier may soothe irritation with croup and bronchiolitis. Make sure you clean it daily.

- Over-the-counter cough medicine is not recommended for infants and may have harmful side effects. The use of prescription medicines depends on the cause of the cough and may include antibiotics, steroids, bronchodilator medication in a nebulized form, or allergy medications.

- To help drain mucus from your baby's head, elevate the head of his bed with blocks, or place a folded blanket or towel under the head of the mattress.

Cradle Cap
(Seborrhoeic Dermatitis)

Description

A noncontagious skin and/or scalp condition that features oily, yellowish scales or crusted patches with possible redness.

What You Need to Know

- Cradle cap is most common in babies but occurs in children as old as six years.

- It usually appears on the scalp but may appear as reddish scales wherever there's a concentration of oil-producing glands (forehead, eyebrows, behind the ears, or groin).

- It can be a recurring condition, but will often improve by itself during the first month.

- It isn't harmful, isn't related to poor hygiene, and will eventually disappear on its own. It doesn't itch or cause discomfort.

- It can be treated, but treatment isn't necessary.

Supplies

Washcloth, soap and water, baby shampoo, fine-tooth comb or brush, baby oil, towel

Symptoms

- Yellowish scales

- Crusty skin patches surrounded by slight redness

Get Professional Help If…

- The condition persists after several weeks of home treatment.

- Your baby's skin becomes infected.

What to Check

Watch for signs of skin infection.

Treatment

- Use a washcloth, soap, and water to wash the affected areas daily. For the scalp, shampoo the hair frequently (daily if necessary).

- Remove scales with a fine-tooth comb, brush, or soft toothbrush.

- For stubborn cases, try rubbing a little baby oil into the affected areas and cover with a warm towel for fifteen minutes. Then shampoo, work scales loose with a comb, and rinse.

- If nothing else works, talk with your baby's caregiver about using a medicated shampoo that helps dissolve the scales or a cortisone cream or lotion.

Crossed Eyes
(Strabismus)

Description

Inward or outward turning of one or both eyes rather than parallel eye motion or position. It's caused by an imbalance of the muscles that control eye movement, resulting in an inability to focus on the same point at the same time.

What You Need to Know

- Many newborns have eyes that periodically wander. The condition usually improves markedly by the time a baby is two to three months old.

- Premature babies are at a higher risk for developing crossed eyes than full-term babies

Supplies

None

Symptoms

For a baby older than two to three months...

- One or both eyes crossing most or all of the time

- Eyes not tracking together

Get Professional Help If...

Your baby's eyes seem crossed, appear to wander, or don't seem to track together after the first few months. Even intermittent crossed eyes after age three months need evaluation. If you have any concerns, see an ophthalmologist or eye specialist recommended by your baby's caregiver. If your baby's condition is serious, it must be treated to prevent vision problems.

What to Check

If the bridge of your baby's nose is flat and he has skin folds on the insides of his eyes, it may seem as though he has crossed eyes. He doesn't; this is a condition called pseudostrabismus. No treatment is necessary, and the appearance will improve over time.

Treatment

- There aren't any home remedies. If you suspect your baby has crossed eyes, have your baby's caregiver recommend an eye specialist to evaluate your baby.

- Medical treatment may involve eye drops, wearing a patch over one eye, wearing prescription glasses, or undergoing surgery.

Croup

Description

A barking cough and/or labored breathing caused by inflammation and swelling of the windpipe (trachea) and voicebox (larynx).

What You Need to Know

- A croup attack may be preceded by a fever and nasal stuffiness but often appears suddenly (usually at night), for no apparent reason. It requires immediate home treatment.

- Children between the ages of three months and three years are the most susceptible because their airways are narrow.

- If the attack is severe and doesn't respond to home treatment, it may require medical treatment.

- A virus almost always causes croup, but allergies may be a factor as well.

- Croup most frequently appears in the late fall and winter.

- If your child has recurrent bouts of croup, discuss further treatment with his care provider.

Supplies

Thermometer, cool-mist humidifier or vaporizer, infant acetaminophen or ibuprofen, liquids

Symptoms

- A hacking cough that sounds like a dog's or seal's bark
- Difficulty breathing
- Fever (See pages 134–37.)

Get Professional Help If...

- Symptoms rapidly worsen and home treatment doesn't help enough to let your baby fall asleep.

- Your baby's fever is higher than 103°F (39.4°C).

- He turns blue, drools, or struggles to breathe.

- He can't vocalize.

What to Check

Don't leave your baby alone during an attack. Because an attack may occur several nights in a row, watch him closely for three nights.

Treatment

- Although you can treat most cases at home, contact your baby's caregiver if your baby's breathing doesn't improve.

- Take your baby into the bathroom, close the door, and run a hot shower to generate steam while you sit with your baby for fifteen to twenty minutes.

- Instead of steam or if steam doesn't help, take your baby into cool, moist outside air for twenty minutes. If there's still no improvement, call 911 or his caregiver immediately.

- If the caregiver prescribes a home treatment, put a cool-mist humidifier or vaporizer in the room, and give him liquids and infant acetaminophen or ibuprofen. (See page 136 for dosage information.)

- Your caregiver may prescribe oral or injectable steroids to help decrease the inflammation and swelling.

- Don't give your baby cough syrup.

- Don't try to open your baby's airway by putting your finger in his mouth. The swollen tissue causing the obstruction can't be cleared away.

Dehydration

Description

A condition in which there's an insufficient amount of fluid in the body. It can range from mild to severe.

What You Need to Know

- The most common causes of dehydration are diarrhea and vomiting.

- Other causes are excessive sweating and urination. With a fever (see pages XXX–XX), the body loses extra fluid through the skin.

- Body fluids contain important salts and minerals that must be replaced along with water when a baby's dehydrated.

Supplies

Thermometer; breast milk or other clear liquids (specifically oral rehydration solutions or electrolyte mixes)

Symptoms

- Very dry mouth and lips
- Sunken eyes and fontanel (soft spot on the head)
- Drowsiness
- Lack of energy
- Dry skin or skin with a doughy texture
- Decreased urine output
- Decreased or absent tears when crying
- Fever (See pages 134–37.)
- Weight loss

Get Professional Help If...

- Your baby's symptoms are severe and he's either excessively sleepy or fussy.

- He has persistent vomiting or diarrhea (see pages 158–59) and can't keep down liquids.

- Home remedies don't improve his condition.

- He has diabetes and shows signs of dehydration.

What to Check

Is your baby urinating infrequently (no wet diapers in six hours or fewer than eight wet diapers in twenty-four hours)?

Treatment

Nurse your baby more often or offer him more bottles of clear liquids. If the cause is vomiting, give him one teaspoon (5 milliliters) of breast milk or other clear liquid—preferably a commercially prepared electrolyte mix. Offer breast milk frequently and increase the amount gradually as able. After he's last vomited, let your baby rest before starting treatment. Your baby should consume extra fluids to compensate for the fluid lost in the diarrhea or vomiting. The total amount depends on his size.

Diaper Rash

Description

A rash on the skin that's covered by a diaper.

What You Need to Know

- Constant skin contact with urine and stool causes the rash. One simple—although often impractical—cure: letting your baby go diaper free. (If you'd like to try this, see http://www.diaper freebaby.org for more information.)

- Yeast (candida) is a common cause of persistent diaper rash and requires medication for treatment. If your baby's taking an antibiotic, he has an increased chance of getting a yeast infection.

- Plastic pants or tight disposable diapers can aggravate diaper rash.

- Most babies get some form of diaper rash before they're toilet trained. The peak age seems to be about eight to ten months.

- Diaper rash often occurs when a baby has diarrhea or when more frequent stools are passed.

Supplies

Water; a diaper rash ointment or cream, or barrier jelly that's recommended by your baby's caregiver

Symptoms

Redness or red patches, with or without tiny pimples, on skin that's covered by a diaper. Open sores or blisters may develop in more severe cases.

Get Professional Help If...

- Your baby's diaper rash starts looking severe or pimples develop whiteheads or blisters.

- Home treatment fails to improve his rash in a few days.

- Fever is present.

- The rash is painful.

What to Check

Is your baby allergic to something that comes in contact with the affected skin? Possible allergens include plastic pants, disposable diapers, detergents, powders, lanolin, perfumes, alcohol, lotions, and fabric softeners.

Treatment

- Change your baby's diapers more frequently, and use plain water to carefully clean him after each change. If you use disposable wipes, they shouldn't contain fragrance or alcohol. Let the wet spots air-dry, or pat them dry before putting on a fresh diaper. Rubbing may be painful and may delay healing.

- Apply a thick layer of diaper rash ointment or cream, or barrier jelly, between the skin and diaper.

- If possible, let your baby go without a diaper for as long as possible.

- If a yeast infection is causing the rash, have your baby's caregiver recommend a treatment.

Diarrhea

Description

Frequent loose, watery bowel movements that are yellowish, light brown, or green.

What You Need to Know

- Causes of diarrhea include bacteria, parasites, diet change, food or milk allergy, food poisoning, antibiotics, intolerance to milk or soy, or viruses. Rotavirus is one of the most common causes of diarrhea during the first year. (An oral vaccination is available to help prevent this cause of diarrhea). It usually appears in the winter and often produces unusually foul-smelling stools. Infections outside the intestinal tract, such as ear, urine, and respiratory infections can also present with diarrhea as a symptom.

- Breastfed infants normally will have up to twelve loose bowel movements each day in the first few months.

- Diarrhea often accompanies colds, sore throats, or infections of the stomach and intestines.

- When accompanied by vomiting, diarrhea can cause dehydration.

Supplies

Thermometer; breast milk or other clear liquids, like electrolyte mixes

Symptoms

- Liquid bowel movements
- More bowel movements than usual

Get Professional Help If...

- Your baby has loose bowel movements more than once every hour or two, for more than twelve hours.

- He has a fever of 102.5°F (39.2°C) or higher for more than one to two days. (See pages 134–37.)

- He has blood in his stools.

- He shows signs of dehydration. (See page 156.)

- He seems to be in pain.

- He has even mild diarrhea for more than two weeks.

- He refuses to eat or drink anything.

What to Check

- Are there signs of dehydration? (See page 156.)

- Is he urinating normally?

- How frequent are his bowel movements and what's their consistency?

- Has his diet changed recently?

- Does he have a fever? (See pages 134–37.)

Treatment

- If the diarrhea is mild (fewer than six to eight watery stools a day), you can usually keep your baby on his normal diet.

- For more severe diarrhea (or if vomiting accompanies the diarrhea), rest your baby's intestinal tract by withholding formula and solid foods for no more than twenty-four hours. You should try to continue breastfeeding.

- While his intestinal tract rests, frequently give your baby small amounts of breast milk or clear electrolyte solutions to satisfy thirst and prevent dehydration. (Don't use heavily sugared beverages like juice, and never use boiled skim milk.) Don't force him to drink the liquids, and don't withhold other foods longer than necessary—certainly not longer than twenty-four hours.

- After twenty-four hours of withholding solid foods (if your baby eats solids), begin feeding him rice, applesauce, pears, bananas, crackers, toast, flavored gelatin, or cereal. If you are formula-feeding, you may want to temporarily use a soy formula. Diarrhea can shed the enzymes that normally help digest the milk sugar lactose.

- On the third day, resume his normal diet.

- Put zinc oxide or another type of topical barrier on the skin covered by a diaper, if it's sore.

- Never use over-the-counter antidiarrheal medications. They can actually worsen the diarrhea.

- You may want to discuss the use of prebiotics (natural food substances that promote a healthy intestinal lining) or probiotics ("friendly" bacteria) with your care provider.

Ear Infection

Description

An inflammation or accumulation of fluid in the middle ear, usually caused by bacterial or viral infection.

What You Need to Know

- Two out of three babies experience at least one ear infection by age two years.

- Ear infections are most frequent between six months and three years of age. Boys have a higher frequency of ear infections than girls.

- A family history of ear infections makes a baby more susceptible.

- Colds often cause the Eustachian tubes (that connect the throat and nose and middle ear space) to swell and close, especially in babies. In babies, the Eustachian tube is shorter and positioned so that the nose and throat communicate easily with the middle ear space. Fluids build up in the middle ear, causing pain and sometimes temporary hearing loss.

- Ear infections occur more often in the winter and early spring.

- Daycare attendance and exposure to secondhand smoke increase risk.

- A baby who drinks a bottle while lying flat on his back may increase his risk of developing an ear infection.

Supplies

Thermometer, infant acetaminophen or ibuprofen, prescribed ear drops, heating pad or hot-water bottle

Symptoms

- Chills and fever (See pages 134–37.)

- Congestion, runny nose

- Ear discharge (may be blood-tinged or yellow; results from a perforation of the eardrum that usually self-heals)

- Fussiness

- Inability to sleep

- Apparent hearing loss

- Rubbing/tugging at ear

- Crying during feeding

- Matter in eyes or discharge from eyes

Get Professional Help If...

- His temperature is higher than 101°F (38.3°C).

- Your baby tugs or rubs his ear(s) and he has other symptoms. (Some babies tug on their ears out of habit.)

- He has trouble balancing or develops an apparent hearing loss.

- He has yellow to red discharge draining from the ear. This may mean his eardrum has ruptured.

What to Check

Monitor your baby's fever.

Treatment

- Apply heating pad or hot water bottle to your baby's ear.

- Pain-relieving ear drops may be helpful in some circumstances. Check with your provider to see if these should be used.

- Have your baby's caregiver examine your baby, even if treatment relieves his pain. It's important to follow the findings. If it's suspected that bacteria has caused the infection, the caregiver may prescribe antibiotics to clear the infection. Make sure you follow the medication instructions, even after your baby's symptoms subside.

- Give your baby infant acetaminophen or ibuprofen—check first with his caregiver.

- To treat discharge, your caregiver may prescribe antibiotic ear drops. Warm the bottle; lay your baby on his back with his head turned to his side, affected ear up; pull out, down, and back on the earlobe. Trickle ear drops into the ear so the liquid runs in.

- After an ear infection clears up, have the caregiver check your baby for any complications that may have arisen. Persistent fluid and potential hearing problems need to be monitored.

Eczema
(Atopic Dermatitis)

Description

An often inherited condition that's characterized by dry, scaly skin and intense itching. The skin can be bumpy and moist at times. Eczema can present by one month of age and often improves by two to three years.

What You Need to Know

- Eczema's cause is unknown. Too-frequent bathing, an allergic reaction, or dry heat can trigger outbreaks.

- Babies with eczema are also more likely to have food sensitivities, asthma, and allergies.

- Eczema often disappears with the use of proper lotions or creams.

- Infant eczema usually occurs on the face, in the bends of the elbows, and behind the knees.

- Touching an irritant or allergen can cause a similar-appearing type of rash at the site, called contact dermatitis. Contact dermatitis is treated much like eczema (with topical creams), but avoiding the irritant or allergen is important, too.

Supplies

Fragrance-free moisturizers, nonprescription or prescription hydrocortisone ointment, mild soap, cool-mist vaporizer or humidifier, baby nail clippers

Symptoms

- Pink or red rash
- Intense itching
- Irritability
- When scratched, a rash oozes a moist substance that dries and aggravates itching.

Get Professional Help If…

- Home treatment doesn't improve your baby's rash within a week.

- The rash appears infected.

What to Check

- Was a new food, clothing, or substance recently exposed to your baby's skin or environment?

- Is soap rinsed thoroughly from your baby's body after baths?

- Do other relatives have eczema?

Treatment

- Use mild soap and reduce the frequency and lengths of your baby's baths. Use fragrance-free moisturizers immediately after bathing your baby.

- Relieve your baby's itching with a hydrocortisone ointment or other topical medication.

- Cut your baby's fingernails (see page 36) to reduce irritation from scratching. Keep air moist with a cool-mist vaporizer or humidifier. Make sure you clean it regularly.

- If a particular food is causing the eczema, eliminate it from your baby's diet; however, don't change his diet extensively without his caregiver's supervision.

- Avoid dressing your baby in wool clothing or in clothing made of other irritating fabrics.

- If the eczema is severe, your baby's caregiver may suggest over-the-counter or prescription oral anti-itching medications.

Flat Heads
(Plagiocephaly, Positional Head Deformity, Torticollis)

Description

The back of a baby's skull (the occiput) appears flattened or misshapen. This can involve the entire back of the head or one side more than the other.

What You Need To Know

- Babies have soft, pliable skulls to allow for the important brain growth that continues to take place after birth. While in utero, the confines of the womb may make the skull asymmetrical. Tight neck muscles (torticollis) may also cause misshapen heads or heads that turn more one way than the other.

- The incidence of flat heads has increased significantly since experts began to recommend that babies sleep on their backs to help prevent Sudden Infant Death Syndrome (SIDS) in 1994. It's of utmost importance that babies remain on their backs while they sleep, but they should spend time on their stomachs ("tummy time") during the day to help develop their neck muscles and prevent flat heads.

- Brain growth and development are *not* affected by a misshapen head.

Supplies

Colorful toys and mobiles, craniocap

Symptoms

The flattened area of your baby's head might not have as much hair growing over it as the rest of his scalp. Looking from above, his head may appear more diamond-shaped than square. His neck muscles may be shorter or tighter on one side versus the other.

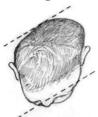 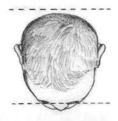

Get Professional Help If...

- Flattening is not improving over the first few months or your baby cries and protests during attempts to turn his head in the other direction. Evaluation by four to six months of age is best.

- There is a ridge along a skull suture line or the skull is unusually long and thin, or flat and wide. This may indicate a rare early fusion of the skull bones called craniosynostosis, and require surgery.

What to Check

- Are you doing enough tummy time with your baby when he is awake?

- Are you placing various objects around your baby, and positioning the crib so he is encouraged to look in different directions?

Treatment

- Reposition your baby often and be sure to practice "tummy time." The American Academy of Pediatrics (AAP) suggests starting with three to five minutes each day and gradually increasing the time he spends on his tummy, up to thirty minutes.

- Use colorful toys and mobiles to encourage your baby to move his head in more than one direction.

- Don't use wedges to position your baby's head. His head could get caught between the wedge and bed, causing suffocation.

- If your baby's neck muscles are tight, physical therapy can help relax them. See a trained specialist before you try anything at home.

- In more severe cases, a caregiver may prescribe and fit a molding device or helmet (called a craniocap) to be worn until your baby's head returns to an acceptable shape.

Food Allergy

Description

An exaggerated response of the immune system to otherwise harmless proteins in foods. The reaction reoccurs with each exposure to the food.

What You Need To Know

- Food allergies are more common in children than adults, occurring in 2 to 8 percent of children under three years of age. Children often outgrow food allergies as their immune systems mature. The tendency to have food allergies is likely genetically inherited.

- Allergies are different from intolerances, sensitivities, or food poisoning.

- Cow milk, eggs, and peanuts are the most common allergies in babies and children. Soy and wheat allergies are the next most common.

- It's not clear whether a breastfeeding mother can transfer allergy potential to her infant through the foods she ingests. If your baby has a reaction when you eat a certain food, avoid it.

- Delaying the introduction of solid foods may help your baby avoid food allergies and allergic conditions like eczema and asthma. If your baby's digestive tract isn't mature enough, the large proteins found in solid foods can sometimes get through the lining of his intestinal wall. If this happens, his immune system kicks in and produces antibodies, resulting in an allergic reaction.

- If your family has a history of allergies, wait until your baby is older to try possibly allergenic foods.

Supplies

Epinephrine (EpiPen)

Symptoms

Symptoms may range from mild to severe and may involve the gastrointestinal, integumentary (skin), and respiratory systems.

- Gastrointestinal
  - Vomiting
  - Cramps
  - Diarrhea
- Integumentary (skin)
  - Eczema
  - Hives
- Respiratory
  - Sneezing
  - Wheezing
- Anaphylaxis (rare but life-threatening): swelling of the tongue and throat, breathing trouble (may include wheezing), blue skin, decrease in blood pressure and thready pulse, loss of consciousness. (See page 140 for more information.)

Get Professional Help If...

- You believe a reaction may be anaphylaxis. Call 911 immediately.

- You need help figuring out if a food allergy is present and how to avoid reactions in the future.

What to Check

- How does your baby react after you introduce a new food?

Treatment

- Introduce solid foods one at a time. Wait at least two to four days after each new food to make sure it doesn't cause an allergic reaction. If your family has a history of allergies, wait a full week before offering the food again. Avoid stews, soups, or multigrain cereals; if any of these causes an allergic reaction in your baby, you won't know exactly which ingredient is to blame.

- If a food causes a reaction, avoid it. You can try serving the food again in very small amounts when your child is older, but only under the direction of a physician. You also can get blood or skin tests done to help evaluate allergies, though skin tests may be more helpful when your child is older than twelve months.

- Your baby's caregiver should prescribe an epinephrine injection device (EpiPen) and train you to use it in case of any food allergy resulting in an anaphylactic reaction. In an emergency, administer the medicine and call 911.

- Your baby may need to wear a medical identification bracelet.

Gastroesophageal Reflux (GER) and Gastroesophageal Reflux Disease (GERD)

Description

Gastroesophageal reflux (GER) is when the stomach contents travel back into the esophagus or feeding tube. This occurs when the muscles at the junction of the esophagus and stomach (called the sphincter) relax at the wrong time or are too weak. Gastroesophageal reflux disease (GERD) occurs when GER causes symptoms or complications.

What You Need to Know

- Babies with GER often spit up (which leads many to call them "happy spitters"). This is a very common condition, because the sphincter muscles are often immature in young infants. The spitting up usually peaks when a GER baby is around four months old and stops most often when he's around seven months old—and almost always by his first birthday. GER babies may spit up less if their food is thickened or if they're kept upright after feedings. Most GER babies outgrow their reflux without problems.

- Premature babies and babies who have a family history of GERD are at higher risk of developing the disease.

Supplies

Some baby equipment, including slings, can help keep a baby upright. Check with your baby's caregiver before using any such equipment. The caregiver may suggest thickening your baby's formula with baby cereal.

Symptoms

GER

- Spitting up

GERD

- Vomiting, possibly painful or forceful
- Cough
- Poor weight gain
- Abdominal or lower chest pain
- Difficult or painful swallowing
- Heartburn (esophagitis)
- Respiratory problems
- Irritability
- Arching of the back

Get Professional Help If...

- Your baby's vomiting green or yellow material, or blood.

- Irritability is significant.

- Vomiting is forceful and frequent, after most feedings. Your baby's caregiver may need to evaluate for pyloric stenosis (a narrowing of the pylorus, the opening from the stomach into the small intestine).

What to Check

- Have your baby's caregiver examine your baby if he has GER or GERD symptoms. Most times, a medical professional can diagnose GER or GERD by taking a careful history of the symptoms and thoroughly examining a baby to rule out other problems. In severe cases, he or she may do other diagnostic testing for further evaluation.

- Some babies who are allergic to cow milk or soy may mimic GER or GERD symptoms. If your baby consumes cow milk or soy formula, his caregiver may suggest giving him a hypoallergenic (hydrolyzed-protein) formula.

Treatment

- If your baby breastfeeds, continue nursing him. Most babies spit up breast milk less often than they do formula.

- If your baby's formula-fed, adding rice cereal to thicken his formula may help alleviate GER or GERD symptoms. Check with his caregiver first.

- Keeping your baby upright for at least thirty minutes after eating often helps alleviate GER or GERD symptoms. You could also try elevating the head of his bed with blocks, or a folded blanket or towel under the head of the mattress. Don't put your baby on his stomach to sleep—this position increases the risk of sudden infant death syndrome (SIDS) and puts pressure on your baby's belly.

- Placing your baby in a car seat to keep him upright is not recommended. The "bent" position will put pressure on his belly and possibly aggravate GER or GERD symptoms.

- Don't overfeed your baby. Burp him often so gas won't put pressure on his belly. Keep his diaper and clothes loose at the waist.

- Your baby's caregiver may prescribe acid suppressant medications, which consist either of histamine H2-receptor antagonists or proton pump inhibitors.

- Surgery for GER and GERD is controversial and rarely needed except for severe cases.

Hearing Loss

Description

A partial or total loss of hearing caused by a congenital defect, illness, or injury. There are two main types of hearing loss. Conductive hearing loss results from problems in the outer or middle ear, and is often medically or surgically treatable. Sensorineural loss (nerve deafness) comes from an inner ear problem or nerve problems between the inner ear and brain, and is often permanent, though using a hearing aid may help.

What You Need to Know

- A sudden loss of hearing is usually temporary and probably means a foreign object, infection, or earwax is blocking the eardrum. (Letting some water get into your baby's ears during regular bathing can help prevent excessive earwax buildup.)

- Your baby may be at more risk of a sensorineural hearing loss if there's a history of deafness in your family.

- A baby needs to be able to hear in order to understand spoken language and, later, to produce clear speech. Thus, hearing problems are important to detect in order for a child to have normal language development.

- Mild hearing loss is common when a baby has a cold or allergies due to fluid accumulating in the middle ear space. This is usually temporary.

Supplies

None

Symptoms

Birth to Age 3 Months

- Awakens to your touch but not to your voice
- Doesn't smile when spoken to
- Doesn't startle at loud noises
- Doesn't seem to recognize your voice or quiet down when crying

Age 4 to 6 Months

- Doesn't try to turn toward a sound made at eye level
- Responds to comforting only when held
- Doesn't pay attention to music
- Shows little interest in babbling or imitating sounds
- Doesn't respond to speech sounds, footsteps, or noise-producing toys by stopping his activities to listen

Age 7 to 12 Months

- Doesn't turn and look in the direction of sounds
- Doesn't respond when spoken to
- Ignores a ringing telephone or doorbell
- Seems startled to see a person nearby

Get Professional Help If...

- Your baby has any of the above symptoms.
- You have any reason to suspect that your baby has trouble hearing.

What to Check

- Was a newborn hearing test done before your baby left the hospital or birth center? If so, what were the results? (The majority of states mandate hearing screening be done before a newborn is discharged from the hospital.)

- Have you observed the startle reflex in your baby? (See page 16.)

- Does your baby react when you squeeze a squeak toy near him?

- If you have any concerns about your baby's hearing, have his caregiver schedule a formal hearing test with an audiologist.

Treatment

Have your baby's caregiver...

- treat all conditions that cause an ear infection or other suspected cause of hearing loss.

- remove a foreign object from your baby's ear—do not remove the object yourself.

- remove earwax buildup at your baby's next checkup; do not insert any object—even a cotton swab—into your baby's ear.

- refer you to an ear, nose, and throat specialist for consideration of ear ventilation tube insertion, if persistent hearing issues are of concern. You may also need to get a formal hearing evaluation from an audiologist to be able to accurately assess the hearing loss and decide if hearing aids are indicated.

Heat Rash/Sunburn

Description

Heat rash, also known as prickly heat or miliaria, appears as small red bumps in the folds of skin, especially on the neck and upper chest. Sunburn appears as red, painful skin, and feels hot to the touch.

What You Need to Know

- Heat rash is very common and causes only minor discomfort. It occurs most often in the summer, when it's humid, and can improve in a few hours or days.

- Heat rash is caused when pores that lead to sweat glands are blocked.

- Never leave a baby in a vehicle, but especially a closed one.

- To prevent sunburn, dress your baby in long-sleeved clothing made of natural fibers and a hat, and apply a PABA-free sunblock (at least SPF 15). Midday sunlight is the strongest, so try not to expose your baby to the sun between 11 A.M. and 3 P.M.

- A severe sunburn could lead to heatstroke, a serious condition. See page 171.

Supplies

Equipment needed for cool baths, thermometer

Symptoms

- Many tiny red bumps in folds of the skin, most often on cheeks, neck, shoulders, and diaper area

- Hot, red skin

- Signs of dehydration, including decreased urine output, decreased or absent tears, dry lips and mouth, sunken soft spots, and lethargy

Get Professional Help If…

- Blisters appear on the bumps.

- Your baby develops a fever after being overheated.

- He has a sunburn that blisters.

What to Check

- Is your washing machine thoroughly rinsing his clothing? Some detergents and bleaches aggravate heat rash.

- Is your baby overdressed? Excess clothing may contribute to heat rash.

- Are oily skin products blocking his pores?

- Does he have a fever? A sunburn with a fever may be an indication of heatstroke.

Treatment

- Move your baby to a cool place immediately.

- Keep your baby's skin as cool and dry as possible.

- Give frequent, cool baths or sponge baths to help open skin pores. Fanning him may help as well.

- Dress him in as little clothing as possible, and make sure the clothing is made of natural fibers. Put him in an air-conditioned environment if possible.

Heatstroke

Description

A life-threatening condition that occurs when a person becomes excessively over-heated. It's caused by external heat, not internal heat (fever). Heatstroke can occur when a baby is in a hot place, like a beach or a closed vehicle, for too long.

What You Need to Know

- Heatstroke is a medical emergency. Call 911 if you suspect your baby has heatstroke.

- Never leave a baby in a vehicle, but especially a closed one.

- To prevent sunburn (which can cause heatstroke), dress your baby in long-sleeved clothing made of natural fibers and a hat, and apply a PABA-free sun-block (at least SPF 15). Midday sunlight is the strongest, so try not to expose your baby to the sun between 11 A.M. and 3 P.M.

Supplies

Equipment needed for cool baths, thermometer

Symptoms

- High fever (See pages 134–37.)

- Hot, red, dry skin

- Rapid pulse

- Restlessness

- Dizziness

- Vomiting

- Rapid, shallow breathing

- Unconsciousness

- Signs of dehydration, including decreased urine output, decreased or absent tears, dry lips and mouth, sunken soft spots, and lethargy

Get Professional Help If...

- Your baby develops a fever after being overheated.

- He has a sunburn that blisters.

What to Check

- Does he have a fever?

- Is he lethargic?

- Does he seem dehydrated?

Treatment

- Call 911 right away.

- Move your baby to a cool place immediately.

- Keep your baby's skin as cool and dry as possible.

- Give frequent, cool baths or sponge baths. Fanning him may help as well.

- Dress him in as little clothing as possible, and make sure the clothing is made of natural fibers. Put him in an air-conditioned environment if possible.

Impetigo

Description

A contagious bacterial infection of the skin, often around the nose, mouth, eyes, and ears.

What You Need to Know

- Impetigo can spread rapidly from one part of the body to another or from person-to-person contact.
- Although not serious, impetigo must be treated persistently.

Supplies

Soap and water, compresses, prescription or over-the-counter antibiotic ointment or cream, baby nail clippers

Symptoms

- Yellowish bumps or scabs on the skin, often in groups, with or without a honey-colored fluid or crust
- Possible blisters

Get Professional Help If…

- The infection spreads or doesn't respond to home treatment after five days.
- Your baby's urine turns red or brownish—a symptom of a rare kidney complication.

What to Check

- Because impetigo is contagious, check other family members for signs of infection.
- Make sure each family member uses his or her own towel and washcloth.

Treatment

- Gently clean the sores with soap and water, then put a compress on them for ten minutes.
- Rub away the crust and pus when the crust softens.
- Cover sores with over-the-counter antibiotic ointment or cream three times a day. Continue treatment three to four times a day until all sores lose their scabs. Your baby's caregiver may prescribe an antibiotic ointment or cream.
- Clip your baby's nails (see page 36) to discourage scratching, which spreads the infection.
- In severe cases, your baby's caregiver may prescribe an oral antibiotic.

Influenza
(Flu)

Description

A viral respiratory illness that may affect both the upper respiratory tract (nose and throat) and lower respiratory tract (bronchial tubes and lungs). It is more severe than the common cold and strikes almost every child from time to time.

What You Need to Know

- Symptoms can include nausea, vomiting, and abdominal pain. However, influenza should not be confused with gastroenteritis, something called the "stomach flu," which presents with vomiting and diarrhea as the main symptoms.

- Influenza is highly contagious, spreading from coughing and sneezing droplets into the air, as well as by touching a contaminated surface or object. It is most frequent in the winter and early spring.

- There are subtypes of influenza, with A and B types responsible for most infections. The terms avian flu and swine flu or H1N1 refer to types of influenza that are within the type A and B categories.

Supplies

If your baby is in pain or discomfort and/or has a high fever, give acetaminophen or ibuprofen to comfort him. (Babies younger than six months should not take ibuprofen.) See pages 135-36 for dosage information.

Symptoms

- High fever (103° F to 105° F, or 39.4° C to 40.6° C)
- Chills and sweating

- Decreased energy
- Dry cough
- Runny or stuffy nose
- May be accompanied by ear infections, croup, bronchiolitis, and pneumonia.

Get Professional Help If…

- You suspect your baby has influenza. Contact your caregiver early in the illness, as a prescribed antiviral medication may shorten the course of the illness and help prevent the spread of infection to others.

- Your baby has underlying health problems, such as heart or lung disease, a weakened immune system or a malignancy. There is increased risk of severe complications from influenza.

- There are signs of secondary infection such as ear pain, persistent cough or a cough that turns phlegm, or sharp pain with breathing. Your caregiver may need to prescribe antibiotics.

What to Check

Watch for difficulty breathing or a bluish color to your baby's skin. If either occurs, call 911.

Treatment

Encourage good fluid intake and monitor for signs of dehydration, including decreased urine output, decreased or absent tears, dry lips and mouth, sunken soft spots, and lethargy. Once your baby is six months old, he can receive the influenza vaccine. See page 132 for more information.

Insect, Animal, or Human Bites

Description

An impression or break in the skin resulting from a bite or sting.

What You Need to Know

- Don't use insect repellents that contain DEET (diethyl toluamide) on babies younger than two months. Instead, dress your baby in long sleeves and pants to cover as much of his skin as possible. If you use a DEET repellent on your child, choose one that contains no more than 30 percent DEET, don't apply it more than once a day, apply to clothes and sparingly on skin, and don't apply it to your child's hands or around his nose, eyes, or mouth. Don't apply it on cuts, wounds, or irritated skin. Wash treated skin and clothing after returning indoors. Avoid spraying DEET in enclosed areas or near food. If you want to use a DEET-free insect repellent, choose those containing eucalyptus oil and/or soybean oil; another option to ask your care provider about is picaridin. Unfortunately, all of these repellants offer protection against the common biting insects but no protection against stinging insects (bees, hornets, and wasps).

- Most animal bites come from family or neighborhood pets. Always supervise your baby when he's in a room with animals. Watch for any aggressive or defensive behaviors.

- Human bites become infected more often than animal bites.

- Deep bite wounds may require stitches, and stitches increase the chances of infection.

- Insect bites usually cause only mild, local reactions; however, in rare cases, they can cause more severe allergic reactions, such as anaphylaxis. (See page 140).

- Scented soaps attract insects.

Supplies

Soap and water, washcloth, a bee-sting kit for allergic infants, calamine lotion, baby nail clippers

Symptoms

Signs of an infected wound include:

- Pus or drainage coming from the bite

- Swelling, tenderness, and warmth around the bite

- Red streaks spreading from the affected area

- Swollen glands in the area of the bite

Get Professional Help If...

- Your baby's been bitten on the face, hands, feet, or genital area.

- The bite wound is large.

- A deep puncture wound has occurred, especially if it can involve bone, tendons, or joints.

- There's any concern that a rabies-infected animal bit your baby. If this is the case, try to have the animal captured and checked for rabies. Wild animals most likely to transmit rabies are bats, skunks, raccoons, coyotes, and foxes. Domestic cats and dogs need to have been vaccinated for rabies to be considered safe from transmission.

- The wound appears infected or extremely swollen.

- Your baby has trouble breathing after an insect bite. (See page 140.)

- His itching is severe or hives appear.

What to Check

Keep an eye on your baby after a bite and watch for signs of infection or trouble breathing. Make sure vaccinations for tetanus and hepatitis B are up to date.

Treatment

- To stop bleeding, apply firm pressure to the wound for up to five minutes.

- Wash the wound with soap and water.

- Use calamine lotion to soothe insect bites.

- For a bee or wasp sting, apply pressure to the wound with a cold, wet washcloth to reduce swelling. If you can see the stinger, try to remove it by scraping your fingernail gently across the wound.

- Trim your baby's nails to prevent scratching.

Meningitis

Description

A rare, serious disease in which a bacterium or virus inflames and infects the membranes surrounding the brain and spinal cord.

What You Need to Know

- A medical professional should diagnose and treat meningitis as soon as possible.

- Good hygiene, like frequent hand-washing, can help prevent the spread of meningitis.

- Vaccinations can help prevent the most serious cases of meningitis.

Supplies

Thermometer

Symptoms

- Moderate to high-grade fever (See pages 134–37.)

- Vomiting

- Decreased appetite

- Extreme listlessness or irritability, or extreme sleepiness

- Stiff neck (babies sometimes don't have this symptom)

- Sometimes, purple spots on body

- Bulging soft spot on head

- Seizures

Get Professional Help If…

- Your baby is less than two months old and has a fever.

- Your baby has meningitis symptoms. No single symptom suggests the disease; look for a combination of the above symptoms.

- You're unsure whether your baby has meningitis symptoms.

What to Check

Do you know whether your baby has been exposed to meningitis? Meningitis is often spread like a cold virus. But it can be spread through contact with stool, such as during diaper changes.

Treatment

Meningitis is a serious disease that always requires medical care. See your baby's caregiver immediately if you suspect your baby has meningitis.

- A spinal tap is necessary to confirm a diagnosis. This test involves using a special needle inserted into the lower back to obtain a sample of spinal fluid. Blood testing will also be done.

- Hospital admission and intravenous (IV) antibiotics, along with early diagnosis, usually results in full recovery.

Pinkeye
(Conjunctivitis)

Description

An irritation or infection of the conjunctiva, or eyelid lining.

What You Need to Know

- Pinkeye is only one cause of red eyes and discharge. Other causes include allergies, colds, chlorinated swimming pool water, dust, and injury to the eye.

- Babies with blocked tear ducts may be more susceptible to eye infections. If your baby has discharge in his eyes and sticky eyelashes, see his caregiver to learn whether he needs prescribed antibiotics.

- Ear infections often accompany conjunctivitis.

- An eye infected with pinkeye will have discharge as well as be bloodshot and pinkish.

- Pinkeye can be very contagious.

Supplies

Prescribed antibiotics, cotton balls

Symptoms

- Red eyes
- Discharge from the eyes, often more abundant after sleep
- Swelling of eyelids

Get Professional Help If...

- Your baby has irritated or swollen eyes, and you're not sure of the cause.

- Your baby has recurrent eye irritations or discharge.

- There is suspicion of an ear infection.

What to Check

- Has your baby had contact with someone with pinkeye?

- Has he had increased tearing since birth in one or both eyes?

Treatment

- Some forms of pinkeye require prescription antibiotic eye drops that you will need to get from your provider.

- To wipe away discharge from your baby's eyes, use a cotton ball that's dampened with clean water. Dispose of the cotton ball after each wipe through the eye.

- Wash your baby's hands frequently, and wash your hands after touching someone with pinkeye.

- To protect other family members, keep your baby's washcloth and towel separate from other clothing.

- Discourage your baby from rubbing his eyes.

Pneumonia

Description

An infection of the lungs, usually viral but sometimes bacterial.

What You Need to Know

- Pneumonia has several different causes, and its severity can vary greatly.

- Some forms of pneumonia are contagious; others aren't.

- Pneumonia occurs most commonly when a viral cold spreads into the lungs

- It is most frequent in the fall, winter, and early spring.

- Going out in the cold does *not* cause pneumonia.

- Pneumonia is more likely to occur if the immune system is weakened or there is an underlying lung abnormality.

Supplies

Thermometer, prescribed antibiotics (for some pneumonia), infant acetaminophen or ibuprofen

Symptoms

- Cough
- Fever (see pages 134-37) with sweating or chills
- Apparent stomach or chest pain
- Fast or labored breathing, possibly accompanied by flaring nostrils or wheezing
- "Sucked in" appearance of the breathing muscles between and below the ribs and above the collarbone

- Decreased appetite

- Possible vomiting

- A bluish tint to lips or nails may indicate decreased oxygen flow in the blood.

Get Professional Help If...

You suspect your baby has pneumonia. His caregiver will diagnose the cause of the infection and may prescribe treatment, possibly with antibiotics. The caregiver may x-ray your baby's chest to confirm the diagnosis. If your baby is very ill, he may need to be hospitalized.

What to Check

Does your baby have trouble breathing? Does he have a fever?

Treatment

- If your baby's caregiver diagnoses pneumonia, he or she may treat your baby with antibiotics.

- Rest is important; make sure your baby gets lots.

- Don't use a cough suppressant. Coughing helps move and clear the secretions associated with pneumonia.

- If your baby has a fever, give him infant acetaminophen or ibuprofen. (See pages 135-36 for dosage information.) Contact his caregiver if the fever is persistent.

Poisoning

Description

Swallowing, breathing in, or making skin contact with certain medicines, cleaning products, petroleum-based products, or other toxic substances can cause poisoning. Half of all poisonings occur in children less than six years of age.

What You Need to Know

- Medicines, cleaners, houseplants, and other common items are the main causes of poisoning. (See pages 96–97.)

- Safe storage can prevent poisoning, but be ready for emergencies by posting the phone number of the national poison control center (800-222-1222) near every telephone.

Supplies

Water or milk, if instructed to give

Symptoms

- Abdominal pain, cramps, and diarrhea
- Blackouts and unconsciousness
- Convulsions or seizures
- Choking or difficulty breathing
- Confusion and drowsiness
- Nausea, vomiting, and coughing up blood
- Behavior change
- Rash or burns, especially on the lips or mouth
- Excessive drooling or a strange odor on the breath
- Throat pain
- Stains on clothing without an apparent explanation

Get Professional Help If...

You suspect your baby has swallowed or put any toxic substance in his mouth.

What to Check

- Have any medicines, cleaners, or other harmful substances been opened, or are any missing? If you find your baby near an empty or open container of a dangerous substance, suspect poisoning.

- Does your home have lead-based paint in it? Lead-based paint chips can poison a baby who swallows them. (See page 96.)

Treatment

- Get the poisonous substance away from your baby. If some of the substance is in his mouth, try to help him spit it out or try to remove it with your fingers.

- Call the national poison control center (800-222-1222) immediately. Be ready to give your name and phone number, your baby's name, age and weight, the name of the poisonous substance, and the time you think it was swallowed.

- Don't make your baby vomit unless instructed to do so.

- If your baby has a poisonous substance on his skin, remove clothing and rinse the skin with lukewarm water.

- If your baby has a poisonous substance in his eye, hold his eyelid open and pour a steady stream of lukewarm water into the inner corner of the eye.

- If you or your baby is exposed to toxic fumes, get into fresh air immediately and then call for help.

- Take the container of the substance and a sample of any vomit to the emergency room with your baby. Make sure you keep both safely away from him.

Roseola

Description

A fever and subsequent rash caused by a virus called human herpesvirus 6 (HHV-6).

What You Need to Know

- Roseola is common in babies six to twelve months old.

- There's no prevention or cure, but it disappears on its own.

- The roseola rash usually appears after three to seven days of moderate to high-grade fever.

- Your baby is usually well when the rash disappears, a day or two after it first appears. By that point, he is likely not contagious.

Supplies

Thermometer, infant acetaminophen or ibuprofen, equipment for cool baths

Symptoms

- A high-grade fever of 103°F to 105°F (39.4°C to 40.6°C). (See pages 134–37.) Rarely, convulsions may accompany high-grade fever.

- Decreased appetite

- Mild crankiness or increased sleepiness

- A slight cough, runny nose, or diarrhea may be present.

- Slightly raised, distinct red spots

- Rash generally appearing on trunk, upper arms, and neck

- The rash appears after the fever disappears.

Get Professional Help If…

- The rash seems especially severe.

- Coughing, vomiting, or diarrhea accompany roseola symptoms.

- Low-grade fever lasts longer than four days without other symptoms.

What to Check

Any high-grade fever requires close observation. Roseola can be diagnosed only when the rash appears. If the rash doesn't appear, something else caused the fever and complications could have already occurred.

Treatment

- Treat your baby's fever. (See pages 134–37.) Dress your baby in light clothing.

- Watch your baby closely for other symptoms.

- Permit moderate activity if your baby feels like moving about.

Sudden Infant Death Syndrome
(SIDS or Crib Death)

Description

The sudden death of an apparently normal, healthy baby during sleep for unknown reasons.

What You Need to Know

- SIDS most often occurs when babies are between two and four months old.

- SIDS is more common in boys than girls. Premature infants, low birth weight infants, multiples, those with a family history of SIDS, and those whose mothers smoke are also at risk. SIDS is less common in breastfed infants.

- To decrease the frequency of SIDS, the American Academy of Pediatrics (AAP) recommends that babies sleep on their backs. Research indicates that fewer SIDS deaths occur when babies sleep exclusively on their backs.

- A disproportionate number of SIDS deaths, about one in five cases, happen in daycares. Always make sure your childcare providers—including baby-sitters—put your baby on his back to sleep. Babies who are "unaccustomed" to sleeping on their tummies because they are put to sleep by their parents on their backs and then suddenly put to sleep on their tummies by others have an eighteen times chance of SIDS.

- It isn't conclusive if swaddling a baby has an effect on the incidence of SIDS. Some believe it helps prevent SIDS by keeping a baby on his back, but others think it may actually increase the risk, as it can be more difficult to wake up a swaddled baby if he isn't used to the practice. If your baby is swaddled early and is not trying to turn, swaddling is likely safe.

- Once your baby learns to roll repeatedly from his back to his belly, it's okay to let him sleep on his stomach.

- Pacifiers may reduce the incidence of SIDS. Make sure you've established breastfeeding before you introduce a pacifier, however.

Supplies

A sleeping area that has a firm surface, meets safety guidelines, and is free of thick blankets, stuffed animals, pillows, and so on. Cribs need to be safety approved and sheets need to be well-fitting. Try not to use blankets and certainly never put them over your baby's head. If you do use blankets, they must be light and tucked in on all sides on the bottom half of the crib mattress. Having your baby sleep in the same room as you in a co-sleeper could reduce your baby's risk of SIDS, but having your baby sleep in the same bed as you could increase the risk. See the section on sleeping in Chapter 2 about the safest place for your baby to sleep.

Symptoms

None

Get Professional Help If...

- Your baby has sleep apnea—periods of twenty seconds or more when breathing stops.

- Your baby turns blue while sleeping.

What to Check

- Is your baby's mattress too soft? Soft surfaces and bedding may increase risk.

- Is your baby's sleeping area too warm? Make sure the temperature is one in which you'd feel comfortable sleeping with light clothes on. If your baby sweats, has flushed cheeks, heat rash or rapid breathing, the room is likely too warm.

Treatment

None. Parents of SIDS victims should contact their healthcare provider to find local support.

Teething

Description

Tenderness of the gums, often accompanied by drooling, caused by the emergence and eruption of teeth.

What You Need to Know

- Not all babies teethe at the same time. (See pages 132–33.) Your baby's teething schedule will be different from any other baby's.

- Never let your baby go to sleep with a bottle of milk or any liquid containing sugar. These increase the risk of tooth decay when coating the teeth during sleep.

Supplies

Thermometer, infant acetaminophen or ibuprofen, teething objects (rings, pacifiers, biscuits, and toys), ice wrapped in a cloth

Symptoms

- Fussiness
- Drooling
- Chewing fingers or other objects
- Crying
- Low-grade fever, usually less than 100°F (37.8°C) (See pages 134–37.)
- Tender, swollen gums
- Irritability
- Loose stools may accompany teething.

Get Professional Help If...

Signs of illness, like vomiting, accompany teething symptoms. Teething shouldn't cause a high-grade fever; if your baby has one, consider other causes and, if necessary, contact your baby's caregiver for a diagnosis and treatment.

What to Check

Consider other causes of your baby's symptoms—hunger, thirst, boredom, ear infection, a need for attention.

Treatment

- You can't do much to ease your baby's teething discomfort, but rubbing his gums with a clean finger may help. Hugs and kisses work as well as anything else.

- If your baby is weaning well and suddenly suffers from teething, he'll probably want to nurse or drink from the bottle instead of a cup. Don't deny him this comfort while he's miserable. When he starts to feel better, you can resume weaning.

- To relieve gum soreness, give your baby infant acetaminophen or ibuprofen. (See pages 135-36 for dosage information.)

- Offer your baby teething rings, pacifiers, biscuits, or toys to gnaw on. (See Chapter 5 for more information on teething toys.) Some teething babies like to chew ice wrapped in cloth. If you choose this option, supervise your baby carefully as he chews on the ice. It can be a choking hazard.

- Avoid giving your baby medications that claim to relieve teething pain; their effectiveness hasn't been proven. Medications that you rub on your baby's gums may numb the back of the throat if overused, which could interfere with your baby's normal gag reflex.

- Once they've erupted, clean your baby's teeth with a soft, infant-sized toothbrush or wipe them with gauze.

Thrush

Description

An infection of the mouth and tongue caused by the fungus candida (yeast).

What You Need to Know

- Thrush's only symptoms are white patches on the mouth and tongue. They may disappear if ignored, but most parents want to treat them.

- Some babies may be fussy or have trouble feeding, though this is unusual.

- Thrush occurs more commonly in infants less than six months old, when the immune system is not fully developed.

Supplies

Prescribed medication, usually an oral antifungal medication

Symptoms

- White, creamy patches on the insides of the cheeks, behind the lips, or on the tongue

- Although they look like dried milk, patches don't wipe off

Get Professional Help If...

Your baby has thrush or you suspect he does—however, thrush isn't an urgent condition.

What to Check

Are there blisters inside your baby's mouth? If so, he may have some other condition.

Treatment

- If your baby's caregiver has prescribed medication, apply it to the patches as directed.

- If you're breastfeeding your baby, you may need to apply medicated ointment to your nipples to prevent passing the infection back to your baby. (See page 66.) If you're bottle-feeding your baby, sterilize all bottle nipples to prevent reinfection.

- If your baby uses a pacifier, thoroughly clean it with hot water daily while treating thrush.

Urinary Tract Infection (UTI)

Description

An infection of the urinary system that can lead to various problems or can be a symptom of other illnesses. There are two main subtypes of urinary tract infections: pyelonephritis, when the infection involves the kidneys, and cystitis, when it involves the bladder. Infants usually get pyelonephritis.

What You Need to Know

- Urinary tract infections can be challenging to detect and treat, especially in babies. Fever may be the only symptom.
- As newborns, boys and girls can get UTIs. When older, girls are more at risk.
- If there's no other cause of persistent high-grade fevers, a healthcare provider will often look for a UTI.

Supplies

Thermometer, infant acetaminophen or ibuprofen, fluids

Symptoms

- Frequent, painful, or bloody urination
- Foul-smelling urine
- Apparent abdominal or back pain
- Fever (See pages 134–37.)
- Nausea
- Possible vomiting

Get Professional Help If…

- You detect any sign of urinary tract infection or blockage.
- Your baby has a fever higher than 101°F (38.3°C) or appears very ill.

What to Check

If there's a family history of bladder or kidney problems, let your baby's caregiver know.

Treatment

- Until you see your baby's caregiver, give your baby infant acetaminophen or ibuprofen for pain (see pages 135–36 for dosage information) and give him lots of fluids to keep flushing out his system.
- Your baby's caregiver will test a urine sample to confirm whether your baby has an infection. This may involve inserting a catheter (a small tube) through the urethra into the bladder, to obtain a specimen for culture. If he has a bacterial UTI, further tests can determine any underlying causes. The caregiver will prescribe an antibiotic if he or she detects a bacterial infection. For young infants, this antibiotic is often given intravenously in a hospital.

Vomiting

Description

The forceful expelling of stomach contents through the nose and mouth—a common symptom with many causes.

What You Need to Know

- By far, the most common cause of vomiting is a contagious viral infection in the stomach.

- Infections outside the gastrointestinal tract such as respiratory infections (ear infections, pneumonia), urinary tract infections, or meningitis may also cause vomiting. (See page 138 for cross references.)

- Babies often spit up. Spitting up is not vomiting. With spitting up, the stomach contents come up easily and often accompany a burp.

- Dehydration is the main concern with vomiting.

- A baby's vomiting in the first few months may have some specific underlying causes:

  - If it occurs fifteen to thirty minutes after every feeding, he may have pyloric stenosis, a condition in which food can't pass out of the stomach into the small intestine. This condition requires surgery.

  - Muscles at the entrance to the stomach may be especially relaxed, resulting in a condition called gastroesophageal reflux (or GER) that allows upwards movement of the stomach contents into the mouth. There are various treatments for this condition. (See pages 166–67.)

Supplies

Thermometers; clear liquids, like breast milk or electrolyte mixes

Get Professional Help If...

- Any vomiting doesn't stop within twenty-four hours or is combined with drowsiness, irritability, apparent abdominal pain, high fever (see pages 134–37), or labored breathing.

- Vomit is bloody, or yellow or green (called bile), more than once or twice.

- Your baby forcefully vomits shortly after being fed.

What to Check

Look for signs of dehydration: listlessness, dry mouth, sunken eyes or soft spot, crying without tears, infrequent urination.

Treatment

- Closely watch your baby when he's vomiting, especially if he's younger than five months. Call his caregiver if vomiting persists.

- A short time after he vomits, offer your baby one teaspoon to one tablespoon (4.9 to 14.8 milliliters) of breast milk or other clear electrolyte solutions every ten minutes. Your provider can recommend which are the best electrolyte solutions.

- Gradually give him more clear liquids. Don't feed him chicken broth, which contains fat and may be difficult to digest.

- Give your baby clear liquids for a day. Then, if he's eating solid foods, give him light foods (applesauce, dry toast, rice, bananas). After three days, resume his regular diet.

Appendix

Guide to Resources

Books

Agnew, Connie, Alan Klein, and Jill Alison Ganon. *Twins! Pregnancy, Birth, and the First Year of Life.* 2006.

American Academy of Pediatrics, The. *Caring for Your Baby and Young Child: Birth to Age 5.* 2009.

Brazelton, T. Berry. *Touchpoints: Your Child's Emotional and Behavioral Development: Birth to 3: The Essential Reference for the Early Years.* 1992.

Brott, Armin A. *The New Father: A Dad's Guide to the First Year.* 2005.

Editors of Good Housekeeping. *The Good Housekeeping Illustrated Book of Pregnancy and Baby Care.* 2004.

Gottman, John and Julie Schwartz Gottman. *And Baby Makes Three: The Six-Step Plan for Preserving Marital Intimacy and Rekindling Romance After Baby Arrives.* 2008.

Huggins, Kathleen. *The Nursing Mother's Companion: Revised Edition.* 2005.

Klaus, Marshall and Phyllis Klaus. *Your Amazing Newborn.* 2000.

La Leche League International. *The Womanly Art of Breastfeeding.* 2010.

Leach, Penelope. *Your Baby and Child: From Birth to Age Five.* 1997.

Lothian, Judith and Charlotte DeVries. *The Official Lamaze Guide: Giving Birth with Confidence.* 2010.

Newman, Jack. *The Ultimate Breastfeeding Book of Answers: The Most Comprehensive Problem-Solution Guide to Breastfeeding from the Foremost Expert in North America.* 2000.

Pantell, Robert H. *Taking Care of Your Child: A Parent's Guide to Complete Medical Care.* 2009.

Peterson, Gayle. *Making Healthy Families.* 2000.

Satter, Ellyn. *Child of Mine: Feeding with Love and Good Sense.* 2000.

Simkin, Penny, April Bolding, Ann Keppler, Janelle Durham, and Janet Walley. *Pregnancy, Childbirth, and the Newborn: The Complete Guide.* 2010.

Sloan, Mark. *Birth Day: A Pediatrician Explores the Science, the History, and the Wonder of Childbirth.* 2009.

Spock, Benjamin. *Dr. Spock's Baby and Child Care.* 2011.

Zuchora-Walske, Christine and Maureen Bard. *Getting Organized for Your New Baby.* 2004.

Magazines

American Baby
www.parents.com/american-baby-magazine/
This magazine is for expectant and new parents, covering baby issues from preconception to age two years.

Babytalk
www.parenting.com/Babytalk/babytalk.jsp?genID=7
This magazine offers articles, tips, and chats on raising your baby.

Consumer Reports
www.consumerreports.org
This magazine reviews baby products, and its accompanying website issues important information about safety standards and recalls.

Mothering
www.mothering.com
This magazine features philosophical inspiration and practical advice about natural family living.

Parenting
www.parenting.com
This magazine offers articles, tips, and chats on all topics concerning pregnancy and raising a child.

Parents
www.parents.com
This magazine is written to help parents raise healthy, happy families.

Working Mother
www.workingmother.com
This magazine is dedicated to the lives of working women and mothers.

Resource Groups

Low-Cost Care Resources

Child Welfare League of America
www.cwla.org/programs/health/healthstate.htm
877-KIDS-NOW (877-543-7669)
This organization has information about low-cost medical
care. Medicaid funds are available for pregnant women
and children younger than six years old whose family
income is less than a certain amount. Contact them to find
the phone numbers for Medicaid agencies in your state.
Your state agency can tell you whether you qualify for
medical assistance.

Women, Infants, and Children (WIC)
www.fns.usda.gov/wic
The WIC program offers food for pregnant women and
breastfeeding help for new mothers whose income is
less than a certain amount. They can also help you find
parenting help and support. Also, your caregiver may help
you find your local WIC office.

Pregnancy Resources

Baby Friendly USA
www.babyfriendlyusa.org/
This source provides a list of "baby friendly" hospitals
and birth centers that have policies to encourage
breastfeeding.

Centers for Disease Control (CDC) on Pregnancy
www.cdc.gov/ncbddd/pregnancy_gateway/before.html
This CDC web page features tips for staying healthy before
and during pregnancy.

Childbirth Connection
www.childbirthconnection.org
This non-profit's website features a discussion of maternity
care options.

International Cesarean Awareness Network (ICAN)
www.ican-online.org
This organization has information for mothers about cesarean births, and how to best recover from them.

March of Dimes
www.marchofdimes.com
March of Dimes seeks to prevent premature birth and
birth defects. You can find helpful information about staying healthy during pregnancy, and preparing and caring
for your baby on their website.

National Newborn Screening and Genetics Regulation
Center (NNSGRC)
http://genes-r-us.uthscsa.edu
This resource can help you learn about specific newborn
screenings and tests.

Baby Care Resources

American Academy of Pediatrics
www.aap.org
847-434-4000
This organization offers information about parenting,
keeping your child healthy, and finding a pediatrician.

American SIDS Institute
www.sids.org/nprevent.htm
800-232-SIDS (800-232-7437)
This organization's provides information about ways to
reduce the risk of SIDS.

Automotive Safety Program
www.preventinjury.org/index.asp
800-543-6227
If your child has special needs, he may need a car seat
that's custom-designed for his situation.

Centers for Disease Control (CDC) on Vaccination Safety
www.cdc.gov/vaccinesafety/Concerns/Index.html
This CDC web page has information on vaccination
schedules and common concerns.

Child care Aware
http://childcareaware.org/
800-424-2246
Child Care Aware is a resource to find high-quality
child care.

Consumer Product Safety Commission (CPSC)
www.cpsc.gov
301-504-7923
This agency offers information about home safety and
unsafe baby care products.

Environmental Protection Agency (EPA)
www.epa.gov/
202-272-0167
This agency has helpful guidelines for making your home
baby-friendly.

Immunization Action Coalition
www.immunize.org
651-647-9009 (Hotline for questions about vaccines:
800-232-2522)
This organization offers information about vaccinations to
keep your baby healthy.

Juvenile Products Manufacturers Association (JPMA)
www.jpma.org
This national trade organization is dedicated to the safe
use of juvenile products. Use their website to find out
whether baby gear has their safety certification.

KidsHealth
www.kidshealth.org
This website includes information for parents and kids
about children's health and development. It features
individual articles on such issues as developmental
disabilities, medical problems, first aid, and nutrition.

National Highway Traffic Safety Administration (NHTSA)
www.nhtsa.gov/CPS
888-DASH-2-DOT (888-327-4236)
Their Child Passenger Safety (CPS) department offers
information about infant and child car seats.

National Association for the Education of Young Children (NAEYC)
www.naeyc.org
You can find daycare guidelines and contact information here.

National Association of Child Care Resource and Referral Agencies
www.naccrra.org
This organization works with referral agencies to provide parents with safe child-care options.

National Vaccine Center
www.nvic.org
This organization provides parents with information on vaccine safety.

Safe Kids USA
www.safekids.org
This website provides safety guidelines for individual age groups and includes information on product recalls.

Seat Check
www.seatcheck.org
866-SEAT-CHECK
This national campaign to help parents properly secure their children in motor vehicles features a free child safety seat inspection, available at their website or by calling their toll-free phone number.

SIDS Alliance (First Candle)
www.sidsalliance.org
800-221-7437
This organization provides information about sudden infant death syndrome (SIDS) and other causes of infant death. They offer suggestions about safe sleeping.

United States Agriculture Department
www.nutrition.gov
http://choosemyplate.gov
This agency's websites include information on nutrition, healthy eating, physical activity, and food safety.

Breastfeeding Resources

Human Milk Banking Association of North America (HMBANA)
www.hmbana.org
This association of milk banks carefully screens and pasteurizes donated breast milk before sending it out to mothers and babies in need.

International Lactation Consultant Association (ILCA)
www.ilca.org/i4a/pages/index.cfm?pageid=1
919-861-5577
This association keeps records of breastfeeding professionals who are International Board Certified Lactation Consultants (IBCLC). Contact them to find a breastfeeding expert in your area.

La Leche League (LLL)
www.lalecheleague.org/WebIndex.html
847-519-7730
This organization offers mother-baby groups for breastfeeding support. Contact them to find a LLL group near you. Or ask them to help you find breastfeeding consultants in your area.

National Women's Health Information Center
www.4woman.gov/breastfeeding
800-944-9662
This agency answers breastfeeding questions.

Parenting Resources

County, State, or City Public Health Department
These departments can give you information about agencies that offer help with parenting issues. Contact the health department for your state, county, or city to learn more about parenting resources near you.

Attachment Parenting International (API)
www.attachmentparenting.org
API is a non-profit organization that supports the philosophy of attachment parenting. Their website features links to support groups and literature.

Autism Speaks
www.autismspeaks.org/
This autism advocacy group has a resource library and updated information for parents of children with autism.

Family Equality Council
www.familyequality.org/site/PageServer?pagename=resources_groups
The Family Equality Council is a source for LGBTQ-headed families and the local groups that support them.

National Healthy Mothers, Healthy Babies Coalition
www.hmhb.org/family.html
703-836-6110
This organization offers help with breastfeeding and parenting.

National Information Center for Children and Youth with Disabilities (NICHCY)
www.nichcy.org
800-695-0285
This organization provides information on disabilities in children and youth; programs and services for infants, children, and youth with disabilities; and more.

National Organization of Mothers of Twins Clubs, Inc.
www.nomotc.org/welcome/zipsearch.htm
877-540-2200
This organization provides information and support for families having more than one baby. Contact them to learn the names of local groups for parents of multiples.

National Organization of Single Mothers, Inc.
www.singlemothers.org
This website includes articles, message boards, and links to support groups for single mothers.

Parents Anonymous, Inc.
www.parentsanonymous.org
909-621-6184
This organization works toward the prevention and treatment of child abuse. Treatment blends support groups with self-help.

Parents Without Partners
www.parentswithoutpartners.org/chapterfind.asp
561-391-8833
This organization provides information and support for single parents and their children. Contact them to find a group in your area.

Planned Parenthood
www.plannedparenthood.org/bc
800-230-PLAN (800-230-7526)
This organization can tell you about methods to avoid getting pregnant.

Prevent Child Abuse America
www.preventchildabuse.org/index.shtml
877-224-8223
This volunteer-based coalition's goals are to foster awareness of the problem and to develop effective child abuse prevention programs.

4MyChild
www.cerebralpalsy.org/
This organization for parents of children with cerebral palsy includes information about medical care, financial assistance, and other important topics.

Your Local Community College
Many community colleges have classes for parents. Contact the family life education department at your local community college.

Postpartum Depression and Loss Resources

Postpartum Support International
www.postpartum.net
800-944-4773
This group offers help to women with postpartum mood disorders. Contact them to learn about a mothers' support group in your area.

Share Pregnancy & Infant Loss Support, Inc.
www.nationalshareoffice.com
800-821-6819
This group offers support for families who have lost a baby by early pregnancy loss, stillbirth, or newborn death.

Solace for Mothers
http://solaceformothers.org/
This organization provides help for mothers who have had a traumatic birth experience.

Online Support Groups

MotheringDotCommune
www.mothering.com/discussions

Parenting Forums
www.parentingforums.com

Talk About Parenting
www.talkaboutparenting.com

190

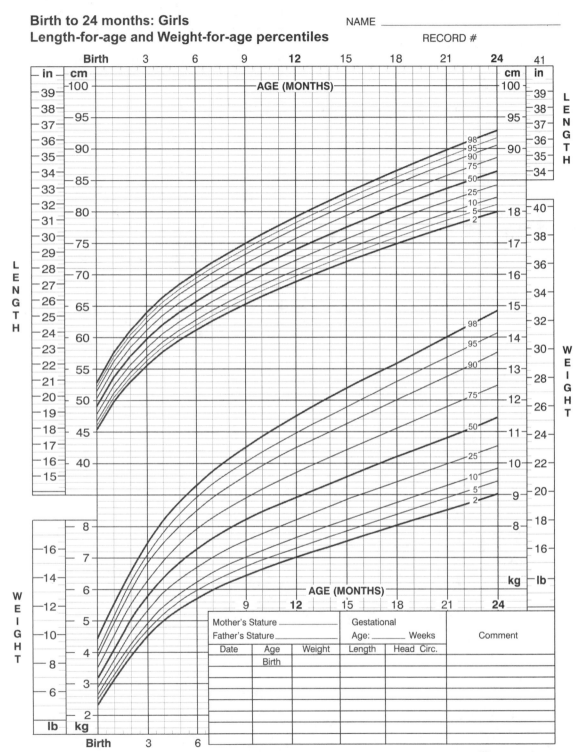

Birth to 24 months: Girls
Length-for-age and Weight-for-age percentiles

NAME _____

RECORD # _____

Birth to 24 months: Boys
Length-for-age and Weight-for-age percentiles

NAME _____

RECORD # _____

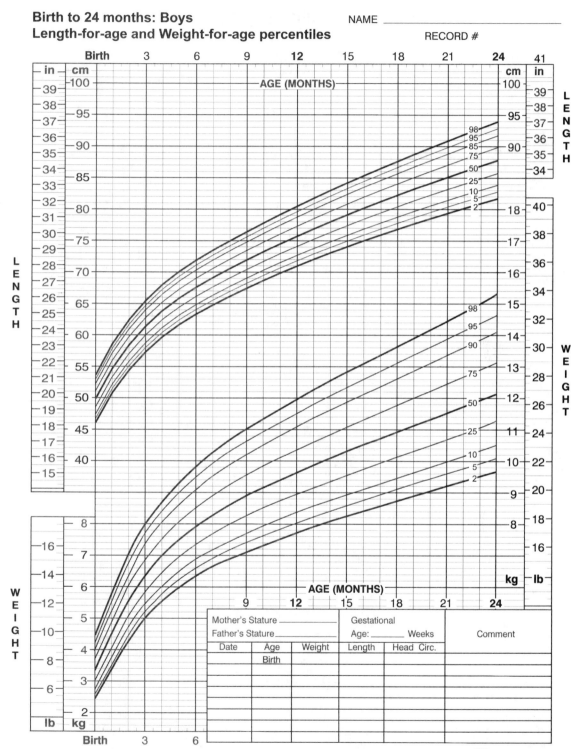

Published by the Centers for Disease Control and Prevention, November 1, 2009
SOURCE: WHO Child Growth Standards (http://www.who.int/childgrowth/en)

Index

A

Accessory nipples, 6
Acetaminophen, 135, 136
Acne, newborn, 139
AED (automated external defibrillator), 142
African descent, newborns of, 6
"Afterpains," 61
Air travel, 112–13
Alcohol intake, ix, 38, 39, 69
Allergies
 anaphylaxis, 140
 food, 84, 164–65
 to protein in cow milk, 69, 73
American Academy of Family Physicians (AAFP), xi
American Academy of Pediatric Dentistry (AAPD), 133
American Academy of Pediatrics (AAP)
 on automated external defibrillators, 142
 on baby walkers, 108
 on breastfeeding, 55
 car seat guidelines by, 98
 on circumcision, xiii
 on cord blood banking, 11
 on co-sleeping, 39, 103
 on dental visits, 133
 finding a pediatric caregiver through, x
 on flat heads, 106, 163
 on formula, 73
 on introducing solid foods, 24, 83
 on mercury thermometers, 136
 on newborn hearing screening, 13
 on sleep positions and SIDS, 21, 40, 181
 on television, 125
 on vitamin supplements for breastfed baby, 62–63
American Dental Association (ADA), 43, 133
American Heart Association, 141
American Medical Association (AMA), xi
Anaphylaxis/anaphylactic shock, 140, 141, 164
Anemia, 13
"Angel kisses," 7
Angie's List, xi
Animal bites, 174–75
Anterior fontanel, 5
Antibiotics
 colds and, 146
 before delivery, ix
 for ear infections, 161
 for impetigo, 172
 for pinkeye, 177
 for pneumonia, 178
 for urinary tract infections, 184
 for yeast infection, 66
Apgar scale/tests, 12
Apnea, 143, 181
Arm cross exercise, 126
Arm raising exercise, 126
Arms, newborn, 6
Asian descent, newborns of, 6
Aspirin, 97, 135
Atopic dermatitis, 162
Attachment parenting, 14
Auditory brainstem response (ABR), 13
Autism, 116, 131

B

Baby. See also Newborn
 bathing, 31–34
 changes for, after birth, 4
 clothing for, 44–48
 comforting a crying, 41–42
 diapering. See Diapers/diapering
 elimination by, 23–24
 feeding. See Breastfeeding; Formula-feeding; Solid foods
 holding, 20
 picking up, 21
 shaking your, 22, 42
 shoes and socks for, 46
 skin care for, 35–36
 sleep for. See Sleeping
 swaddling and rocking, 22
Baby bounce exercise, 127
Baby carriers, 104–05
Baby food
 commercially prepared, 87
 warming, 87
Baby gear, 98–109
 baby carriers, 104–05
 baby swing/jumper, 107–08
 bassinets, 102–03
 bedside co-sleeper, 103
 bouncer seats, 105–06
 car seats, 98–101
 changing tables, 102
 cradles, 102–03
 cribs, 101–02
 high chairs, 106
 monitors, 107
 play yards, 103–04
 stationary walkers/play centers, 108–09
 strollers, 104
Baby lotions and oils, 31, 35, 36
Baby massage, 36
Baby monitors, 107
Babysitters, 110–11
Baby swing/jumper, 107–08
Backpacks, baby, 104–05
Back position, picking baby up from, 21
Back position, sleeping on, 21, 40, 117, 181
Balls, 125
Barbecue grills, 96
Bare feet, baby walking on, 46
Bassinets, 37, 102–03
Bathroom, childproofing, 94–95
Baths/bathing
 sponge, 31–32
 tub, 33–34
Bedding, 38
Bed-sharing, 37, 39
Bedside co-sleepers, 38, 103
Beds, types of, 37–38
Bellybuttons, 6
Bibs, 47
Bicycle seats, 109
Bilirubin, 8, 9
Birth defects, preventing, ix
Birthmarks, 7
Birthplace, choosing the right, x
Birth plans, x
Bites (animal, insect, or human), 174–75
Biting, breastfeeding and, 66
Blankets, 38, 48, 102
Blinking reflex, 17
Blisters, lip, 5, 7
Blocks, 125
Body, of newborn, 6
Bonnets, 47
Books, for baby, 124
Boredom, in baby, 41
Bottle-feeding. See Formula-feeding
Bottles
 dental care and, 133
 different types of, 74, 75
 features of, 75
 storing expressed milk in, 63–64
 used for supplemental feedings, 63
 warmed in microwaves, 64, 75, 79, 94
Botulism, 43
Bouncer seats, 105–06
Bowel movements
 constipation, 150
 diarrhea, 158–59
 during early weeks, 23
 during first year, 24
 of newborn, 6
 right after birth, 23
Breastfeeding, xi–xii
 baby's bowel movements and, 24
 benefits of, 55, 56
 biting and, 66
 breast care and, 64–65
 breast infections, 66
 childhood obesity and, 90
 clogged milk ducts and, 65–66
 colostrum and, 60
 on demand, 61–62
 disadvantages of, 57
 emotional and mental preparations for, 59
 engorgement and, 65
 first feeding, 59–60
 frequency of, 61–62
 interrupting nursing session, 62
 jaundice and, 9
 latching and, 60
 length of feeding, 62
 "let-down" reflex for, 60–61
 milk production, 61
 mother's needs and support for, 67–69
 night wakings and, 40
 nipple soreness with, 65
 nursing positions for, 70–71
 on one or both breasts, 62
 physical preparation for, 59
 with premature, ill, or multiple babies, 67
 recommendations on, 55
 supplemental feedings with, 63–64
 vitamin supplements for babies and, 62–63
 weaning and, 69, 72
Breast milk
 colostrum, 60
 expressed, 63–64
 in milk banks, 67
 transitioning to mature, 60
Breast pumps, 63, 64
Breasts (mother)
 caring for, for breastfeeding, 64–65
 clogged milk ducts, 65–66
 mastitis, 66
 yeast infection of, 66
Breasts (newborn), 6
Breathing emergency, 141
"Brick dust" urine, 23
Bronchiolitis, 143
Bubble-free bottles, 75
Bumper pads, 38, 102
Burping, 41, 81, 82

C

Café-au-lait spots, 7
Caffeine intake, ix, 69
Calamine lotion, 174, 175
Calcium, ix, 133
Caps, for baby, 47
Caput succedaneum, 8
Carbon monoxide detectors, 92
Cardiac arrest, 141
Caregivers, medical
 choosing for baby, x–xi
 interviewing, xi
 resources for finding, x–xi
 types of, x
 vaccinations and, 131
 well-child checkups with, 130
 when to contact for high fever, 136
Caregiver-to-child ratios, 53
Carrying baby, 20
Car safety, 101
Car seats, 98–101, 112, 113
Centers for Disease Control (CDC), xii, 131
Cephalhematoma, 8
Cerebral palsy, 116
Cesarean births, 11, 57, 60, 71
Chambered bottles, 75
Changing pads, 26
Changing tables, 25, 102
Checkups, ix, 129, 130
Childcare. See Daycare providers
Child Care Aware hotline, 49

Childhood obesity, 90
Child passenger safety (CPS) technician, 98
Childproofing, 53, 92–97
Choking, 141, 144–45
Circumcision, xii–xiii, 31, 35
Clavicle, broken, 8
Clogged milk ducts, 65–66
Cloth diapers, 25, 28
Clothing
    checklist, 47
    comfort features on, 45
    dressing baby, 46
    practical features on, 44–45
    safety features on, 45
    sizing, 44
    strategies for stretching your budget with,
        44
    temperature changes and, 45
"Cluster feeding," 61
Colds, 146
Colic, 42, 147–48
Collarbone, broken, 8
Colostrum, 60
Comforting, for crying baby, 41–42
Commercially prepared baby foods, 87
Concentrated liquid formula, 74
Concussion/head injury, 149
Congenital adrenal hyperplasia, 13
Conjunctivitis (pinkeye), 177
Constipation, 24, 150
Consumer Product Safety Commission
    (CPSC), 103, 104
Consumer Reports, 98,104
Convulsion, 151
Cord blood, xi, 11
Cornstarch, 35
Co-sleeping, 37
Coughs, 152
Coveralls/stretchies, 47
CPR (cardiopulmonary resuscitation), 141
Cradle cap, 5, 153
Cradle hold, 70
Cradles, 37, 102–03
Creams, 26, 35
Crib gym/exerciser, 125
Cribs, 37, 101–02
Crossed eyes, 154
Croup, 155
Crying, 40, 41–42, 147
Cytomegalovirus (CMV), ix

D
Dacryostenosis, 7
Daycare providers, 49–53
    checking references of, 50
    choosing type of, 49
    interviewing, 50–53
    steps in finding, 49–50
DEET (diethyl toluamide), 174
Dehydration, 156
Demand feeding, 61–62, 78
Dental care, 132–133
Developmental dysplasia of the hips, 8
Development, baby, 115–27
    abilities, birth to one year old, 91
    birth through two months, 117
    six through nine months, 119–20
    ten through twelve months, 121–22
    three through five months, 118
    toys and, 123–25
    warning signs and, 116
Diaper pails, 26
Diaper rash, 157
Diapers/diapering, 25–30
    care of, 27–28
    changing area for, 25–26
    cloth, 25
    crying baby and, 41
    daycare and, 52
    disposable, 25
    knowing your baby is getting enough
        breast milk and, 61, 62
    step-by-step instructions, 30
    supplies and materials for, 29
    supplies for, 26

tips for, 29
Diaper wipes, 26
Diarrhea, 158–59
Diet, of mother, ix, 68, 69
Digital thermometer, 137
Dimple, on newborn, 9
Dining room, childproofing, 94
Diseases, screening newborn for, 12–13
Disposable bottles, 75
Disposable diapers, 25, 28
Doctor of Osteopathy, x
Dresses, for baby, 47
Drug use, recreational, ix, 38, 39
Drying off newborn, 11
DTaP vaccine, 132

E
Ear infections, 160–61
Ear thermometer, 137
Eczema, 162
Electric shock, 141
Electric space heaters, 93
Elimination. See Bowel movements; Dia-
        pers/diapering; Urination
Engorgement, 65, 72
Environmental hazards, ix, 97
EpiPen (epinephrine injection device), 140,
        165
Epstein pearl, 5
Erythema toxicum, 9
Erythromycin ointment, 11
Examinations, newborn, xii, 11–13
Exercises, baby, 126–27
Expressed milk, 63–64
Eye care, for newborn, 11
Eyes
    crossed, 154
    of newborn, 5
    pinkeye, 177

F
Face, of newborn, 5
Family
    changes in, after baby's birth, 2–3
    not fitting the traditional mold, 3
Family history, assessing, x
Family nurse practitioner, x
Family physician, x
Fathers, changes for, 2–3
Federal Aviation Administration (FAA), 112
Feeding. See Breastfeeding; Formula-
        feeding; Solid foods
Feet, misshapen, 10
Fencing reflex, 17
Fevers
    after vaccination, 131
    convulsions with, 151
    levels of, 134–35
    reaction to vaccinations and, 131
    with roseola, 180
    treatment of, 135–36
Fifth disease, ix
Finger food, 87
Fingernails
    of newborn, 6
    trimming baby's, 36
Finger sucking, 43
Fire escape plan, 93
Fish, ix
Flat angiomata, 7
Flat heads, 163
Fluids, for nursing moms, 68
Fluoride, 63, 132
Folic acid, ix
Fontanels, 5, 20
Food allergies, 84, 140, 164–65
Food and Drug Administration (FDA), 131
Football hold position, for breastfeeding, 71
Foremilk, 62
Formula-feeding, xi–xii
    advantages of, 58
    amount of formula for, 78
    baby's bowel movements and, 24
    breastfeeding vs., 55
    burping and spitting up with, 81
    demand, 78

disadvantages of, 58
    equipment for, 74–76
    giving bottle to baby, 79
    packaging of formula, 73–74
    preparing formula, 74, 77
    storing formula, 74
    types of formula, 73
    weaning from, 80
    weaning from breastfeeding to, 72
Frenulum, 10
Front packs, 104–05
Furniture, safety edges on, 93

G
Gagging reflex, 17
Galactosemia, 13
Gastroesophageal reflux (GER), 166–67, 185
Gastroesophageal reflux disease (GERD),
        166–67
General practitioner, x
Genitalia
    bathing and, 32
    of newborn, 6
German measles, ix, 132
Glass bottles, 75
Glass thermometers, 136
"Goose eggs," 8
Grasp exercise, 126
Groin hernia, 9–10
Group B streptococcus (GBS) bacteria, ix
Growth spurts, 61–62, 83

H
Hair, newborn, 5
Hands-free bottles, 75, 79
Hardwood floors, 93
Hats, for baby, 47, 96
Head
    of newborn, 5
    supporting your baby's, 21
Head injury, 149
Head-tilt/chin-lift method of CPR, 141
Health caregiver. See Caregivers, medical
Health issues. See also Medical care
    breastfeeding and, 56
    daycare and, 51–52
    mastitis, 66
Hearing loss, 116, 168–69
Hearing, of newborn, 15
Hearing tests, 13
Heat rash, 8, 170
Heatstroke, 171
Height, growth in baby's, 44
Hemangiomas, 7
Hemoglobinopathy, 13
Hepatitis B vaccination, 12, 132
Herbicides, 96
Hernia, 9–10
    groin, 9–10
    inguinal, 9–10
    umbilical, 10
HiB vaccine, 132
Hiccups, breastfeeding and, 66
High chairs, 106
Hindmilk, 62
Hips, developmental dysplasia of, 8
Holding baby, 20
Home daycare, 53
Home healthcare, xiii
Homemade baby food, 88–89
Honey, 43, 85
Household products, toxic, 97
Human bites, 174–75
Human herpesvirus 6 (HHV-6), 180
Human Milk Banking Association of North
        America (HMBANA), 67
Humidifiers, 38, 95, 146, 152, 155, 162
Hunger, in baby, 41
Hydrolyzed-protein formula, 73, 147, 166
Hydrocele, 10
Hypospadias, 10
Hypothyroidism, 13

I
Ibuprofen, 65, 66, 135, 136–37, 146
Identification bracelet, 12

Ill babies, breastfeeding, 67
Impetigo, 172
Inactivated poliovirus vaccine, 132
Inchworm exercise, 127
Influenza (flu), 173
Influenza vaccine, 132
Inguinal hernia, 9–10
Insect bites, 174–75
Intelligence, of newborn, 15
International Lactation Consultant
    Association (ILCA), 59
Interviewing
    babysitters, 110
    child's caregiver, xi
    daycare providers, 49–53
Intoeing, 10
Inverted nipples, 59
Iron-fortified formula, 73
Iron intake, ix

J
Jacket, for baby, 47
Jaundice, 8–9, 62
Jaw thrust technique of CPR, 141, 142
Juice, 85, 86
Jumpers, baby, 108

K
Kitchen, childproofing, 94

L
"Lactose-free" formula, 13, 73
La Leche League (LLL), 59, 63, 67
Lanolin, 65
Lanugo, 5–6
Latching, for breastfeeding, 60
LATCH (Lower Anchors and Tethers for
    Children) system, 99
Latex nipples, 76
Laundering diapers, 27, 28
Laundry room, childproofing, 95
Lead, ix, 93
Leg bending exercise, 127
Legs, newborn, 6, 10
"Let-down" reflex, 60–61
Lip blisters, 5, 7
Liquids, for nursing moms, 68
Litter boxes, ix
Lunch meats, ix
Lying down position, for breastfeeding, 71
Lymphocytic choriomeningitis virus, ix

M
March of Dimes website, x, 12–13
Massage, baby, 36
Mastitis, 66
Mattresses, 38, 39
Mattress pads, 38
Meconium, 23
Medical care
    basic supplies for, 134
    dental, 132–133
    fevers and, 134–36
    taking baby's temperature, 136–37
    vaccinations, 130–32
    well-child checkups, 129, 130
Medical caregivers. See Caregivers, medi-
    cal
Medical conditions. See also Skin/skin
    conditions
    anaphylaxis, 140
    bites, 174–75
    breathing emergency/cardiac arrest,
      141
    bronchiolitis, 143
    choking, 144–45
    cold/upper respiratory infection, 146
    colic, 147–48
    concussion/head injury, 149
    constipation, 150
    convulsions, 151
    coughs, 152
    CPR, 141, 142
    crossed eyes, 154
    croup, 155
    dehydration, 156
    diarrhea, 158–59

ear infections, 160–61
flat heads, 163
food allergies. See Food allergies
gastroesophageal reflux, 166–67
handling common problems, 133–34
hearing loss, 168–69
heatstroke, 171
impetigo, 172
influenza, 173
meningitis, 176
pneumonia, 178
poisoning, 179
sudden infant death syndrome (SIDS).
    See Sudden infant death syndrome
    (SIDS)
symptoms index, 138
teething, 182
thrush, 183
urinary tract infection (UTI), 184
vomiting, 185
Medications
    for baby's fever, 135–36
    breastfeeding and, 69
    childproofing and, 94–95
    cough medicine, 152
    for nursing moms, 68
    taken during pregnancy, ix
    for teething, 182
Mediterranean descent, newborns of, 6
Meningitis, 176
Mercury thermometers, 136
Metabolic disorders, screening newborn
    for, 13
Microwaves, 64, 75, 79, 94
Milia, 8
Miliaria, 8, 170
Milk banks, 67
Milk-based formula, 73
Mirrors, 124
Misshapen feet, 10
Mittens, for baby, 48
Mobiles, 38, 102, 123, 124, 163
Moles, on newborn, 7
Mongolian spots, 7
Monitors, baby, 107
Moro reflex, 16
Mothers
    benefits of breastfeeding to, 56
    changes for, after baby's birth, 2
    support for nursing, 67
    taking care of themselves, ix–x
    vitamin supplements for, 63
Mucus, 146
Multiple births, breastfeeding and, 67, 69
Music, for getting baby to sleep, 39

N
Nails, 6, 36
Napping, 37
Natal teeth, 5
National Association for the Education
    of Young Children (NAEYC), 53
National Highway Traffic Safety
    Administration, 98–99
National Newborn Screening and Genetics
    Regulation Center (NNSGRC), 12
National poison control center, 96, 97,
    135–36, 179
National Vaccine Center, 131
Naturopathic physician, x
Navel, caring for, 35
Neck, of newborn, 5
Neonatal pustular melanosis, 9
Neonatologist, x
Nesting toys, 125
Nevi (moles), 7
Newborn. See also Baby
    changes in family after arrival of, 2–3
    exams and procedures for, xii–xiii, 11–13
    hearing of, 15
    intelligence of, 15
    physical appearance of, 5–6
    possible conditions of, 7–10
    reflexes of, 16–17
    sense of smell and taste in, 15

sight of, 14–15
sociability of, 15
touch of, 14
Nipples (bottle), 76
Nipples (breast)
    babies born with extra, 6
    care for, 64
    leaking, 65
    preparing for breastfeeding, 59
    sore, 65
Non-accidental head trauma (NAHT), 42
Nose, of newborn, 5
Nursery, childproofing, 95
Nursing. See Breastfeeding

O
Obesity, pediatric, 90
Oils, for baby, 35
Omega-3 fatty acid, ix
Onesies, 47
Oral thermometer, 137
Orthodontic nipples, 76
Otoacoustic emissions (OAE), 13
Outdoors, safety issues and, 96
Outlet safety covers, 92, 93
Overalls, 47
Overdressing, 45
Overstimulation of senses, 41
Oxytocin, 56, 60

P
Pacifiers, 41, 43, 60, 61, 148, 181
Pails, diaper, 26
Paint, lead in, 93
Pajamas, 47
Palmar reflex, 16
Parachute reflex, 17
Parents, changes for, 2–3
Parvovirus B19, ix
Pediatric caregivers. See Caregivers,
    medical
Pediatricians, x
Pediatric nurse practitioner, x
Pediatric obesity, 90
Penis, caring for, 35–36
Perinatologist, x
Personal flotation device (PFD), 109
Pesticides, 96
Pet safety, 109
Phenylketonuria (PKU), 13
Physical contact, inadequate, 41
Physician's assistant, x
Pictures, for baby, 124
"Pigeon toed," 10
Pillows, for baby, 38
Pinkeye, 177
Placing reflex, 16
Plagiocephaly, 106, 163
Plantar reflex, 16
Plants, poisonous, 97
Plastic bags, 92
Plastic bottles, 75
Play centers, stationary, 108–09
Play yards/playpens, 38, 103–04
Pneumococcal conjugate vaccine, 132
Pneumonia, 178
Poisoning, 95, 96, 97, 179
Poisonous plants, 97
Popcorn, 85
Port-wine stains, 7
Positional head deformity, 163
Positions
    for breastfeeding, 65–66
    nursing, 70–71
    sleep, 40
Posterior fontanel, 5
Postpartum support, xiii–xiv
Powdered formula, 73
Powders, 26, 35
Pregnancy, taking care of yourself during,
    ix–x
Premature babies
    backpacks for, 105
    breastfeeding, 56, 67
    circumcising, xiii
    crossed eyes and, 154

developmental milestones for, 115
SIDS and, 181
transporting, 100
Prenatal vitamins, ix, 63
Prescription medications. See Medications
Primary teeth, 132, 133
Procedures, for newborn, 11–13
Prune juice, 150
Pseudostrabismus, 154
Pull toys, 125

Q
Qualifications, daycare provider, 51
R
Rashes
diaper, 157
heat, 8, 170
newborn, 9
Rattles, 124
Raw fish, ix
Ready-to-feed formula, 73
Receiving blankets, 48
Recreational drug use, ix, 38, 39
Rectal temperatures, 134, 136–37
References
for babysitter, 111
for daycare providers, 50
Reflexes, 16–17
Relaxation, for nursing moms, 68
Respiratory syncytial virus (RSV), 143
Rest, for nursing moms, 68
Reusable bottles, 75
Reverse-cycle feeding, 64
Reye's syndrome, 135
Rocking motion, 4, 22
Rodent feces, ix
"Rooming in," xii, 14
Rooming-in policy, x, 14
Rooting reflex, 16
Roseola, 180
Rotavirus vaccine, 132
Rubella, ix, 132

S
Sacral dimple, 9
Safety issues
baby food, 88–89
baby gear and, 98–109
baby's development and, 91
bicycle seats, 109
boating and life jackets, 109
childproofing, 92–96
daycare and, 51–52
feeding solid foods, 87
with pets, 109
poisonous plants, 97
shopping carts, 109
toxic substances, 96–97
travel, 112–13
"Salmon patches," 7
Salt intake, ix
Screening tests, 12–13
Seafood, ix
Seizures, 151
Self-weaning, 72
Senses
hearing, 15
overstimulation of, 41
sight, 14–15
smell, 15
taste, 15
touch, 14
Shaken baby syndrome, 42
Shaking your baby, 22, 42
Sheets, bed, 38
Shellfish, ix
Shoes, baby's, 46
Shopping carts, 109
Siblings, 3
Sickle cell disease, 13
SIDS. See Sudden infant death syndrome (SIDS)
Sight, of newborn, 14–15
Silicone nipples, 76

Skin/skin conditions
caring for baby's, 35–36
cradle cap, 153
diaper rash, 157
eczema, 162
heat rash, 170
impetigo, 172
of newborn, 5–6
newborn acne, 139
newborn rashes, 9
roseola, 180
Skin-to-skin contact, 11, 14
Sleeping
bed options for, 37–38
co-sleeping, 37
daycare and, 52
environment for, 38–39
needs and habits, 37
night waking and, 40
positions for, 40
preparing baby for, 39
SIDS and, 181
Slings, 105
Smell, of newborn, 15
Smoke detectors, 92
Smoking
breastfeeding and, 69
childhood obesity and, 90
during pregnancy, ix
while caring for baby, 92
Snowsuit, for baby, 48
Sociability, of newborn, 15
Socks, for baby, 46, 47
Soft spots (fontanels), 5, 20
Solid foods
amount to give, 86
bowel movements and, 24
commercially prepared, 87
finger food, 87
food allergies and, 84
foods to avoid, 85
homemade, 88–89
how to introduce, 84
safety issues, 88–89
schedules for feeding, 85
spoon-feeding for, 86
when to introduce, 83
Sounds, experienced by newborn, 4
Soy-based formula, 73
Spinal tap, 176
Spitting up, 81
Sponge baths, 31–32, 135
Spoon-feeding, 86
Squeak toy, 124
Stacking rings, 125
Stairs, childproofing, 95
Startle reflex, 16
Stationary walkers/play centers, 108–09
Stepping reflex, 16
Stomach position, picking baby up from, 21
Stomachs, babies on their, 21
Stools. See Bowel movements
Storage
of expressed breast milk, 63–64
of formula, 74
"Stork bites," 7
"Strawberry" marks, 7
Strollers, 104
Stuffed animals, 124
Sucking
breastfeeding and, 60
as a comforting measure, 41
non-nutritive, 43
weaning and, 72
Sucking reflex, 16
Sudden infant death syndrome (SIDS), 37, 181
bedding and, 38
breastfeeding and, 56
sleep positions and, 40, 163
Sunblock, for baby, 96
Supernumerary nipples, 6
Swaddling, 22, 181
Swallowing reflex, 17
Sweaters, for baby, 47

Swings, baby, 107–08
Symptoms (medical) index, 138
T
Taste, of newborn, 15
Tears/tear ducts, 7–8
Teething, 80, 132, 182
Teething toys, 125
Teeth, of newborn, 5
Television, 125
Temperature. See also Fevers
baby's clothing and, 45
of baby's room, 38
extremes in, 41
of newborn, 4
Thimerosal, 131
Thrush, 183
Thumb sucking, 43
Toenails, trimming baby's, 36
Tongue thrust reflex, 16
Tongue-tie, 10
Tonic neck reflex, 17
Tooth, baby's first, 132
Torticollis, 163
Touch, of newborn, 14
Toxic substances, 96–97
Toxoplasmosis, ix
Toys, 123–125
Travel, 112–13
Tub baths, 33–34
U
Umbilical cord
bathing and, 31, 32
blood banking, 11
caring for, 35
clamping, xii, 6, 11
Umbilical granuloma, 35
Umbilical hernia, 10
Underarm temperatures, 134
Undescended testes, 10
United States Department of Agriculture, ix
Unpasteurized milk, ix
Upper respiratory infection, 146
Urinary tract infections, 184
Urination
during early weeks, 23
during first year, 23
of newborn, 6
V
Vaccinations, ix, 12, 130–32
Vaccine Adverse Event Reporting System (VAERS), 131
Vagina, secretions from baby's, 36
Vaporizers, 38
Vernix caseosa, 5
Vitamin D, ix, 62–63, 73, 132
Vitamin K shot, 11
Vitamins
prenatal, ix, 63
preserved in baby food, 88
Vitamin supplements, 62–63, 86
Vomiting, 185
W
Walkers, stationary, 108–09
Warming baby food, 87
Weaning
from breastfeeding, 69, 72
with formula-feeding, 80
Weight gain, in baby, 44, 55, 62
Weight, of newborn, 4
Well-child checkups, 129, 130
Wheezing, 143
"White noise," 148
Wipes, diaper, 26
"Witch's milk," 6
Withdrawal reflex, 17
World Health Organization (WHO), 55
Wrist lesions, 10
Y
Yeast infection, 66, 157

Also from Meadowbrook Press

Baby Play & Learn Child-development expert Penny Warner offers 160 ideas for games and activities that provide hours of developmental learning opportunities. It includes bulleted lists of skills baby learns through play, step-by-step instructions for each game and activity, and illustrations that demonstrate how to play many of the games.

Baby & Child Emergency First Aid edited by Mitchell J. Einzig, MD. This user-friendly book is the next best thing to 911, with a quick-reference index, large illustrations, and easy-to-read instructions on handling the most common childhood emergencies.

Feed Me! I'm Yours is an easy-to-use, economical guide to making baby food at home. More than 200 recipes cover everything a parent needs to know about teething foods, nutritious snacks, and quick, pleasing lunches. Now revised.

100,000+ Baby Names is the #1 baby name book and the most complete guide for helping you name your baby. It contains more than 100,000 popular and unusual names from around the world, complete with origins, meanings, variations, and famous namesakes. It also includes the most recently available top 100 names for girls and boys, as well as over 300 helpful lists of names to consider and avoid.

Pregnancy, Childbirth, and the Newborn, 4th Edition This book covers all aspects of childbearing, from conception through early infancy. It offers detailed information, suggestions, and advice to help make pregnancy, childbirth, and new parenthood an enjoyable, healthy experience. It presents the latest research-based information, including new information on complementary medicine approaches, updated information on interventions during childbirth, and new advice to help you make informed decisions about your care. It's the most authoritative, yet easy to use.
Extra information, resources, and worksheets are located on PCNGuide.com.

The ICEA Guide to Pregnancy & Birth In this new guide, the International Childbirth Education Association (ICEA) presents the best available evidence-based research on pregnancy, childbirth, and newborn care. Its goal is to help expectant parents understand their options in maternity care, and to guide them as they make informed decisions that are best for them and their families. Written in plain English and organized for easy reference, this is a great resource for any childbirth class.

We offer many more titles written to delight, inform, and entertain.
To browse our full selection of titles, visit our web site at:

www.MeadowbrookPress.com

For quantity discounts, please call: 1-800-338-2232

Ⅷ Meadowbrook Press